David McDowall was educated at
Sandhurst and St John's College,
Oxford, where he read history.
Between 1972 and 1979, he worked for
the British Council and the United
Nations in India, Iraq, Beirut and
Vienna.

David McDowall is now a full-time
writer. As well as a number of
publications on the Middle East, both
for adults and children, he has written
two books on the Armada. He now
lives in Britain, and is married with two
children.

AN ILLUSTRATED
HISTORY OF
BRITAIN

David McDowall

Longman

Longman Group UK Limited,
Longman House, Burnt Mill, Harlow,
Essex CM20 2JE, England
and Associated Companies throughout the world.

First published 1989

British Library Cataloguing in Publication Data
McDowall, David
   An illustrated history of Britain.
   1. Great Britain—History
   I. Title
   941   DA30

Paperback 0-582-74914-X
Cased 0-582-04432-4

Set in 11/13 pt Goudy Old Style

Produced by Longman Group (FE) Ltd
Printed in Hong Kong

Acknowledgements

We are grateful to Penguin Books Ltd for permission to reproduce an extract from *The Canterbury Tales* by Geoffrey Chaucer, translated by Nevill Coghill (Penguin Classics, 1951, 1958, 1960), copyright (c) Nevill Coghill, 1951, 1958, 1960.

We are grateful to the following for permission to reproduce copyright photographs:
Aerofilms for page 6 (left) and 24 (top left); Barnaby's Picture Library for page 170 and 176 (bottom); BBC Hulton Picture Library for pages 141, 144, 151, 154, 163 and 165; Bibliothèque Royale Albert ler, Brussels (Ms 13076/77 fo 24v) for page 47; Bodleian Library, Oxford (Ms Bodley 764 f 41v) for page 38 (right); Janet and Colin Bord for page 4; The Bridgeman Art Library/British Museum, London for page 98; The Bridgeman Art Library/Tichborne Park, Hampshire for pages 102–103 and The Bridgeman Art Library/Victoria and Albert Museum for page 78; City of Bristol Museum and Art Gallery for page 106; Britain on View for pages 20 and 70; British Library for pages 14, 22, 24 (bottom right), 27, 42, 46, 50, 57, 60, 64, 75 and 146; Trustees of the British Museum for pages 3, 5, 7, 12 and 91; Camera Press London for pages 175, 179 and 183 (Albert Watson); J. Allan Cash Photolibrary for page 178; The Governing Body of Christ Church, Oxford for pages 45 and 62; Christie's for page 139 (top); City Council of Bristol and City of Bristol Record Office – 04720(1) for page 59; Courtesy of the Library of Congress for page 112; Presidents and Fellows of Corpus Christi College, Oxford for page 38 (top and bottom left); Crown copyright, published by permission of the Ministry of Defense and of the Controller of Her Majesty's Stationery Office/Cambridge University Collection for page 117; Courtesy of the Dean and Chapter of Westminster for page 33; In the Collection of the Duke of Buccleuch and Queensberry, K.T. for page 92; Stanley Gibbons for page 135 (left); *The Guardian* for page 96; Copyright reserved. Reproduced by gracious permission of Her Majesty the Queen for pages 86, 111 and 135 (right); Royal Commission on the Historical Monuments of England for page 24 (top right); Michael Holford for page 17; Illustrated London News Picture Library for page 148; Imperial War Museum for page 160; A.F. Kersting for pages 31, 41, 58, 65 and 81; Lambeth Palace Library for page 54; Linen Hall Library, Belfast for page 122 (top); Lloyd's of London for page 104; London Docklands Development Corporation for page 181; London Transport Museum Photographic Archive for page 158; Manchester City Art Galleries for page 137; Mansell Collection for pages 90, 98, 115 (left), 127 (top), 136 and 140; The Marquess of Bath, Longleat House, Warminster, Wiltshire for page 83; The Marquess of Salisbury for page 82; The Marquess of Tavistock and the Trustees of the Bedford Estates, Woburn Abbey for page 74; Marylebone Cricket Club for page 153; Kenneth McNally for page 19; Museum of London for page 142; Director of the National Army Museum, Chelsea, London for page 147; National Gallery of Canada, Ottawa for page 124; Reproduced by courtesy of the Trustees, National Gallery, London for page 115 (right) and 119; National Library of Ireland, Lawrence Collection 11566 for page 150; The National Maritime Museum, London for pages 66 and 126–7 (bottom); National Portrait Gallery for pages 51, 53, 67, 68, 71, 87, 94 and 139 (bottom); The National Trust Photographic Library for page 130; North Yorkshire County Library for page 152; Popperfoto for page 167; David Redfern for page 171; Dr P.J. Reynolds for page 6 (right); Trustees of the Science Museum, London for page 100; Sheffield City Libraries for page 133; Shell for page 176 (top); The Board of Trinity College, Dublin for page 19; Tony Stone Photolibrary – London for page 2; University Museum of National Antiquities, Oslo, Norway for page 16; Board of Trustees of the Victoria and Albert Museum for pages 101 and 110; The Victoria Art Gallery, Bath City Council for page 116; Wales Tourist Board for page 52; Walker Art Gallery, Liverpool for page 122 (bottom); Weald and Downland Open Air Museum, Singleton, Chichester, West Sussex for page 63; West Stow Anglo-Saxon Village trust for page 13; Windsor Castle, Royal Library © Her Majesty the Queen for page 30; Woodmansterne/Museum of London for page 10.

Cover photographs by: Bodleian Library, Oxford (Ms Bodley 764 f 41v) (top right); A.F. Kersting (middle left); The Marquess of Tavistock and the Trustees of the Bedford Estates, Woburn Abbey (middle right); The National Maritime Museum, London (middle top & bottom right); National Portrait Gallery, London (top left); Popperfoto (bottom left); Tony Stone Photolibrary-London for the background.

Picture Research by Sandra Assersohn

Contents

Earliest times

Chapter 1	**The foundation stones**	3
	The island · Britain's prehistory · The Celts · The Romans · Roman life	
Chapter 2	**The Saxon invasion**	11
	The invaders · Government and society · Christianity: the partnership of Church and state · The Vikings · Who should be king?	
Chapter 3	**The Celtic kingdoms**	18
	Wales · Ireland · Scotland	

The early Middle Ages

Chapter 4	**Conquest and feudal rule**	23
	The Norman Conquest · Feudalism · Kingship: a family business · Magna Carta and the decline of feudalism	
Chapter 5	**The power of the kings of England**	29
	Church and state · The beginnings of Parliament · Dealing with the Celts	
Chapter 6	**Government and society**	34
	The growth of government · Law and justice · Religious beliefs · Ordinary people in country and town · The growth of towns as centres of wealth · Language, literature and culture	

The late Middle Ages

Chapter 7	**The century of war, plague and disorder**	43
	War with Scotland and France · The age of chivalry · The century of plagues · The poor in revolt · Heresy and orthodoxy	
Chapter 8	**The crisis of kings and nobles**	51
	The crisis of kingship · Wales in revolt · The struggle in France · The Wars of the Roses · Scotland	
Chapter 9	**Government and society**	57
	Government and society · The condition of women · Language and culture	

The Tudors

Chapter 10	**The birth of the nation state**	67
	The new monarchy · The Reformation · The Protestant–Catholic struggle	
Chapter 11	**England and her neighbours**	73
	The new foreign policy · The new trading empire · Wales · Ireland · Scotland and England · Mary Queen of Scots and the Scottish Reformation · A Scottish king for England	
Chapter 12	**Government and society**	79
	Tudor parliaments · Rich and poor in town and country · Domestic life · Language and culture	

The Stuarts

Chapter 13	**Crown and Parliament**	87
	Parliament against the Crown · Religious disagreement · Civil war	
Chapter 14	**Republican and Restoration Britain**	92
	Republican Britain · Catholicism, the Crown and the new constitutional monarchy · Scotland and Ireland · Foreign relations	
Chapter 15	**Life and thought**	98
	The revolution in thought · Life and work in the Stuart age · Family life	

The eighteenth century

Chapter 16	**The political world**	107
	Politics and finance · Wilkes and liberty · Radicalism and the loss of the American colonies · Ireland · Scotland	
Chapter 17	**Life in town and country**	114
	Town life · The rich · The countryside · Family life	
Chapter 18	**The years of revolution**	121
	Industrial revolution · Society and religion · Revolution in France and the Napoleonic Wars	

The nineteenth century

Chapter 19	**The years of power and danger**	131
	The danger at home, 1815–32 · Reform · Workers revolt · Family life	
Chapter 20	**The years of self-confidence**	138
	The railway · The rise of the middle classes · The growth of towns and cities · Population and politics · Queen and monarchy · Queen and empire · Wales, Scotland and Ireland	
Chapter 21	**The end of an age**	151
	Social and economic improvements · The importance of sport · Changes in thinking · The end of "England's summer" · The storm clouds of war	

The twentieth century

Chapter 22	**Britain at war**	159
	The First World War · The rise of the Labour Party · The rights of women · Ireland · Disappointment and depression · The Second World War	
Chapter 23	**The age of uncertainty**	168
	The new international order · The welfare state · Youthful Britain · A popular monarchy · The loss of empire · Britain, Europe and the United States · Northern Ireland · Scotland and Wales · The years of discontent · The new politics · Britain: past, present and future	

Author's acknowledgement

I could not possibly have written this brief account of Britain's history
without considerable help from a number of other books. Notable among these
are the following:

Maurice Ashley: *The People of England* (Weidenfeld and Nicolson 1982)
Maurice Ashley: *England in the Seventeenth Century* (Penguin 1961)
S.T. Bindoff: *Tudor England* (Penguin 1965)
Asa Briggs: *A Social History of England* (Weidenfeld and Nicolson 1983)
Valerie Chancellor: *Medieval and Tudor Britain* (Penguin 1967)
Dorothy George: *England in Transition* (Penguin 1962)
J.D. Mackie: *A History of Scotland* (Penguin 1984)
K.O. Morgan (ed.): *The Oxford Illustrated History of Britain* (Oxford University
    Press 1984)
A.L. Morton: *A People's History of England* (Lawrence and Wishart 1984)
Maire and Conor Cruise O'Brien: *A Concise History of Ireland* (Thames and
    Hudson 1972)
A.J. Patrick: *The Making of a Nation, 1603–1789* (Penguin 1982)
J.H. Plumb: *England in the Eighteenth Century* (Penguin 1966)
M.M. Postan: *The Medieval Economy and Society* (Weidenfeld and Nicolson 1972)
Jasper Ridley: *The History of England* (Routledge and Kegan Paul 1981)
Alan Sked and Chris Cook: *Post-War Britain* (Penguin 1984)
D.M. Stenton: *English Society in the Early Middle Ages* (Penguin 1967)
Lawrence Stone: *The Family, Sex and Marriage in England 1500–1800* (Weidenfeld and
    Nicolson 1977)
David Thomson: *England in the Nineteenth Century* (Penguin 1970)
David Thomson: *England in the Twentieth Century* (Penguin 1983)
G.M. Trevelyan: *A Shortened History of England* (Penguin 1983)
Gwynn Williams: *When was Wales?* (Penguin 1985)

I owe an entirely different kind of debt to my wife, Elizabeth. She not only
persuaded me to write this book, but in many places suggested an elegance
and clarity quite beyond my own ability. To her, then, I dedicate the end-product,
with my love and thanks.

Earliest times

1 The foundation stones
The island · Britain's prehistory · The Celts · The Romans · Roman life

The island

However complicated the modern industrial state may be, land and climate affect life in every country. They affect social and economic life, population and even politics. Britain is no exception. It has a milder climate than much of the European mainland because it lies in the way of the Gulf Stream, which brings warm water and winds from the Gulf of Mexico. Within Britain there are differences of climate between north and south, east and west. The north is on average 5°C cooler than the south. Annual rainfall in the east is on average about 600 mm, while in many parts of the west it is more than double that. The countryside is varied also. The north and west are mountainous or hilly. Much of the south and east is fairly flat, or low-lying. This means that the south and east on the whole have better agricultural conditions, and it is possible to harvest crops in early August, two months earlier than in the north. So it is not surprising that southeast Britain has always been the most populated part of the island. For this reason it has always had the most political power.

Britain is an island, and Britain's history has been closely connected with the sea. Until modern times it was as easy to travel across water as it was across land, where roads were frequently unusable. At moments of great danger Britain has been saved from danger by its surrounding seas. Britain's history and its strong national sense have been shaped by the sea.

Stonehenge is the most powerful monument of Britain's prehistory. Its purpose is still not properly understood. Those who built Stonehenge knew how to cut and move very large pieces of stone, and place horizontal stone beams across the upright pillars. They also had the authority to control large numbers of workers, and to fetch some of the stone from distant parts of Wales.

Britain's prehistory

Britain has not always been an island. It became one only after the end of the last ice age. The temperature rose and the ice cap melted, flooding the lower-lying land that is now under the North Sea and the English Channel.

The Ice Age was not just one long equally cold period. There were warmer times when the ice cap retreated, and colder periods when the ice cap reached as far south as the River Thames. Our first evidence of human life is a few stone tools, dating from one of the warmer periods, about 250,000 BC. These simple objects show that there were two different kinds of inhabitant. The earlier group made their tools from flakes of flint, similar in kind to stone tools found across the north European plain as far as Russia. The other group made tools from a central core of flint, probably the earliest method of human tool making, which spread from

A hand axe, made from flint, found at Swanscombe in north Kent.

3

Africa to Europe. Hand axes made in this way have been found widely, as far north as Yorkshire and as far west as Wales.

However, the ice advanced again and Britain became hardly habitable until another milder period, probably around 50,000 BC. During this time a new type of human being seems to have arrived, who was the ancestor of the modern British. These people looked similar to the modern British, but were probably smaller and had a life span of only about thirty years.

Around 10,000 BC, as the Ice Age drew to a close, Britain was peopled by small groups of hunters, gatherers and fishers. Few had settled homes, and they seemed to have followed herds of deer which provided them with food and clothing. By about 5000 BC Britain had finally become an island, and had also become heavily forested. For the wanderer–hunter culture this was a disaster, for the cold-loving deer and other animals on which they lived largely died out.

About 3000 BC Neolithic (or New Stone Age) people crossed the narrow sea from Europe in small round boats of bent wood covered with animal skins. Each could carry one or two persons. These people kept animals and grew corn crops, and knew how to make pottery. They probably came from either the Iberian (Spanish) peninsula or even the North African coast. They were small, dark, and long-headed people, and may be the forefathers of dark-haired inhabitants of Wales and Cornwall today. They settled in the western parts of Britain and Ireland, from Cornwall at the southwest end of Britain all the way to the far north.

These were the first of several waves of invaders before the first arrival of the Romans in 55 BC. It used to be thought that these waves of invaders marked fresh stages in British development. However, although they must have brought new ideas and methods, it is now thought that the changing pattern of Britain's prehistory was the result of local economic and social forces.

The great "public works" of this time, which needed a huge organisation of labour, tell us a little of how prehistoric Britain was developing. The earlier of these works were great "barrows", or burial mounds, made of earth or stone. Most of these barrows are found on the chalk uplands of south Britain. Today these uplands have poor soil and few trees, but they were not like that then. They were airy woodlands that could easily be cleared for farming, and as a result were the most

There were Stone Age sites from one end of Britain to the other. This stone hut, at Skara Brae, Orkney, off the north coast of Scotland, was suddenly covered by a sandstorm before 2000 BC. Unlike southern sites, where wood was used which has since rotted, Skara Brae is all stone, and the stone furniture is still there. Behind the fireplace (bottom left) there are storage shelves against the back wall. On the right is probably a stone sided bed, in which rushes or heather were placed for warmth.

easily habitable part of the countryside. Eventually, and over a very long period, these areas became overfarmed, while by 1400 BC the climate became drier, and as a result this land could no longer support many people. It is difficult today to imagine these areas, particularly the uplands of Wiltshire and Dorset, as heavily peopled areas.

Yet the monuments remain. After 3000 BC the chalkland people started building great circles of earth banks and ditches. Inside, they built wooden buildings and stone circles. These "henges", as they are called, were centres of religious, political and economic power. By far the most spectacular, both then and now, was Stonehenge, which was built in separate stages over a period of more than a thousand years. The precise purposes of Stonehenge remain a mystery, but during the second phase of building, after about 2400 BC, huge bluestones were brought to the site from south Wales. This could only have been achieved because the political authority of the area surrounding Stonehenge was recognised over a very large area, indeed probably over the whole of the British Isles. The movement of these bluestones was an extremely important event, the story of which was passed on from generation to generation. Three thousand years later, these unwritten memories were recorded in Geoffrey of Monmouth's *History of Britain*, written in 1136.

Stonehenge was almost certainly a sort of capital, to which the chiefs of other groups came from all over Britain. Certainly, earth or stone henges were built in many parts of Britain, as far as the Orkney Islands north of Scotland, and as far south as Cornwall. They seem to have been copies of the great Stonehenge in the south. In Ireland the centre of prehistoric civilisation grew around the River Boyne and at Tara in Ulster. The importance of these places in folk memory far outlasted the builders of the monuments.

After 2400 BC new groups of people arrived in southeast Britain from Europe. They were round-headed and strongly built, taller than Neolithic Britons. It is not known whether they invaded by armed force, or whether they were invited by

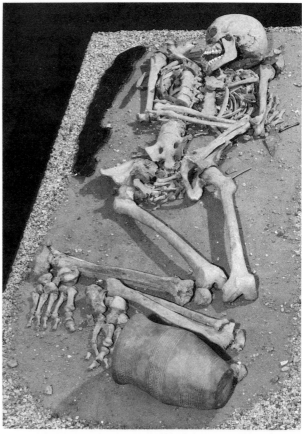

The grave of one of the "Beaker" people, at Barnack, Cambridgeshire, about 1800 BC. It contains a finely decorated pottery beaker and a copper or bronze dagger. Both items distinguished the Beaker people from the earlier inhabitants. This grave was the main burial place beneath one of a group of "barrows", or burial mounds.

Neolithic Britons because of their military or metal-working skills. Their influence was soon felt and, as a result, they became leaders of British society. Their arrival is marked by the first individual graves, furnished with pottery beakers, from which these people get their name: the "Beaker" people.

Why did people now decide to be buried separately and give up the old communal burial barrows? It is difficult to be certain, but it is thought that the old barrows were built partly to please the gods of the soil, in the hope that this would stop the chalk upland soil getting poorer. The Beaker people brought with them from Europe a new cereal, barley, which could grow almost anywhere. Perhaps they felt it was no longer necessary to please the gods of the chalk upland soil.

Maiden Castle, Dorset, is one of the largest Celtic hill-forts of the early Iron Age. Its strength can still be clearly seen, but even these fortifications were no defence against disciplined Roman troops.

A reconstructed Iron Age farm. Farms like this were established in southeast Britain from about 700 BC onwards. This may have been the main or even only building; large round huts increasingly took the place of smaller ones. "Their houses are large, round, built of planks and wickerwork, the roof being a dome of thatch," wrote the Greek philosopher Strabo. In most of Celtic Europe huts were square.

The Beaker people probably spoke an Indo-European language. They seem to have brought a single culture to the whole of Britain. They also brought skills to make bronze tools and these began to replace stone ones. But they accepted many of the old ways. Stonehenge remained the most important centre until 1300 BC. The Beaker people's richest graves were there, and they added a new circle of thirty stone columns, this time connected by stone lintels, or cross-pieces. British society continued to be centred on a number of henges across the countryside.

However, from about 1300 BC onwards the henge civilisation seems to have become less important, and was overtaken by a new form of society in southern England, that of a settled farming class. At first this farming society developed in order to feed the people at the henges, but eventually it became more important and powerful as it grew richer. The new farmers grew wealthy because they learned to enrich the soil with natural waste materials so that it did not become poor and useless. This change probably happened at about the same time that the chalk uplands were becoming drier. Family villages and fortified enclosures appeared across the landscape, in lower-lying areas as well as on the chalk hills, and the old central control of Stonehenge and the other henges was lost.

From this time, too, power seems to have shifted to the Thames valley and southeast Britain. Except for short periods, political and economic power has remained in the southeast ever since. Hill-forts replaced henges as the centres of local power, and most of these were found in the southeast, suggesting that the land successfully supported more people here than elsewhere.

There was another reason for the shift of power eastwards. A number of better-designed bronze swords have been found in the Thames valley, suggesting that the local people had more advanced metalworking skills. Many of these swords have been found in river beds, almost certainly thrown in for religious reasons. This custom may be the origin of the story of the legendary King Arthur's sword, which was given to him from out of the water and which was thrown back into the water when he died.

The Celts

Around 700 BC, another group of people began to arrive. Many of them were tall, and had fair or red hair and blue eyes. These were the Celts, who probably came from central Europe or further east, from southern Russia, and had moved slowly westwards in earlier centuries. The Celts were technically advanced. They knew how to work with iron, and could make better weapons than the people who used bronze. It is possible that they drove many of the older inhabitants westwards into Wales, Scotland and Ireland. The Celts began to control all the lowland areas of Britain, and were joined by new arrivals from the European mainland. They continued to arrive in one wave after another over the next seven hundred years.

The Celts are important in British history because they are the ancestors of many of the people in Highland Scotland, Wales, Ireland, and Cornwall today. The Iberian people of Wales and Cornwall took on the new Celtic culture. Celtic languages, which have been continuously used in some areas since that time, are still spoken. The British today are often described as Anglo-Saxon. It would be better to call them Anglo-Celt.

Our knowledge of the Celts is slight. As with previous groups of settlers, we do not even know for certain whether the Celts invaded Britain or came peacefully as a result of the lively trade with Europe from about 750 BC onwards. At first most of Celtic Britain seems to have developed in a generally similar way. But from about 500 BC trade contact with Europe declined, and regional differences between northwest and southeast Britain increased. The Celts were organised into different tribes, and tribal chiefs were chosen from each family or tribe, sometimes as the result of fighting matches between individuals, and sometimes by election.

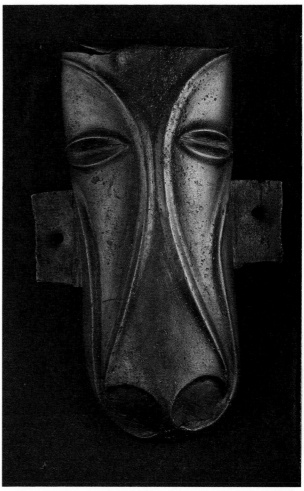

The Stanwick horse mask shows the fine artistic work of Celtic metalworkers in about AD 50. The simple lines and lack of detail have a very powerful effect.

The last Celtic arrivals from Europe were the Belgic tribes. It was natural for them to settle in the southeast of Britain, probably pushing other Celtic tribes northwards as they did so. At any rate, when Julius Caesar briefly visited Britain in 55 BC he saw that the Belgic tribes were different from the older inhabitants. "The interior is inhabited", he wrote, "by peoples who consider themselves indigenous, the coast by people who have crossed from Belgium. Nearly all of these still keep the names of the [European] tribes from which they came."

The Celtic tribes continued the same kind of agriculture as the Bronze Age people before them. But their use of iron technology and their introduction of more advanced ploughing methods made it possible for them to farm heavier soils. However, they continued to use, and build, hill-forts. The increase of these, particularly in the southeast, suggests that the Celts were highly successful farmers, growing enough food for a much larger population.

The hill-fort remained the centre for local groups. The insides of these hill-forts were filled with houses, and they became the simple economic capitals and smaller "towns" of the different tribal areas into which Britain was now divided. Today the empty hill-forts stand on lonely hilltops. Yet they remained local economic centres long after the Romans came to Britain, and long after they went.

Within living memory certain annual fairs were associated with hill-forts. For example, there was an annual September fair on the site of a Dorset hill-fort, which was used by the writer Thomas Hardy in his novel *Far from the Madding Crowd*, published in 1874.

The Celts traded across tribal borders and trade was probably important for political and social contact between the tribes. Trade with Ireland went through the island of Anglesey. The two main trade outlets eastwards to Europe were the settlements along the Thames River in the south and on the Firth of Forth in the north. It is no accident that the present-day capitals of England and Scotland stand on or near these two ancient trade centres. Much trade, both inside and beyond Britain, was conducted by river and sea. For money the Celts used iron bars, until they began to copy the Roman coins they saw used in Gaul (France).

According to the Romans, the Celtic men wore shirts and breeches (knee-length trousers), and striped or checked cloaks fastened by a pin. It is possible that the Scottish tartan and dress developed from this "striped cloak". The Celts were also "very careful about cleanliness and neatness", as one Roman wrote. "Neither man nor woman," he went on, "however poor, was seen either ragged or dirty."

The Celtic tribes were ruled over by a warrior class, of which the priests, or Druids, seem to have been particularly important members. These Druids could not read or write, but they memorised all the religious teachings, the tribal laws, history, medicine and other knowledge necessary in Celtic society. The Druids from different tribes all over Britain probably met once a year. They had no temples, but they met in sacred groves of trees, on certain hills, by rivers or by river sources. We know little of their kind of worship except that at times it included human sacrifice.

During the Celtic period women may have had more independence than they had again for hundreds of years. When the Romans invaded Britain two of the largest tribes were ruled by women who fought from their chariots. The most powerful Celt to stand up to the Romans was a woman, Boadicea. She had become queen of her tribe when her husband had died. She was tall, with long red hair, and had a frightening appearance. In AD 61 she led her tribe against the Romans. She nearly drove them from Britain, and she destroyed London, the Roman capital, before she was defeated and killed. Roman writers commented on the courage and strength of women in battle, and leave an impression of a measure of equality between the sexes among the richer Celts.

The Romans

The name "Britain" comes from the word "Pretani", the Greco-Roman word for the inhabitants of Britain. The Romans mispronounced the word and called the island "Britannia".

The Romans had invaded because the Celts of Britain were working with the Celts of Gaul against them. The British Celts were giving them food, and allowing them to hide in Britain. There was another reason. The Celts used cattle to pull their ploughs and this meant that richer, heavier land could be farmed. Under the Celts Britain had become an important food producer because of its mild climate. It now exported corn and animals, as well as hunting dogs and slaves, to the European mainland. The Romans could make use of British food for their own army fighting the Gauls.

The Romans brought the skills of reading and writing to Britain. The written word was important for spreading ideas and also for establishing power. As early as AD 80, as one Roman at the time noted, the governor Agricola "trained the sons of chiefs in the liberal arts ... the result was that the people who used to reject Latin began to use it in speech and writing. Further the wearing of our national dress came to be valued and the toga [the Roman cloak] came into fashion." While the Celtic peasantry remained illiterate and only Celtic-speaking, a number of town dwellers spoke Latin and Greek with ease, and the richer landowners in the country almost certainly used Latin. But Latin completely disappeared both in its spoken and written forms when the Anglo-Saxons invaded

Britain in the fifth century AD. Britain was probably more literate under the Romans than it was to be again until the fifteenth century.

Julius Caesar first came to Britain in 55 BC, but it was not until almost a century later, in AD 43, that a Roman army actually occupied Britain. The Romans were determined to conquer the whole island. They had little difficulty, apart from Boadicea's revolt, because they had a better trained army and because the Celtic tribes fought among themselves. The Romans considered the Celts as war-mad, "high spirited and quick for battle", a description some would still give the Scots, Irish and Welsh today.

The Romans established a Romano-British culture across the southern half of Britain, from the River Humber to the River Severn. This part of Britain was inside the empire. Beyond were the upland areas, under Roman control but not developed. These areas were watched from the towns of York, Chester and Caerleon in the western peninsula of Britain that later became known as Wales. Each of these towns was held by a Roman legion of about 7,000 men. The total Roman army in Britain was about 40,000 men.

The Romans could not conquer "Caledonia", as they called Scotland, although they spent over a century trying to do so. At last they built a strong wall along the northern border, named after the Emperor Hadrian who planned it. At the time, Hadrian's wall was simply intended to keep out raiders from the north. But it also marked the border between the two later countries, England and Scotland. Eventually, the border was established a few miles further north. Efforts to change it in later centuries did not succeed, mainly because on either side of the border an invading army found its supply line overstretched. A natural point of balance had been found.

Roman control of Britain came to an end as the empire began to collapse. The first signs were the attacks by Celts of Caledonia in AD 367. The Roman legions found it more and more difficult to stop the raiders from crossing Hadrian's wall. The same was happening on the European mainland as

Germanic groups, Saxons and Franks, began to raid the coast of Gaul. In AD 409 Rome pulled its last soldiers out of Britain and the Romano-British, the Romanised Celts, were left to fight alone against the Scots, the Irish and Saxon raiders from Germany. The following year Rome itself fell to raiders. When Britain called to Rome for help against the raiders from Saxon Germany in the mid-fifth century, no answer came.

Roman life

The most obvious characteristic of Roman Britain was its towns, which were the basis of Roman administration and civilisation. Many grew out of Celtic settlements, military camps or market centres. Broadly, there were three different kinds of town in Roman Britain, two of which were towns established by Roman charter. These were the *coloniae*, towns peopled by Roman settlers, and the *municipia*, large cities in which the whole population was given Roman citizenship. The third kind, the *civitas*, included the old Celtic tribal capitals, through which the Romans administered the Celtic population in the countryside. At first these towns had no walls. Then, probably from the end of the second century to the end of the third century AD, almost every town was given walls. At first many of these were no more than earthworks, but by AD 300 all towns had thick stone walls.

The Romans left about twenty large towns of about 5,000 inhabitants, and almost one hundred smaller ones. Many of these towns were at first army camps, and the Latin word for camp, *castra*, has remained part of many town names to this day (with the ending chester, caster or cester): Gloucester, Leicester, Doncaster, Winchester, Chester, Lancaster and many others besides. These towns were built with stone as well as wood, and had planned streets, markets and shops. Some buildings had central heating. They were connected by roads which were so well built that they survived when later roads broke up. These roads continued to be used long after the Romans left, and became the main roads of modern Britain. Six of these Roman roads met in London, a capital city of about 20,000

The reconstruction of a Roman kitchen about AD 100 shows pots and equipment. The tall pots, or amphorae, were for wine or oil. The Romans produced wine in Britain, but they also imported it from southern Europe.

people. London was twice the size of Paris, and possibly the most important trading centre of northern Europe, because southeast Britain produced so much corn for export.

Outside the towns, the biggest change during the Roman occupation was the growth of large farms, called "villas". These belonged to the richer Britons who were, like the townspeople, more Roman than Celt in their manners. Each villa had many workers. The villas were usually close to towns so that the crops could be sold easily. There was a growing difference between the rich and those who did the actual work on the land. These, and most people, still lived in the same kind of round huts and villages which the Celts had been living in four hundred years earlier, when the Romans arrived.

In some ways life in Roman Britain seems very civilised, but it was also hard for all except the richest. The bodies buried in a Roman graveyard at York show that life expectancy was low. Half the entire population died between the ages of twenty and forty, while 15 per cent died before reaching the age of twenty.

It is very difficult to be sure how many people were living in Britain when the Romans left. Probably it was as many as five million, partly because of the peace and the increased economic life which the Romans had brought to the country. The new wave of invaders changed all that.

2 The Saxon invasion

The invaders · Government and society · Christianity: the partnership of Church and state · The Vikings · Who should be king?

The invaders

The wealth of Britain by the fourth century, the result of its mild climate and centuries of peace, was a temptation to the greedy. At first the Germanic tribes only raided Britain, but after AD 430 they began to settle. The newcomers were warlike and illiterate. We owe our knowledge of this period mainly to an English monk named Bede, who lived three hundred years later. His story of events in his *Ecclesiastical History of the English People* has been proved generally correct by archaeological evidence.

Bede tells us that the invaders came from three powerful Germanic tribes, the Saxons, Angles and Jutes. The Jutes settled mainly in Kent and along the south coast, and were soon considered no different from the Angles and Saxons. The Angles settled in the east, and also in the north Midlands, while the Saxons settled between the Jutes and the Angles in a band of land from the Thames Estuary westwards. The Anglo-Saxon migrations gave the larger part of Britain its new name, England, "the land of the Angles".

The British Celts fought the raiders and settlers from Germany as well as they could. However, during the next hundred years they were slowly pushed westwards until by 570 they were forced west of Gloucester. Finally most were driven into the mountains in the far west, which the Saxons called "Weallas", or "Wales", meaning "the land of the foreigners". Some Celts were driven into Cornwall, where they later accepted the rule of Saxon lords. In the north, other Celts were driven into the lowlands of the country which became

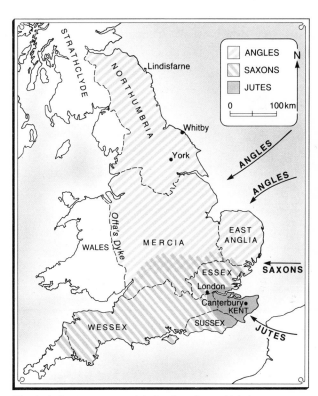

The Anglo-Saxon invasions and the kingdoms they established.

known as Scotland. Some Celts stayed behind, and many became slaves of the Saxons. Hardly anything is left of Celtic language or culture in England, except for the names of some rivers, Thames, Mersey, Severn and Avon, and two large cities, London and Leeds.

The strength of Anglo-Saxon culture is obvious even today. Days of the week were named after Germanic gods: Tig (Tuesday), Wodin (Wednesday), Thor (Thursday), Frei (Friday). New place-names appeared on the map. The first of

11

these show that the earliest Saxon villages, like the Celtic ones, were family villages. The ending -ing meant folk or family, thus "Reading" is the place of the family of Rada, "Hastings" of the family of Hasta. *Ham* means farm, *ton* means settlement. Birmingham, Nottingham or Southampton, for example, are Saxon place-names. Because the Anglo-Saxon kings often established settlements, Kingston is a frequent place-name.

The Anglo-Saxons established a number of kingdoms, some of which still exist in county or regional names to this day: Essex (East Saxons), Sussex (South Saxons), Wessex (West Saxons), Middlesex (probably a kingdom of Middle Saxons), East Anglia (East Angles). By the middle of the seventh century the three largest kingdoms, those of Northumbria, Mercia and Wessex, were the most powerful.

Left: A silver penny showing Offa, king of Mercia (AD 757–896). Offa was more powerful than any of the other Anglo-Saxon kings of his time or before him. His coins were of a higher quality than any coins used since the departure of the Romans four hundred years earlier.

Right: A gold coin of King Offa, a direct copy of an Arab dinar of the year AD 774. Most of it is in Arabic, but on one side it also has "OFFA REX". It tells us that the Anglo-Saxons of Britain were well aware of a more advanced economic system in the distant Arab empire, and also that even as far away as Britain and northern Europe, Arab-type gold coins were more trusted than any others. It shows how great were the distances covered by international trade at this time.

It was not until a century later that one of these kings, King Offa of Mercia (757–96), claimed "kingship of the English". He had good reason to do so. He was powerful enough to employ thousands of men to build a huge dyke, or earth wall, the length of the Welsh border to keep out the troublesome Celts. But although he was the most powerful king of his time, he did not control all of England.

The power of Mercia did not survive after Offa's death. At that time, a king's power depended on the personal loyalty of his followers. After his death the next king had to work hard to rebuild these personal feelings of loyalty. Most people still believed, as the Celts had done, that a man's first

duty was to his own family. However, things were changing. The Saxon kings began to replace loyalty to family with loyalty to lord and king.

Government and society

The Saxons created institutions which made the English state strong for the next 500 years. One of these institutions was the King's Council, called the *Witan*. The Witan probably grew out of informal groups of senior warriors and churchmen to whom kings like Offa had turned for advice or support on difficult matters. By the tenth century the Witan was a formal body, issuing laws and charters. It was not at all democratic, and the king could decide to ignore the Witan's advice. But he knew that it might be dangerous to do so. For the Witan's authority was based on its right to choose kings, and to agree the use of the king's laws. Without its support the king's own authority was in danger. The Witan established a system which remained an important part of the king's method of government. Even today, the king or queen has a *Privy Council*, a group of advisers on the affairs of state.

The Saxons divided the land into new administrative areas, based on *shires*, or counties. These shires, established by the end of the tenth century, remained almost exactly the same for a thousand years. "Shire" is the Saxon word, "county" the Norman one, but both are still used. (In 1974 the counties were reorganised, but the new system is very like the old one.) Over each shire was appointed a *shire reeve*, the king's local administrator. In time his name became shortened to "sheriff".

Anglo-Saxon technology changed the shape of English agriculture. The Celts had kept small, square fields which were well suited to the light plough they used, drawn either by an animal or two people. This plough could turn corners easily. The Anglo-Saxons introduced a far heavier plough which was better able to plough in long straight lines across the field. It was particularly useful for cultivating heavier soils. But it required six or eight oxen to pull it, and it was difficult to turn. This heavier plough led to changes in land ownership and organisation. In order to make the best use of

Reconstruction of an Anglo-Saxon village. Each house had probably only one room, with a wooden floor with a pit beneath it. The pit may have been used for storage, but more probably to keep the house off the damp ground. Each village had its lord. The word "lord" means "loaf ward" or "bread keeper", while "lady" means "loaf kneader" or "bread maker", a reminder that the basis of Saxon society was farming. The duty of the village head, or lord, was to protect the farm and its produce.

village land, it was divided into two or three very large fields. These were then divided again into long thin strips. Each family had a number of strips in each of these fields, amounting probably to a family "holding" of twenty or so acres. Ploughing these long thin strips was easier because it avoided the problem of turning. Few individual families could afford to keep a team of oxen, and these had to be shared on a co-operative basis.

One of these fields would be used for planting spring crops, and another for autumn crops. The third area would be left to rest for a year, and with the other areas after harvest, would be used as common land for animals to feed on. This Anglo-Saxon pattern, which became more and more common, was the basis of English agriculture for a thousand years, until the eighteenth century.

It needs only a moment's thought to recognise that the fair division of land and of teams of oxen, and the sensible management of village land shared out between families, meant that villagers had to work more closely together than they had ever done before.

The Saxons settled previously unfarmed areas. They cut down many forested areas in valleys to farm the richer lowland soil, and they began to drain the wet land. As a result, almost all the villages which appear on eighteenth-century maps already existed by the eleventh century.

In each district was a "manor" or large house. This was a simple building where local villagers came to pay taxes, where justice was administered, and where men met together to join the Anglo-Saxon army, the *fyrd*. The lord of the manor had to organise all this, and make sure village land was properly shared. It was the beginning of the manorial system which reached its fullest development under the Normans.

At first the lords, or *aldermen*, were simply local officials. But by the beginning of the eleventh century they were warlords, and were often called by a new Danish name, *earl*. Both words, alderman and earl, remain with us today: aldermen are elected officers in local government, and earls are high ranking nobles. It was the beginning of a class system, made up of king, lords, soldiers and workers on the land. One other important class developed during the Saxon period, the men of learning. These came from the Christian Church.

Christianity: the partnership of Church and state

We cannot know how or when Christianity first reached Britain, but it was certainly well before Christianity was accepted by the Roman Emperor Constantine in the early fourth century AD. In the last hundred years of Roman government Christianity became firmly established across Britain, both in Roman-controlled areas and beyond. However, the Anglo-Saxons belonged to an older Germanic religion, and they drove the Celts into the west and north. In the Celtic areas Christianity continued to spread, bringing paganism to an end. The map of Wales shows a number of place-names beginning or ending with *llan*, meaning the site of a small Celtic monastery around which a village or town grew.

In 597 Pope Gregory the Great sent a monk, Augustine, to re-establish Christianity in England. He went to Canterbury, the capital of the king of Kent. He did so because the king's wife came from

13

The opening page of St Luke's Gospel, made at the Northumbrian island of Lindisfarne, about AD 698. In his History, Bede wrote how one man told the pagan Northumbrian king, "when you are sitting in winter with your lords in the feasting hall, with a good fire to warm and light it, a sparrow flies in from the storms of rain and snow outside. It flies in at one door, across the lighted room and out through the other door into the darkness and storms outside. In the same way man comes into the light for a short time, but of what came before, or what is to follow, man is ignorant. If this new teaching tells us something more certain, it seems worth following." Christianity gave the Anglo-Saxon world new certainty.

Europe and was already Christian. Augustine became the first Archbishop of Canterbury in 601. He was very successful. Several ruling families in England accepted Christianity. But Augustine and his group of monks made little progress with the ordinary people. This was partly because Augustine was interested in establishing Christian authority, and that meant bringing rulers to the new faith.

It was the Celtic Church which brought Christianity to the ordinary people of Britain. The Celtic bishops went out from their monasteries of Wales, Ireland and Scotland, walking from village to village teaching Christianity. In spite of the differences between Anglo-Saxons and Celts, these bishops seem to have been readily accepted in Anglo-Saxon areas. The bishops from the Roman Church lived at the courts of the kings, which they made centres of Church power across England. The two Christian Churches, Celtic and Roman, could hardly have been more different in character. One was most interested in the hearts of ordinary people, the other was interested in authority and organisation. The competition between the Celtic and Roman Churches reached a crisis because they disagreed over the date of Easter. In 663 at the Synod (meeting) of Whitby the king of Northumbria decided to support the Roman Church. The Celtic Church retreated as Rome extended its authority over all Christians, even in Celtic parts of the island.

England had become Christian very quickly. By 660 only Sussex and the Isle of Wight had not accepted the new faith. Twenty years later, English teachers returned to the lands from which the Anglo-Saxons had come, bringing Christianity to much of Germany.

Saxon kings helped the Church to grow, but the Church also increased the power of kings. Bishops gave kings their support, which made it harder for royal power to be questioned. Kings had "God's approval". The value of Church approval was all the greater because of the uncertainty of the royal succession. An eldest son did not automatically become king, as kings were chosen from among the members of the royal family, and any member who had enough soldiers might try for the throne. In addition, at a time when one king might try to conquer a neighbouring kingdom, he would probably have a son to whom he would wish to pass this enlarged kingdom when he died. And so when King Offa arranged for his son to be crowned as his successor, he made sure that this was done at a Christian ceremony led by a bishop. It was good political propaganda, because it suggested that kings were chosen not only by people but also by God.

There were other ways in which the Church increased the power of the English state. It established monasteries, or *minsters*, for example

Westminster, which were places of learning and education. These monasteries trained the men who could read and write, so that they had the necessary skills for the growth of royal and Church authority. The king who made most use of the Church was Alfred, the great king who ruled Wessex from 871–899. He used the literate men of the Church to help establish a system of law, to educate the people and to write down important matters. He started the *Anglo-Saxon Chronicle*, the most important source, together with Bede's *Ecclesiastical History of the English People*, for understanding the period.

During the next hundred years, laws were made on a large number of matters. By the eleventh century royal authority probably went wider and deeper in England than in any other European country.

This process gave power into the hands of those who could read and write, and in this way class divisions were increased. The power of landlords, who had been given land by the king, was increased because their names were written down. Peasants, who could neither read nor write, could lose their traditional rights to their land, because their rights were not registered.

The Anglo-Saxon kings also preferred the Roman Church to the Celtic Church for economic reasons. Villages and towns grew around the monasteries and increased local trade. Many bishops and monks in England were from the Frankish lands (France and Germany) and elsewhere. They were invited by English rulers who wished to benefit from closer Church and economic contact with Europe. Most of these bishops and monks seem to have come from churches or monasteries along Europe's vital trade routes. In this way close contact with many parts of Europe was encouraged. In addition they all used Latin, the written language of Rome, and this encouraged English trade with the continent. Increased literacy itself helped trade. Anglo-Saxon England became well known in Europe for its exports of woollen goods, cheese, hunting dogs, pottery and metal goods. It imported wine, fish, pepper, jewellery and wheel-made pottery.

The Vikings

Towards the end of the eighth century new raiders were tempted by Britain's wealth. These were the Vikings, a word which probably means either "pirates" or "the people of the sea inlets", and they came from Norway and Denmark. Like the Anglo-Saxons they only raided at first. They burnt churches and monasteries along the east, north and west coasts of Britain and Ireland. London was itself raided in 842.

In 865 the Vikings invaded Britain once it was clear that the quarrelling Anglo-Saxon kingdoms could not keep them out. This time they came to conquer and to settle. The Vikings quickly accepted Christianity and did not disturb the local population. By 875 only King Alfred in the west of Wessex held out against the Vikings, who had already taken most of England. After some serious defeats Alfred won a decisive battle in 878, and eight years later he captured London. He was strong enough to make a treaty with the Vikings.

The Viking invasions and the areas they brought under their control.

The story of the battle of Hastings and the Norman conquest of Saxon England is told in the Bayeux tapestry cartoon. "Harold the king is killed" says the Latin writing, and beneath it stands a man with an arrow in his eye, believed to be King Harold. In the picture strip below the main scene, men are seen stealing the clothing from the dead and wounded, a common practice on battlefields through the centuries.

The Oseberg Viking ship, made in about AD 800, was 21 metres long and carried about 35 men. Although this particular ship was probably only used along the coast, ships of similar size were used to invade Britain. Their design was brilliant. When an exact copy of similar ship was used to cross the Atlantic to America in 1893, its captain wrote, "the finest merchant ships of our day . . . have practically the same type of bottom as the Viking ships."

Viking rule was recognised in the east and north of England. It was called the Danelaw, the land where the law of the Danes ruled. In the rest of the country Alfred was recognised as king. During his struggle against the Danes, he had built walled settlements to keep them out. These were called *burghs*. They became prosperous market towns, and the word, now usually spelt *borough*, is one of the commonest endings to place names, as well as the name of the unit of municipal or town administration today.

Who should be king?

By 950 England seemed rich and peaceful again after the troubles of the Viking invasion. But soon afterwards the Danish Vikings started raiding westwards. The Saxon king, Ethelred, decided to pay the Vikings to stay away. To find the money he set a tax on all his people, called *Danegeld*, or "Danish money". It was the beginning of a regular tax system of the people which would provide the money for armies. The effects of this tax were most heavily felt by the ordinary villagers, because they had to provide enough money for their village landlord to pay Danegeld.

When Ethelred died Cnut (or Canute), the leader of the Danish Vikings, controlled much of England. He became king for the simple reason that the royal council, the Witan, and everyone else, feared disorder. Rule by a Danish king was far better than rule by no one at all. Cnut died in 1035, and his son died shortly after, in 1040. The Witan chose Edward, one of Saxon Ethelred's sons, to be king.

Edward, known as "the Confessor", was more interested in the Church than in kingship. Church building had been going on for over a century, and he encouraged it. By the time Edward died there was a church in almost every village. The pattern of the English village, with its manor house and church, dates from this time. Edward started a new church fit for a king at Westminster, just outside the city of London. In fact Westminster Abbey was a Norman, not a Saxon building, because he had spent almost all his life in Normandy, and his mother was a daughter of the duke of Normandy. As their name suggests, the Normans were people from the north. They were the children and grandchildren of Vikings who had captured, and settled in, northern France. They had soon become

French in their language and Christian in their religion. But they were still well known for their fighting skills.

Edward only lived until 1066, when he died without an obvious heir. The question of who should follow him as king was one of the most important in English history. Edward had brought many Normans to his English court from France. These Normans were not liked by the more powerful Saxon nobles, particularly by the most powerful family of Wessex, the Godwinsons. It was a Godwinson, Harold, whom the Witan chose to be the next king of England. Harold had already shown his bravery and ability. He had no royal blood, but he seemed a good choice for the throne of England.

Harold's right to the English throne was challenged by Duke William of Normandy. William had two claims to the English throne. His first claim was that King Edward had promised it to him. The second claim was that Harold, who had visited William in 1064 or 1065, had promised William that he, Harold, would not try to take the throne for himself. Harold did not deny this second claim, but said that he had been forced to make the promise, and that because it was made unwillingly he was not tied by it.

Harold was faced by two dangers, one in the south and one in the north. The Danish Vikings had not given up their claim to the English throne. In 1066 Harold had to march north into Yorkshire to defeat the Danes. No sooner had he defeated them than he learnt that William had landed in England with an army. His men were tired, but they had no time to rest. They marched south as fast as possible.

Harold decided not to wait for the whole Saxon army, the *fyrd*, to gather because William's army was small. He thought he could beat them with the men who had done so well against the Danes. However, the Norman soldiers were better armed, better organised, and were mounted on horses. If he had waited, Harold might have won. But he was defeated and killed in battle near Hastings.

William marched to London, which quickly gave in when he began to burn villages outside the city. He was crowned king of England in Edward's new church of Westminster Abbey on Christmas Day, 1066. A new period had begun.

3   The Celtic kingdoms
Wales · Ireland · Scotland

England has always played the most powerful part in the history of the British Isles. However, the other three countries, Wales, Ireland and Scotland, have a different history. Until recently few historians looked at British history except from an English point of view. But the stories of Wales, Ireland and Scotland are also important, because their people still feel different from the Anglo-Saxon English. The experience of the Welsh, Irish and Scots helps to explain the feeling they have today.

Wales

By the eighth century most of the Celts had been driven into the Welsh peninsula. They were kept out of England by Offa's Dyke, the huge earth wall built in AD 779. These Celts, called Welsh by the Anglo-Saxons, called themselves *cymry*, "fellow countrymen".

Because Wales is a mountainous country, the *cymry* could only live in the crowded valleys. The rest of the land was rocky and too poor for anything except keeping animals. For this reason the population remained small. It only grew to over half a million in the eighteenth century. Life was hard and so was the behaviour of the people. Slavery was common, as it had been all through Celtic Britain.

Society was based on family groupings, each of which owned one or more village or farm settlement. One by one in each group a strong leader made himself king. These men must have been tribal chiefs to begin with, who later managed to become overlords over neighbouring family groups. Each of these kings tried to conquer the others, and the idea of a high, or senior, king developed.

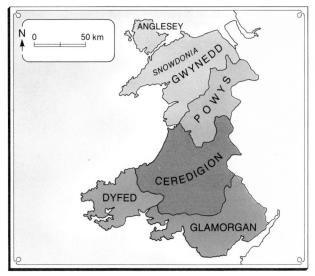

Wales and its Celtic kingdoms.

The early kings travelled around their kingdoms to remind the people of their control. They travelled with their hungry followers and soldiers. The ordinary people ran away into the hills and woods when the king's men approached their village.

Life was dangerous, treacherous and bloody. In 1043 the king of Glamorgan died of old age. It was an unusual event, because between 949 and 1066 no less than thirty-five Welsh rulers died violently, usually killed by a *cymry*, a fellow countryman.

In 1039 Gruffydd ap (son of) Llewelyn was the first Welsh high king strong enough to rule over all Wales. He was also the last, and in order to remain in control he spent almost the whole of his reign fighting his enemies. Like many other Welsh rulers, Gruffydd was killed by a *cymry* while defending Wales against the Saxons. Welsh kings after him were able to rule only after they had promised loyalty to Edward the Confessor, king of England. The story of an independent and united Wales was over almost as soon as it had begun.

Ireland

Ireland was never invaded by either the Romans or the Anglo-Saxons. It was a land of monasteries and had a flourishing Celtic culture. As in Wales, people were known by the family grouping they belonged to. Outside their tribe they had no protection and no name of their own. They had only the name of their tribe. The kings in this tribal society were chosen by election. The idea was that the strongest man should lead. In fact the system led to continuous challenges.

Five kingdoms grew up in Ireland: Ulster in the north, Munster in the southwest, Leinster in the southeast, Connaught in the west, with Tara as the seat of the high kings of Ireland.

Christianity came to Ireland in about AD 430. The beginning of Ireland's history dates from that time, because for the first time there were people who could write down events. The message of Christianity was spread in Ireland by a British slave, Patrick, who became the "patron saint" of Ireland. Christianity brought writing, which weakened the position of the Druids, who depended on memory and the spoken word. Christian monasteries grew up, frequently along the coast.

This period is often called Ireland's "golden age". Invaders were unknown and culture flowered. But it is also true that the five kingdoms were often at war, each trying to gain advantage over the other, often with great cruelty.

A page from the Book of Kells, the finest surviving Irish Celtic manuscript.

The round tower of Devenish is one of only two that still stand at Celtic monastic sites in Ulster, Ireland. This one was built in the twelfth century AD. The entrance is about three metres above ground level, and had a ladder that could be pulled in so that enemies could not enter. This design may well have been introduced after the Viking raids began in the ninth century.

Ireland's Celtic kingdoms.

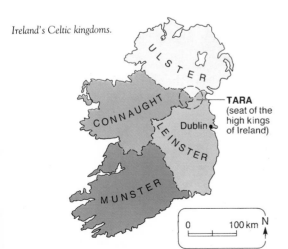

ULSTER

CONNAUGHT

LEINSTER

TARA (seat of the high kings of Ireland)

Dublin

MUNSTER

0   100 km   N

This "golden age" suddenly ended with the arrival of Viking raiders, who stole all that the monasteries had. Very little was left except the stone memorials that the Vikings could not carry away.

The Vikings, who traded with Constantinople (now Istanbul), Italy, and with central Russia, brought fresh economic and political action into Irish life. Viking raids forced the Irish to unite. In 859 Ireland chose its first high king, but it was not an effective solution because of the quarrels that took place each time a new high king was chosen. Viking trade led to the first towns and ports. For the Celts, who had always lived in small settlements, these were revolutionary. Dublin, Ireland's future capital, was founded by the Vikings.

As an effective method of rule the high kingship of Ireland lasted only twelve years, from 1002 to 1014, while Ireland was ruled by Brian Boru. He is still looked back on as Ireland's greatest ruler. He tried to create one single Ireland, and encouraged the growth of organisation – in the Church, in administration, and in learning.

Brian Boru died in battle against the Vikings. One of the five Irish kings, the king of Leinster, fought on the Vikings' side. Just over a century later another king of Leinster invited the Normans of England to help him against his high king. This gave the Normans the excuse they wanted to enlarge their kingdom.

Scotland

As a result of its geography, Scotland has two different societies. In the centre of Scotland mountains stretch to the far north and across to the west, beyond which lie many islands. To the east and to the south the lowland hills are gentler, and much of the countryside is like England, rich, welcoming and easy to farm. North of the "Highland Line", as the division between highland and lowland is called, people stayed tied to their own family groups. South and east of this line society was more easily influenced by the changes taking place in England.

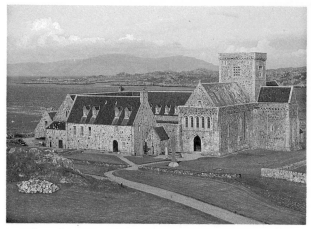

Iona, the western Scottish island on which St Columba established his abbey in AD 563 when he came Ireland. From Iona Columba sent his missionaries to bring Christianity to the Scots. The present cathedral was built in about 1500.

Scotland was populated by four separate groups of people. The main group, the Picts, lived mostly in the north and northeast. They spoke Celtic as well as another, probably older, language completely unconnected with any known language today, and they seem to have been the earliest inhabitants of the land. The Picts were different from the Celts because they inherited their rights, their names and property from their mothers, not from their fathers.

The non-Pictish inhabitants were mainly Scots. The Scots were Celtic settlers who had started to move into the western Highlands from Ireland in the fourth century.

In 843 the Pictish and Scottish kingdoms were united under a Scottish king, who could also probably claim the Pictish throne through his mother, in this way obeying both Scottish and Pictish rules of kingship.

The third group were the Britons, who inhabited the Lowlands, and had been part of the Romano-British world. (The name of their kingdom, Strathclyde, was used again in the county reorganisation of 1974.) They had probably given up their old tribal way of life by the sixth century. Finally, there were Angles from Northumbria who had pushed northwards into the Scottish Lowlands.

Unity between Picts, Scots and Britons was achieved for several reasons. They all shared a

Scotland: its early peoples.

common Celtic culture, language and background. Their economy mainly depended on keeping animals. These animals were owned by the tribe as a whole, and for this reason land was also held by tribes, not by individual people. The common economic system increased their feeling of belonging to the same kind of society and the feeling of difference from the agricultural Lowlands. The sense of common culture may have been increased by marriage alliances between tribes. This idea of common landholding remained strong until the tribes of Scotland, called "clans", collapsed in the eighteenth century.

The spread of Celtic Christianity also helped to unite the people. The first Christian mission to Scotland had come to southwest Scotland in about AD 400. Later, in 563, Columba, known as the "Dove of the Church", came from Ireland. Through his work both Highland Scots and Picts were brought to Christianity. He even, so it is said, defeated a monster in Loch Ness, the first mention of this famous creature. By the time of the Synod of Whitby in 663, the Picts, Scots and Britons had all been brought closer together by Christianity.

The Angles were very different from the Celts. They had arrived in Britain in family groups, but they soon began to accept authority from people outside their own family. This was partly due to

their way of life. Although they kept some animals, they spent more time growing crops. This meant that land was held by individual people, each man working in his own field. Land was distributed for farming by the local lord. This system encouraged the Angles of Scotland to develop a non-tribal system of control, as the people of England further south were doing. This increased their feeling of difference from the Celtic tribal Highlanders further north.

Finally, as in Ireland and in Wales, foreign invaders increased the speed of political change. Vikings attacked the coastal areas of Scotland, and they settled on many of the islands, Shetland, the Orkneys, the Hebrides, and the Isle of Man southwest of Scotland. In order to resist them, Picts and Scots fought together against the enemy raiders and settlers. When they could not push them out of the islands and coastal areas, they had to deal with them politically. At first the Vikings, or "Norsemen", still served the king of Norway. But communications with Norway were difficult. Slowly the earls of Orkney and other areas found it easier to accept the king of Scots as their overlord, rather than the more distant king of Norway.

However, as the Welsh had also discovered, the English were a greater danger than the Vikings. In 934 the Scots were seriously defeated by a Wessex army pushing northwards. The Scots decided to seek the friendship of the English, because of the likely losses from war. England was obviously stronger than Scotland but, luckily for the Scots, both the north of England and Scotland were difficult to control from London. The Scots hoped that if they were reasonably peaceful the Sassenachs, as they called the Saxons (and still call the English), would leave them alone.

Scotland remained a difficult country to rule even from its capital, Edinburgh. Anyone looking at a map of Scotland can immediately see that control of the Highlands and islands was a great problem. Travel was often impossible in winter, and slow and difficult in summer. It was easy for a clan chief or noble to throw off the rule of the king.

The early Middle Ages

4 Conquest and feudal rule
*The Norman Conquest · Feudalism · Kingship: a family business ·
Magna Carta and the decline of feudalism*

The Norman Conquest

William the Conqueror's coronation did not go as planned. When the people shouted "God Save the King" the nervous Norman guards at Westminster Abbey thought they were going to attack William. In their fear they set fire to nearby houses and the coronation ceremony ended in disorder.

Although William was now crowned king, his conquest had only just begun, and the fighting lasted for another five years. There was an Anglo-Saxon rebellion against the Normans every year until 1070. The small Norman army marched from village to village, destroying places it could not control, and building forts to guard others. It was a true army of occupation for at least twenty years. The north was particularly hard to control, and the Norman army had no mercy. When the Saxons fought back, the Normans burnt, destroyed and killed. Between Durham and York not a single house was left standing, and it took a century for the north to recover.

Few Saxon lords kept their lands and those who did were the very small number who had accepted William immediately. All the others lost everything. By 1086, twenty years after the arrival of the Normans, only two of the greater landlords

An argument between King Henry II and his archbishop, Thomas Becket. Behind Becket stand two knights, probably those who killed him to please Henry. The picture illustrates the struggle between Church and state during the early Middle Ages. The Church controlled money, land (including towns and feudal estates), and men. As a result, the kings of England had to be very careful in their dealings with the Church. They tried to prevent any increase in Church power, and tried to appoint bishops who would be more loyal to the king than to the Church. Becket died because he tried to prevent the king from gaining more control of Church affairs.

and only two bishops were Saxon. William gave the Saxon lands to his Norman nobles. After each English rebellion there was more land to give away. His army included Norman and other French land seekers. Over 4,000 Saxon landlords were replaced by 200 Norman ones.

Feudalism

William was careful in the way he gave land to his nobles. The king of France was less powerful than many of the great landlords, of whom William was the outstanding example. In England, as each new area of land was captured, William gave parts of it as a reward to his captains. This meant that they held separate small pieces of land in different parts of the country so that no noble could easily or quickly gather his fighting men to rebel. William only gave some of his nobles larger estates along the troublesome borders with Wales and Scotland. At the same time he kept enough land for himself to make sure he was much stronger than his nobles. Of all the farmland of England he gave half to the Norman nobles, a quarter to the Church, and kept a fifth himself. He kept the Saxon system of sheriffs, and used these as a balance to local nobles. As a result England was different from the rest of Europe because it had one powerful family, instead of a large number of powerful nobles. William, and the kings after him, thought of England as their personal property.

William organised his English kingdom according to the feudal system which had already begun to develop in England before his arrival. The word

Castle Rising in Norfolk, a fine example of the stone-built keeps the Normans built in the early twelfth century. These replaced the earlier Norman "motte and bailey" castles, which were earth mounds surrounded by a wooden fence or pallisade. A stone-built keep of the new kind was extremely difficult to capture, except by surprise. Keeps of this kind had a well, providing fresh water for a long siege.

The great hall in Castle Headingham, built in 1140, gives an idea of the inside of a Norman castle. The floor was covered with rushes or reeds, cut from a nearby marsh or wetland area. The walls were decorated with woven woollen embroidered hangings, for which England was famous. the furniture is of a much later date. In Norman times there was probably a large but simple table and chair for the lord of the castle. Others sat on benches, or might have stood for meals.

"feudalism" comes from the French word *feu*, which the Normans used to refer to land held in return for duty or service to a lord. The basis of feudal society was the holding of land, and its main purpose was economic. The central idea was that all land was owned by the king but it was held by others, called "vassals", in return for services and goods. The king gave large estates to his main nobles in return for a promise to serve him in war for up to forty days. The nobles also had to give him part of the produce of the land. The greater nobles gave part of their lands to lesser nobles, knights, and other "freemen". Some freemen paid for the land by doing military service, while others paid rent. The noble kept "serfs" to work on his own land. These were not free to leave the estate, and were often little better than slaves.

There were two basic principles to feudalism: every man had a lord, and every lord had land. The king was connected through this "chain" of people to the lowest man in the country. At each level a man had to promise loyalty and service to his lord. This promise was usually made with the lord sitting on his chair and his vassal kneeling before him, his hands placed between those of his lord. This was

A thirteenth-century knight pays homage. The nobility of Britain still pay homage to the sovereign during the coronation ceremony. Ever since the Middle Ages, west European Christians have used the feudal homage position when praying, a reminder of their relationship to God, their lord and protector.

called "homage", and has remained part of the coronation ceremony of British kings and queens until now. On the other hand, each lord had responsibilities to his vassals. He had to give them land and protection.

When a noble died his son usually took over his estate. But first he had to receive permission from the king and make a special payment. If he was still a child the king would often take the produce of the estate until the boy was old enough to look after the estate himself. In this way the king could benefit from the death of a noble. If all the noble's family died the land went back to the king, who would be expected to give it to another deserving noble. But the king often kept the land for some years, using its wealth, before giving it to another noble.

If the king did not give the nobles land they would not fight for him. Between 1066 and the mid-fourteenth century there were only thirty years of complete peace. So feudal duties were extremely important. The king had to make sure he had enough satisfied nobles who would be willing to fight for him.

William gave out land all over England to his nobles. By 1086 he wanted to know exactly who owned which piece of land, and how much it was worth. He needed this information so that he could plan his economy, find out how much was produced and how much he could ask in tax. He therefore sent a team of people all through England to make a complete economic survey. His men asked all kinds of questions at each settlement: How much land was there? Who owned it? How much was it worth? How many families, ploughs and sheep were there? And so on. This survey was the only one of its kind in Europe. Not surprisingly, it was most unpopular with the people, because they felt they could not escape from its findings. It so reminded them of the paintings of the Day of Judgement, or "doom", on the walls of their churches that they called it the "Domesday" Book. The name stuck. The Domesday Book still exists, and gives us an extraordinary amount of information about England at this time.

Kingship: a family business

To understand the idea of kingship and lordship in the early Middle Ages it is important to realise that at this time there was little or no idea of nationalism. William controlled two large areas: Normandy, which he had been given by his father, and England, which he had won in war. Both were personal possessions, and it did not matter to the rulers that the ordinary people of one place were English while those of another were French. To William the important difference between Normandy and England was that as duke of Normandy he had to recognise the king of France as his lord, whereas in England he was king with no lord above him.

When William died, in 1087, he left the Duchy of Normandy to his elder son, Robert. He gave England to his second son, William, known as "Rufus" (Latin for red) because of his red hair and red face. When Robert went to fight the Muslims in the Holy Land, he left William II (Rufus) in charge of Normandy. After all, the management of Normandy and England was a family business.

William Rufus died in a hunting accident in 1100, shot dead by an arrow. He had not married, and therefore had no son to take the crown. At the time of William's death, Robert was on his way home to Normandy from the Holy Land. Their younger brother, Henry, knew that if he wanted the English crown he would have to act very quickly. He had been with William at the time of the accident. He rode to Winchester and took charge of the king's treasury. He then rode to Westminster, where he was crowned king three days later. Robert was very angry and prepared to invade. But it took him a year to organise an army.

The Norman nobles in England had to choose between Henry and Robert. This was not easy because most of them held land in Normandy too. In the end they chose Henry because he was in London, with the crown already on his head. Robert's invasion was a failure and he accepted payment to return to Normandy. But Henry wanted more. He knew that many of his nobles would willingly follow him to Normandy so that they

Henry II's empire.

Within the map legend:

lands inherited from his father, Geoffrey Plantagenet, count of Anjou

lands inherited from his mother, Queen Matilda of England

lands gained by his marriage to Eleanor of Aquitaine

lands gained by his son Geoffrey's marriage to Constance of Brittany

lands belonging to, and directly ruled by, the French king

lands which recognised the French king as overlord

boundary of Henry II's French lands

could win back their Norman lands. In 1106 Henry invaded Normandy and captured Robert. Normandy and England were reunited under one ruler.

Henry I's most important aim was to pass on both Normandy and England to his successor. He spent the rest of his life fighting to keep Normandy from other French nobles who tried to take it. But in 1120 Henry's only son was drowned at sea.

During the next fifteen years Henry hoped for another son but finally accepted that his daughter, Matilda, would follow him. Henry had married Matilda to another great noble in France, Geoffrey Plantagenet. Geoffrey was heir to Anjou, a large and important area southwest of Normandy. Henry hoped that the family lands would be made larger by this marriage. He made all the nobles promise to accept Matilda when he died. But then Henry himself quarrelled publicly with Matilda's husband, and died soon after. This left the succession in question.

At the time both the possible heirs to Henry were on their own estates. Matilda was with her husband in Anjou and Henry's nephew, Stephen of Blois, was in Boulogne, only a day's journey by sea from England. As Henry had done before him, Stephen raced to England to claim the crown. Also as before, the nobles in England had to choose between Stephen, who was in England, and Matilda, who had quarrelled with her father and who was still in France. Most chose Stephen, who seems to have been good at fighting but little else. He was described at the time as "of outstanding skill in arms, but in other things almost an idiot, except that he was more inclined towards evil." Only a few nobles supported Matilda's claim.

Matilda invaded England four years later. Her fight with Stephen led to a terrible civil war in which villages were destroyed and many people were killed. Neither side could win, and finally in 1153 Matilda and Stephen agreed that Stephen could keep the throne but only if Matilda's son, Henry, could succeed him. Fortunately for England, Stephen died the following year, and the family possessions of England and the lands in France were united under a king accepted by everyone. It took years for England to recover from the civil war. As someone wrote at the time, "For nineteen long winters, God and his angels slept." This kind of disorder and destruction was common in Europe, but it was shocking in England because people were used to the rule of law and order.

Henry II was the first unquestioned ruler of the English throne for a hundred years. He destroyed the castles which many nobles had built without royal permission during Stephen's reign, and made sure that they lived in manor houses that were undefended. The manor again became the centre of local life and administration.

Henry II was ruler of far more land than any previous king. As lord of Anjou he added his father's lands to the family empire. After his marriage to Eleanor of Aquitaine he also ruled the lands south of Anjou. Henry II's empire stretched from the Scottish border to the Pyrenees.

Four kings of the early Middle Ages: (top row) Henry II, Richard I, (bottom row) John and Henry III. Richard's shield carries the badge of the English kings. The three gold lions (called "leopards" in heraldic language) on a red field still form two of the four "quarters" of the Royal Standard or shield today.

England provided most of Henry's wealth, but the heart of his empire lay in Anjou. And although Henry recognised the king of France as the overlord of all his French lands, he actually controlled a greater area than the king of France. Many of Henry's nobles held land on both sides of the English channel.

However, Henry quarrelled with his beautiful and powerful wife, and his sons, Richard and John, took Eleanor's side. It may seem surprising that Richard and John fought against their own father. But in fact they were doing their duty to the king of France, their feudal overlord, in payment for the lands they held from him. In 1189 Henry died a broken man, disappointed and defeated by his sons and by the French king.

Henry was followed by his rebellious son, Richard. Richard I has always been one of England's most popular kings, although he spent hardly any time in England. He was brave, and a good soldier, but his nickname *Coeur de Lion*, "lionheart", shows that his culture, like that of the kings before him, was French. Richard was everyone's idea of the perfect feudal king. He went to the Holy Land to make war on the Muslims and he fought with skill, courage and honour.

On his way back from the Holy Land Richard was captured by the duke of Austria, with whom he had quarrelled in Jerusalem. The duke demanded money before he would let him go, and it took two years for England to pay. Shortly after, in 1199, Richard was killed in France. He had spent no more than four or five years in the country of which he was king. When he died the French king took over parts of Richard's French lands to rule himself.

Richard had no son, and he was followed by his brother, John. John had already made himself unpopular with the three most important groups of people, the nobles, the merchants and the Church.

John was unpopular mainly because he was greedy. The feudal lords in England had always run their own law courts and profited from the fines paid by those brought to court. But John took many cases out of their courts and tried them in the king's courts, taking the money for himself.

It was normal for a feudal lord to make a payment to the king when his daughter was married, but John asked for more than was the custom. In the same way, when a noble died, his son had to pay money before he could inherit his father's land. In order to enlarge his own income, John increased the amount they had to pay. In other cases when a noble died without a son, it was normal for the land to be passed on to another noble family. John kept the land for a long time, to benefit from its wealth. He did the same with the bishoprics. As for the merchants and towns, he taxed them at a higher level than ever before.

In 1204 King John became even more unpopular with his nobles. The French king invaded Normandy and the English nobles lost their lands there. John had failed to carry out his duty to them as duke of Normandy. He had taken their money but he had not protected their land.

In 1209 John quarrelled with the pope over who should be Archbishop of Canterbury. John was in a weak position in England and the pope knew it. The pope called on the king of France to invade England, and closed every church in the country. At a time when most people believed that without the Church they would go to hell, this was a very serious matter. In 1214 John gave in, and accepted the pope's choice of archbishop.

In 1215 John hoped to recapture Normandy. He called on his lords to fight for him, but they no longer trusted him. They marched to London, where they were joined by angry merchants. Outside London at Runnymede, a few miles up the river, John was forced to sign a new agreement.

Magna Carta and the decline of feudalism

This new agreement was known as "Magna Carta", the Great Charter, and was an important symbol of political freedom. The king promised all "freemen" protection from his officers, and the right to a fair and legal trial. At the time perhaps less than one quarter of the English were "freemen". Most were not free, and were serfs or little better. Hundreds of years later, Magna Carta was used by Parliament to protect itself from a powerful king. In fact Magna Carta gave no real freedom to the majority of people in England. The nobles who wrote it and forced King John to sign it had no such thing in mind. They had one main aim: to make sure John did not go beyond his rights as feudal lord.

Magna Carta marks a clear stage in the collapse of English feudalism. Feudal society was based on links between lord and vassal. At Runnymede the nobles were not acting as vassals but as a class. They established a committee of twenty-four lords to make sure John kept his promises. That was not a "feudal" thing to do. In addition, the nobles were acting in co-operation with the merchant class of towns.

The nobles did not allow John's successors to forget this charter and its promises. Every king recognised Magna Carta, until the Middle Ages ended in disorder and a new kind of monarchy came into being in the sixteenth century.

There were other small signs that feudalism was changing. When the king went to war he had the right to forty days' fighting service from each of his lords. But forty days were not long enough for fighting a war in France. The nobles refused to fight for longer, so the king was forced to pay soldiers to fight for him. (They were called "paid fighters", *solidarius*, a Latin word from which the word "soldier" comes.) At the same time many lords preferred their vassals to pay them in money rather than in services. Vassals were gradually beginning to change into tenants. Feudalism, the use of land in return for service, was beginning to weaken. But it took another three hundred years before it disappeared completely.

5 The power of the kings of England

Church and state · The beginnings of Parliament · Dealing with the Celts

Church and state

John's reign also marked the end of the long struggle between Church and state in England. This had begun in 1066 when the pope claimed that William had promised to accept him as his feudal lord. William refused to accept this claim. He had created Norman bishops and given them land on condition that they paid homage to him. As a result it was not clear whether the bishops should obey the Church or the king. Those kings and popes who wished to avoid conflict left the matter alone. But some kings and popes wanted to increase their authority. In such circumstances trouble could not be avoided.

The struggle was for both power and money. During the eleventh and twelfth centuries the Church wanted the kings of Europe to accept its authority over both spiritual and earthly affairs, and argued that even kings were answerable to God. Kings, on the other hand, chose as bishops men who would be loyal to them.

The first serious quarrel was between William Rufus and Anselm, the man he had made Archbishop of Canterbury. Anselm, with several other bishops, fearing the king, had escaped from England. After William's death Anselm refused to do homage to William's successor, Henry I. Henry, meanwhile, had created several new bishops but they had no spiritual authority without the blessing of the archbishop. This left the king in a difficult position. It took seven years to settle the disagreement. Finally the king agreed that only the Church could create bishops. But in return the Church agreed that bishops would pay homage to the king for the lands owned by their bishoprics. In practice the wishes of the king in the appointment of bishops remained important. But after Anselm's death Henry managed to delay the appointment of a new archbishop for five years while he benefited from the wealth of Canterbury. The struggle between Church and state continued.

The crisis came when Henry II's friend Thomas Becket was appointed Archbishop of Canterbury in 1162. Henry hoped that Thomas would help him bring the Church more under his control. At first Becket refused, and then he gave in. Later he changed his mind again and ran away to France, and it seemed as if Henry had won. But in 1170 Becket returned to England determined to resist the king. Henry was very angry, and four knights who heard him speak out went to Canterbury to murder Becket. They killed him in the holiest place in the cathedral, on the altar steps.

All Christian Europe was shocked, and Thomas Becket became a saint of the Church. For hundreds of years afterwards people not only from England but also from Europe travelled to Canterbury to pray at Becket's grave. Henry was forced to ask the pope's forgiveness. He also allowed himself to be whipped by monks. The pope used the event to take back some of the Church's privileges. But Henry II could have lost much more than he did. Luckily for Henry, the nobles were also involved in the argument, and Henry had the nobles on his side. Usually the Church preferred to support the king against the nobles, but expected to be rewarded for its support. King John's mistake forty years later was to upset both Church and nobles at the same time.

The beginnings of Parliament

King John had signed Magna Carta unwillingly, and it quickly became clear that he was not going to keep to the agreement. The nobles rebelled and soon pushed John out of the southeast. But civil war was avoided because John died suddenly in 1216.

John's son, Henry III, was only nine years old. During the first sixteen years as king he was under the control of powerful nobles, and tied by Magna Carta.

Henry was finally able to rule for himself at the age of twenty-five. It was understandable that he wanted to be completely independent of the people who had controlled his life for so long. He spent his time with foreign friends, and became involved in expensive wars supporting the pope in Sicily and also in France.

Henry's heavy spending and his foreign advisers upset the nobles. Once again they acted as a class, under the leadership of Simon de Montfort, earl of Leicester. In 1258 they took over the government and elected a council of nobles. De Montfort called it a *parliament*, or *parlement*, a French word meaning a "discussion meeting". This "parliament" took control of the treasury and forced Henry to get rid of his foreign advisers. The nobles were supported by the towns, which wished to be free of Henry's heavy taxes.

But some of the nobles did not support the revolutionary new council, and remained loyal to Henry. With their help Henry was finally able to defeat and kill Simon de Montfort in 1265. Once again he had full royal authority, although he was careful to accept the balance which de Montfort had created between king and nobles. When Henry died in 1272 his son Edward I took the throne without question.

Edward I's parliament. Edward sits in front of his nobles, bishops and shire knights. On his right sits Alexander, king of Scots, and on his left is Llewelyn, Prince of Wales. It is unlikely either ever sat in Edward's parliament, but he liked to think of them as under his authority. Beyond Alexander and Llewelyn sit the archbishops of Canterbury and York, and there are more bishops on the left of the picture, a reminder of the political and economic strength of the Church at this time. In the centre are woolsacks, symbolic of England's wealth.

Edward I brought together the first real parliament. Simon de Montfort's council had been called a parliament, but it included only nobles. It had been able to make statutes, or written laws, and it had been able to make political decisions. However, the lords were less able to provide the king with money, except what they had agreed to pay him for the lands they held under feudal arrangement. In the days of Henry I (1100–35), 85 per cent of the king's income had come from the land. By 1272 income from the land was less than 40 per cent of the royal income. The king could only raise the rest by taxation. Since the rules of feudalism did not include taxation, taxes could only be raised with the agreement of those wealthy enough to be taxed.

Several kings had made arrangements for taxation before, but Edward I was the first to create a "representative institution" which could provide the money he needed. This institution became the House of Commons. Unlike the House of Lords it contained a mixture of "gentry" (knights and other wealthy freemen from the shires) and merchants from the towns. These were the two broad classes of people who produced and controlled England's wealth.

In 1275 Edward I commanded each shire and each town (or borough) to send two representatives to his parliament. These "commoners" would have stayed away if they could, to avoid giving Edward money. But few dared risk Edward's anger. They became unwilling representatives of their local community. This, rather than Magna Carta, was the beginning of the idea that there should be "no taxation without representation", later claimed by the American colonists of the eighteenth century.

In other parts of Europe, similar "parliaments" kept all the gentry separate from the commoners. England was special because the House of Commons contained a mixture of gentry belonging to the feudal ruling class and merchants and freemen who did not. The co-operation of these groups, through the House of Commons, became important to Britain's later political and social development. During the 150 years following Edward's death the agreement of the Commons

Harlech Castle, one of several castles built by Edward I in order to control the north and west of Wales. The mountainous country of Snowdonia in the background was a place of safety for the Welsh rebels. While it was extremely difficult for Edward to reach the rebels in these mountains, it was also impossible for such rebels ever to capture castles as strong as Harlech. These hugely expensive castles were so strong that they persuaded the Welsh that another rising against English rule was unlikely to succeed.

became necessary for the making of all statutes, and all special taxation additional to regular taxes.

Dealing with the Celts

Edward I was less interested in winning back parts of France than in bringing the rest of Britain under his control.

William I had allowed his lords to win land by conquest in Wales. These Normans slowly extended their control up the Welsh river valleys and by the beginning of the twelfth century much of Wales was held by them. They built castles as they went forward, and mixed with and married the Welsh during the eleventh, twelfth and thirteenth centuries. A new class grew up, a mixture of the Norman and Welsh rulers, who spoke Norman French and Welsh, but not English. They all became vassals of the English king.

The only Welsh who were at all free from English rule lived around Snowdon, the wild mountainous area of north Wales. They were led by Llewelyn ap Gruffydd, prince of Gwynedd, who tried to become independent of the English. Edward was determined to defeat him and bring Wales completely under his control. In 1282 Llewelyn was captured and killed. Edward then began a programme of castle building which was extremely expensive and took many years to complete.

In 1284 Edward united west Wales with England, bringing the English county system to the newly conquered lands. But he did not interfere with the areas the Normans had conquered earlier on the English–Welsh border, because this would have led to trouble with his nobles.

The English considered that Wales had become part of England for all practical purposes. If the Welsh wanted a prince, they could have one. At a public ceremony at Caernarfon Edward I made his own baby son (later Edward II) Prince of Wales. From that time the eldest son of the ruling king or queen has usually been made Prince of Wales.

Ireland had been conquered by Norman lords in 1169. They had little difficulty in defeating the Irish kings and tribes. Henry II, afraid that his lords might become too independent, went to Ireland himself. He forced the Irish chiefs and Norman lords to accept his lordship. He did so with the authority of the pope, who hoped to bring the Irish Celtic Church under his own control.

Henry II made Dublin, the old Viking town, the capital of his new colony. Much of western Ireland remained in the hands of Irish chiefs, while Norman lords governed most of the east. Edward I took as much money and as many men as he could for his wars against the Welsh and Scots. As a result Ireland was drained of its wealth. By 1318 it was able to provide the English king with only one-third of the amount it had been able to give in 1272. The Norman nobles and Irish chiefs quietly avoided English authority as much as possible. As a result, the English Crown only controlled Dublin and a small area around it, known as "the Pale".

The Irish chiefs continued to live as they always had done, moving from place to place, and eating out of doors, a habit they only gave up in the sixteenth century. The Anglo-Irish lords, on the other hand, built strong stone castles, as they had done in Wales. But they also became almost completely independent from the English Crown, and some became "more Irish than the Irish".

In Scotland things were very different. Although Scottish kings had sometimes accepted the English king as their "overlord", they were much stronger than the many Welsh kings had been. By the eleventh century there was only one king of Scots, and he ruled over all the south and east of Scotland. Only a few areas of the western coast were still completely independent and these all came under the king's control during the twelfth and thirteenth centuries. In Ireland and Wales Norman knights were strong enough to fight local chiefs on their own. But only the English king with a large army could hope to defeat the Scots. Most English kings did not not even try, but Edward I was differen

The Scottish kings were closely connected with England. Since Saxon times, marriages had frequently taken place between the Scottish and English royal families. At the same time, in order to establish strong government, the Scottish kings offered land to Norman knights from England in return for their loyalty. Scotland followed England in creating a feudal state. On the whole Celtic society accepted this, probably because the Normans married into local Celtic noble families. The feudal system, however, did not develop in the Highlands, where the tribal "clan" system continued. Some Scottish kings held land in England, just as English kings held lands in France. And in exactly the same way they did homage, promising loyalty to the English king for that land.

In 1290 a crisis took place over the succession to the Scottish throne. There were thirteen possible heirs. Among these the most likely to succeed were John de Balliol and Robert Bruce, both Norman–Scottish knights. In order to avoid civil war the Scottish nobles invited Edward I to settle the matter.

Edward had already shown interest in joining Scotland to his kingdom. In 1286 he had arranged for his own son to marry Margaret, the heir to the Scottish throne, but she had died in a shipwreck. Now he had another chance. He told both men that they must do homage to him, and so accept his overlordship, before he would help settle the question. He then invaded Scotland and put one of them, John de Balliol, on the Scottish throne.

De Balliol's four years as king were not happy. First, Edward made him provide money and troops for the English army and the Scottish nobles rebelled. Then Edward invaded Scotland again, and captured all the main Scottish castles. During the invasion Edward stole the sacred Stone of Destiny from Scone Abbey on which, so the legend said, all Scottish kings must sit. Edward believed that without the Stone, any Scottish coronation would be meaningless, and that his own possession of the Stone would persuade the Scots to accept him as king. However, neither he nor his successors became kings of Scots, and the Scottish kings managed perfectly well without it.

Edward's treatment of the Scots created a popular resistance movement. At first it was led by William Wallace, a Norman–Scottish knight. But after one victory against an English army, Wallace's "people's army" was itself destroyed by Edward in 1297. The Scots had formed rings of spearmen which stood firm against the English cavalry attacks, but Edward's Welsh longbowmen broke the Scottish formations, and the cavalry then charged down on them.

It seemed as if Edward had won after all. He captured Wallace and executed him, putting his head on a pole on London Bridge. Edward tried to make Scotland a part of England, as he had done with Wales. Some Scottish nobles accepted him, but the people refused to be ruled by the English king. Scottish nationalism was born on the day Wallace died.

A new leader took up the struggle. This was Robert Bruce, who had competed with John de Balliol for the throne. He was able to raise an army and defeat the English army in Scotland. Edward I gathered another great army and marched against Robert Bruce, but he died on the way north in 1307. On Edward's grave were written the words "Edward, the Hammer of the Scots". He had intended to hammer them into the ground and destroy them, but in fact he had hammered them into a nation.

After his death his son, Edward II, turned back to England. Bruce had time to defeat his Scottish enemies, and make himself accepted as king of the Scots. He then began to win back the castles still held by the English. When Edward II invaded Scotland in 1314 in an effort to help the last English-held castles, Bruce destroyed his army at Bannockburn, near Stirling. Six years later, in 1320, the Scots clergy meeting at Arbroath wrote to the pope in Rome to tell him that they would never accept English authority: "for as long as even one hundred of us remain alive, we will never consent to subject ourselves to the dominion of the English."

Edward I's coronation chair. The Scottish Stone of Destiny which Edward took from Scone Abbey is under the seat, a symbol of England's desire to rule Scotland. On either side of the throne stand the symbolic state sword and shield of Edward III.

6 Government and society

The growth of government • Law and justice • Religious beliefs • Ordinary people in country and town • The growth of towns as centres of wealth • Language, literature and culture

The growth of government

William the Conqueror had governed England and Normandy by travelling from one place to another to make sure that his authority was accepted. He, and the kings after him, raised some of the money they needed by trying cases and fining people in the royal courts. The king's "household" was the government, and it was always on the move. There was no real capital of the kingdom as there is today. Kings were crowned in Westminster, but their treasury stayed in the old Wessex capital, Winchester. When William and the kings after him moved around the country staying in towns and castles, they were accompanied by a large number of followers. Wherever they went the local people had to give them food and somewhere to stay. It could have a terrible effect. Food ran out, and prices rose.

This form of government could only work well for a small kingdom. By the time the English kings were ruling half of France as well they could no longer travel everywhere themselves. Instead, they sent nobles and knights from the royal household to act as sheriffs. But even this system needed people who could administer taxation, justice, and carry out the king's instructions. It was obviously not practical for all these people to follow the king everywhere. At first this "administration" was based in Winchester, but by the time of Edward I, in 1290, it had moved to Westminster. It is still there today. However, even though the administration was in Westminster the real capital of England was still "in the king's saddle".

The king kept all his records in Westminster, including the Domesday Book. The king's administration kept a careful watch on noble families. It made sure the king claimed money every time a young noble took over the lands of his father, or when a noble's daughter married. In every possible way the king always "had his hand in his subject's pocket". The administration also checked the towns and the ports to make sure that taxes were paid, and kept a record of the fines made by the king's court.

Most important of all, the officials in Westminster had to watch the economy of the country carefully. Was the king getting the money he needed in the most effective way? Such questions led to important changes in taxation between 1066 and 1300. In 1130 well over half of Henry I's money came from his own land, one-third from his feudal vassals in rights and fines, and only one-seventh from taxes. One hundred and fifty years later, over half of Edward I's money came from taxes, but only one-third came from his land and only one-tenth from his feudal vassals. It is no wonder that Edward called to his parliament representatives of the people whom he could tax most effectively.

It is not surprising, either, that the administration began to grow very quickly. When William I invaded Britain he needed only a few clerks to manage his paperwork. Most business, including feudal homage, was done by the spoken, not written, word. But the need for paperwork grew rapidly. In 1050 only the king (Edward the Confessor) had a seal with which to "sign" official papers. By the time of Edward I, just over two hundred years later, even the poorest man was expected to have a seal in order to sign official papers, even if he could not read. From 1199 the administration in Westminster kept copies of all the letters and documents that were sent out.

The amount of wax used for seals on official papers gives an idea of the rapid growth of the royal administration. In 1220, at the beginning of Henry III's reign, 1.5 kg were used each week. Forty years later, in 1260, this had risen to 14 kg weekly. And government administration has been growing ever since.

Law and justice

The king, of course, was responsible for law and justice. But kings usually had to leave the administration of this important matter to someone who lived close to the place where a crime was committed. In Saxon times every district had had its own laws and customs, and justice had often been a family matter. After the Norman Conquest nobles were allowed to administer justice among the villages and people on their lands. Usually they mixed Norman laws with the old Saxon laws. They had freedom to act more or less as they liked. More serious offences, however, were tried in the king's courts.

Henry I introduced the idea that all crimes, even those inside the family, were no longer only a family matter but a breaking of the "king's peace". It was therefore the king's duty to try people and punish them. At first the nobles acted for the king on their own lands, but Henry wanted the same kind of justice to be used everywhere. So he appointed a number of judges who travelled from place to place administering justice. (These travelling, or "circuit", judges still exist today.) They dealt both with crimes and disagreements over property. In this way the king slowly took over the administration from the nobles.

At first the king's judges had no special knowledge or training. They were simply trusted to use common sense. Many of them were nobles or bishops who followed directly the orders of the king. It is not surprising that the quality of judges

depended on the choice of the king. Henry II, the most powerful English king of the twelfth century, was known in Europe for the high standards of his law courts. "The convincing proof of our king's strength," wrote one man, "is that whoever has a just cause wants to have it tried before him, whoever has a weak one does not come unless he is dragged."

By the end of the twelfth century the judges were men with real knowledge and experience of the law. Naturally these judges, travelling from place to place, administered the same law wherever they went. This might seem obvious now, but since Saxon times local customs and laws had varied from one place to another. The law administered by these travelling judges became known as "common law", because it was used everywhere.

England was unlike the rest of Europe because it used common law. Centuries later, England's common law system was used in the United States (the North American colonies) and in many other British colonial possessions, and accepted when these became nations in their own right. In other parts of Europe legal practice was based on the Civil Law of the Roman Empire, and the Canon Law of the Church. But although English lawyers referred to these as examples of legal method and science, they created an entirely different system of law based on custom, comparisons, previous cases and previous decisions. In this way traditional local laws were replaced by common law all over the land. This mixture of experience and custom is the basis of law in England even today. Modern judges still base their decisions on the way in which similar cases have been decided.

The new class of judges was also interested in how the law was carried out, and what kinds of punishment were used. From Anglo-Saxon times there had been two ways of deciding difficult cases when it was not clear if a man was innocent or guilty. The accused man could be tested in battle against a skilled fighter, or tested by "ordeal". A typical "ordeal" was to put a hot iron on the man's tongue. If the burn mark was still there three days later he was thought to be guilty. It was argued that

God would leave the burn mark on a guilty man's tongue. Such a system worked only as long as people believed in it. By the end of the twelfth century there were serious doubts and in 1215 the pope forbade the Church to have anything to do with trial by ordeal.

In England trial by ordeal was replaced with trial by jury. The jury idea dated back to the Danes of Danelaw, but had only been used in disputes over land. Henry II had already introduced the use of juries for some cases in the second half of the twelfth century. But it was not the kind of jury we know today. In 1179 he allowed an accused man in certain cases to claim "trial by jury". The man could choose twelve neighbours, "twelve good men and true", who would help him prove that he was not guilty. Slowly, during the later Middle Ages, the work of these juries gradually changed from giving evidence to judging the evidence of others. Juries had no training in the law. They were ordinary people using ordinary common sense. It was soon obvious that they needed guidance. As a result law schools grew up during the thirteenth century, producing lawyers who could advise juries about the points of law.

Religious beliefs

The Church at local village level was significantly different from the politically powerful organisation the king had to deal with. At the time of William I the ordinary village priest could hardly read at all, and he was usually one of the peasant community. His church belonged to the local lord, and was often built next to the lord's house. Almost all priests were married, and many inherited their position from their father.

However, even at village level the Church wished to replace the lord's authority with its own, but it was only partly successful. In many places the lord continued to choose the local priest, and to have more influence over him than the more distant Church authorities were able to have.

The Church also tried to prevent priests from marrying. In this it was more successful, and by the end of the thirteenth century married priests were

unusual. But it was still common to find a priest who "kept a girl in his house who lit his fire but put out his virtue."

There were, however, many who promised not to marry and kept that promise. This was particularly true of those men and women who wanted to be monks or nuns and entered the local monastery or nunnery. One reason for entering a religious house was the increasing difficulty during this period of living on the land. As the population grew, more and more people found they could not feed their whole family easily. If they could enter a son or daughter into the local religious house there would be fewer mouths to feed. Indeed, it may have been the economic difficulties of raising a family which persuaded priests to follow the Church ruling. Life was better as a monk within the safe walls of a monastery than as a poor farmer outside. A monk could learn to read and write, and be sure of food and shelter. The monasteries were centres of wealth and learning.

In 1066 there were fifty religious houses in England, home for perhaps 1,000 monks and nuns. By the beginning of the fourteenth century there were probably about 900 religious houses, with 17,500 members. Even though the population in the fourteenth century was three times larger than it had been in 1066, the growth of the monasteries is impressive.

The thirteenth century brought a new movement, the "brotherhoods" of friars. These friars were wandering preachers. They were interested not in Church power and splendour, but in the souls of ordinary men and women. They lived with the poor and tried to bring the comfort of Christianity to them. They lived in contrast with the wealth and power of the monasteries and cathedrals, the local centres of the Church.

Ordinary people in country and town

There were probably between 1.5 and 2 million people living in England in 1066. The Domesday Book tells us that nine-tenths of them lived in the countryside. It also tells us that 80 per cent of the land used for farming at the beginning of the twentieth century was already being ploughed in 1086. In fact it was not until the nineteenth century that the cultivated area became greater than the level recorded in the Domesday Book.

Life in the countryside was hard. Most of the population still lived in villages in southern and eastern parts of England. In the north and west there were fewer people, and they often lived apart from each other, on separate farms. Most people lived in the simplest houses. The walls were made of wooden beams and sticks, filled with mud. The roofs were made of thatch, with reeds or corn stalks laid thickly and skilfully so that the rain ran off easily. People ate cereals and vegetables most of the time, with pork meat for special occasions. They worked from dawn to dusk every day of the year, every year, until they were unable to work any longer. Until a man had land of his own he would usually not marry. However, men and women often slept together before marriage, and once a woman was expecting a child, the couple had no choice but to marry.

The poor were divided from their masters by the feudal class system. The basis of this "manorial system" was the exchange of land for labour. The landlord expected the villagers to work a fixed number of days on his own land, the "home farm". The rest of the time they worked on their small strips of land, part of the village's "common land" on which they grew food for themselves and their family. The Domesday Book tells us that over three-quarters of the country people were serfs. They were not free to leave their lord's service or his land without permission. Even if they wanted to run away, there was nowhere to run to. Anyway, a serf's life, under his lord's protection, was better than the life of an unprotected wanderer. Order and protection, no matter how hard life might be, was always better than disorder, when people would starve.

The manorial system was not the same all over the country, and it did not stay the same throughout the Middle Ages. There were always differences in the way the system worked between one estate and another, one region and another, and between one period and another. Local customs and both local and national economic pressures affected the way things worked.

The manorial system is often thought to be Norman, but in fact it had been growing slowly throughout the Anglo-Saxon period. The Normans inherited the system and developed it to its fullest extent. But the Normans were blamed for the bad aspects of the manorial system because they were foreign masters.

In the early days of the Conquest Saxons and Normans feared and hated each other. For example, if a dead body was found, the Saxons had to prove that it was not the body of a murdered Norman. If they could not prove it, the Normans would burn the nearest village. The Norman ruling class only really began to mix with and marry the Saxons, and consider themselves "English" rather than French, after King John lost Normandy in 1204. Even then, dislike remained between the rulers and the ruled.

Every schoolchild knows the story of Robin Hood, which grew out of Saxon hatred for Norman rule. According to the legend Robin Hood lived in Sherwood Forest near Nottingham as a criminal or "outlaw", outside feudal society and the protection of the law. He stole from the rich and gave to the poor, and he stood up for the weak against the powerful. His weapon was not the sword of nobles and knights, but the longbow, the weapon of the common man.

In fact, most of the story is legend. The only thing we know is that a man called Robert or "Robin" Hood was a wanted criminal in Yorkshire in 1230. The legend was, however, very popular with the common people all through the fourteenth, fifteenth and sixteenth centuries, although the ruling class greatly disliked it. Later the story was changed. Robin Hood was described as a man of noble birth, whose lands had been taken by King John. Almost certainly this was an effort by the authorities to make Robin Hood "respectable".

Left: *Two out of twelve pictures illustrating the occupations of each month, about 1280. Above left February: a man sits cooking and warming his boots by the fire. Above him hang smoked meat and sausages, probably his only meat for the winter. In the autumn most animals were killed, and smoked or salted to keep them from going bad. There was only enough food to keep breeding animals alive through the winter. Below left November: perhaps it is the same man knocking acorns or nuts from a tree for his pigs to eat. The complete set of pictures shows mixed farming, which produced cereals, grapes for wine and pigs.*

Above: *A woman milks a cow, while the cow tenderly licks its calf. Almost all the population lived in the country, but cows were kept by townspeople too. This domestic scene has a touching gentleness about it.*

Most landlords obtained their income directly from the home farm, and also from letting out some of their land in return for rent in crops or money. The size of the home farm depended on how much land the landlord chose to let out. In the twelfth century, for example, many landlords found it more profitable to let out almost all the home farm lands, and thus be paid in money or crops rather than in labour. In fact it is from this period that the word "farm" comes. Each arrangement the landlord made to let land to a villager was a "firma": a fixed or settled agreement.

By 1300 the population was probably just over four million (up to the nineteenth century figures can only be guessed at), about three times what it had been in 1066. This increase, of course, had an effect on life in the country. It made it harder to grow enough food for everyone. The situation was made worse by the Normans' love of hunting. They drove the English peasants out of the forests, and punished them severely if they killed any forest animals. "The forest has its own laws," wrote one man bitterly, "based not on the common law of the kingdom, but on the personal wishes of the king."

The peasants tried to farm more land. They drained marshland, and tried to grow food on high ground and on other poor land. But much of this newly cleared land quickly became exhausted, because the soil was too poor, being either too heavy or too light and sandy. As a result, the effort to farm more land could not match the increase in population, and this led to a decline in individual family land holdings. It also led to an increase in the number of landless labourers, to greater poverty and hunger. As land became overused, so bad harvests became more frequent. And in the years of bad harvest people starved to death. It is a pattern cruelly familiar to many poor countries today. Among richer people, the pressure on land led to an increase in its value, and to an increase in buying and selling. Landowning widows found themselves courted by land-hungry single men.

Unfortunately, agricultural skills improved little during this period. Neither peasants nor landlords had the necessary knowledge or understanding to develop them. In addition, manorial landlords, equally interested in good harvests, insisted that the animals of the peasantry grazed on their own land to enrich it during its year of rest. Many villagers tried to increase their income by other activities and became blacksmiths, carpenters, tilers or shepherds, and it is from the thirteenth century that many villagers became known by their trade name.

Shortage of food led to a sharp rise in prices at the end of the twelfth century. The price of wheat, for example, doubled between 1190 and 1200. A sheep that cost four pence in 1199 fetched ten pence in 1210. Prices would be high in a bad season, but could suddenly drop when the harvest was specially good. This inflation weakened feudal ties, which depended to a great extent on a steady economic situation to be workable. The smaller landed knights found it increasingly difficult to pay for their military duties. By the end of the thirteenth century a knight's equipment, which had cost fifteen shillings in the early twelfth century, now cost more than three times this amount. Although nobles and knights could get more money from their land by paying farm labourers and receiving money rents than by giving land rent free in return for labour, many knights with smaller estates became increasingly indebted.

We know about these debts from the records of the "Exchequer of the Jews". The small Jewish community in England earned its living by lending money, and lived under royal protection. By the late thirteenth century these records show a large number of knights in debt to Jewish money lenders. When a knight was unable to repay the money he had borrowed, the Jewish money lender sold the knight's land to the greater landholding nobility. This did not please Edward I, who feared the growth in power of the greater nobility as they profited from the disappearance of smaller land-holders. He had wanted the support of the knightly class against the greater lords, and it was partly for this reason that he had called on them to be represented in Parliament. Now he saw the danger that as a class they might become seriously weakened. The Jews were middlemen in an economic process which was the result of social forces at work in the countryside. While the economic function of the Jews in providing capital had been useful they had been safe, but once this

was no longer so, the king used popular feeling against them as an excuse to expel them. In 1290 the Jewish community was forced to leave the country.

Feudalism was slowly dying out, but the changes often made landlords richer and peasants poorer. Larger landlords had to pay fewer feudal taxes, while new taxes were demanded from everyone in possession of goods and incomes. As a result many could not afford to pay rent and so they lost their land. Some of these landless people went to the towns, which offered a better hope for the future.

The growth of towns as centres of wealth

England was to a very large degree an agricultural society. Even in towns and cities, many of those involved in trade or industry also farmed small holdings of land on the edge of town. In this sense England was self-sufficient. However, throughout the Middle Ages England needed things from abroad, such as salt and spices. Inside England there was a good deal of trade between different regions. Wool-growing areas, for example, imported food from food-producing areas. However, it is harder to know the extent of this internal trade because it was less formal than international trade, and therefore less recorded.

We know more about international trade, which was recorded because the king obtained a considerable income from customs dues. During the Anglo-Saxon period most European trade had been with the Frisians in the Low Countries, around the mouth of the River Rhine. Following the Viking invasions most trade from the ninth century onwards had taken place with Scandinavia. By the eleventh century, for example, English grain was highly valued in Norway. In return England imported Scandinavian fish and tall timber. However, by the end of the twelfth century this Anglo-Scandinavian trade link had weakened.

This was the result of the Norman Conquest, after which England looked away from the northeast, Scandinavia and Germany, and towards the south, France, the Low Countries, and beyond. The royal family had links with Gascony in southwest France, and this led to an important trade exchange of wine for cloth and cereal. However, easily the most important link was once again with the Low Countries, and the basis of this trade was wool.

England had always been famous for its wool, and in Anglo-Saxon times much of it had been exported to the Low Countries. In order to improve the manufacture of woollen cloth, William the Conqueror encouraged Flemish weavers and other skilled workers from Normandy to settle in England. They helped to establish new towns: Newcastle, Hull, Boston, Lynn and others. These settlers had good connections with Europe and were able to begin a lively trade. However, raw wool rather than finished cloth remained the main export. As the European demand for wool stayed high, and since no other country could match the high quality of English wool, English exporters could charge a price high above the production cost, and about twice as much as the price in the home market. The king taxed the export of raw wool heavily as a means of increasing his own income. It was easily England's most profitable business. When Richard I was freed from his captivity, over half the price was paid in wool. As a symbol of England's source of wealth, a wool sack has remained in the House of Lords ever since this time. Much of the wool industry was built up by the monasteries, which kept large flocks of sheep on their great estates.

The wool trade illustrates the way in which the towns related to the countryside. "Chapmen" or "hucksters", travelling traders, would buy wool at particular village markets. Then they took the wool to town, where it would be graded and bundled up for export or for local spinning. Larger fairs, both in town and country, were important places where traders and producers met, and deals could be made. These were not purely English affairs. For-eign merchants seeking high quality wool frequently attended the larger fairs.

Such trade activities could not possibly have taken place under the restrictions of feudalism. But towns were valuable centres to nobles who wanted to sell their produce and to kings who wished to benefit from the increase in national wealth. As a result, the townspeople quickly managed to free themselves from feudal ties and interference. At the end of the Anglo-Saxon period there were only a few towns, but by 1250 most of England's towns were already established.

Many towns stood on land belonging to feudal lords. But by the twelfth century kings were discouraging local lords from taking the wealth from nearby towns. They realised that towns could become effective centres of royal authority, to balance the power of the local nobility. The kings therefore gave "charters of freedom" to many towns, freeing the inhabitants from feudal duties to the local lord. These charters, however, had to be paid for, and kings sold them for a high price. But it was worth the money. Towns could now raise their own local taxes on goods coming in. They could also have their own courts, controlled by the town merchants, on condition that they paid an annual tax to the king. Inside the town walls, people were able to develop social and economic organisations free from feudal rule. It was the beginnings of a middle class and a capitalist economy.

Within the towns and cities, society and the economy were mainly controlled by "guilds". These were brotherhoods of different kinds of merchants, or of skilled workers. The word "guild" came from the Saxon word "gildan", to pay, because members paid towards the cost of the brotherhood. The merchant guilds grew in the thirteenth century and included all the traders in any particular town. Under these guilds trade was more tightly controlled than at any later period. At least one hundred guilds existed in the thirteenth century, similar in some ways to our modern trade unions. The right to form a guild was sometimes included in a town's charter of freedom. It was from among the members of the guild that the town's leaders were probably chosen. In the course of time entry into these guilds became increasingly difficult as guilds tried to control a particular trade. In some cases entry was only open to the sons of guild members. In other cases entry could be obtained by paying a fee to cover the cost of the training, or apprenticeship, necessary to maintain the high standard of the trade.

During the fourteenth century, as larger towns continued to grow, "craft" guilds came into being. All members of each of these guilds belonged to the same trade or craft. The earliest craft guilds were those of the weavers in London and Oxford. Each guild tried to protect its own trade interests. Members of these guilds had the right to produce, buy or sell their particular trade without having to pay special town taxes. But members also had to make sure that goods were of a certain quality, and had to keep to agreed prices so as not to undercut other guild members.

In London the development of craft guilds went further than elsewhere, with a rich upper level of the craft community, the so-called livery companies, controlling most of the affairs of the city. Over the centuries the twelve main livery companies have developed into large financial institutions. Today they play an important part in the government of the City of London, and the yearly choice of its Lord Mayor.

Language, literature and culture

The growth of literacy in England was closely connected with the twelfth-century Renaissance, a cultural movement which had first started in Italy. Its influence moved northwards along the trade routes, reaching England at the end of the century. This revolution in ideas and learning brought a new desire to test religious faith against reason. Schools of learning were established in many towns and cities. Some were "grammar" schools independent of the Church, while others were attached to a cathedral. All of these schools taught Latin, because most books were written in this language. Although it may seem strange for education to be based on a dead language, Latin was important because it was the educated language of almost all Europe, and was therefore useful in the spread of ideas and learning. In spite of the dangers, the Church took a lead in the new intellectual movement.

In England two schools of higher learning were established, the first at Oxford and the second at Cambridge, at the end of the twelfth century. By the 1220s these two universities were the intellectual leaders of the country.

Few could go to the universities. Most English people spoke neither Latin, the language of the Church and of education, nor French, the language of law and of the Norman rulers. It was a long time before English became the language of the ruling class. Some French words became part of the English language, and often kept a more polite meaning than the old Anglo-Saxon words. For example, the word "chair", which came from the French, describes a better piece of furniture than the Anglo-Saxon word "stool". In the same way, the Anglo-Saxon word "belly" was replaced in polite society by the word "stomach". Other Anglo-Saxon words ceased to be used altogether.

Mob Quad in Merton College is the oldest of Oxford's famous "quadrangles", or courtyards. It was built in the first half of the fourteenth century. Almost all the Oxford colleges were built round quandrangles, with a library on one side (in Mob Quad on the first floor on the left), and living areas for both masters and students on the other sides. Merton College chapel, in the background, is the finest late fourteenth-century example in Oxford.

Es nouuelles d'albyon
S'il vous en plaist escouter
Mon frere & mon compaignon
Sachez qu'a mon retourner
J'ay este deca la mer

Et eu a joyeuse chiere

The late Middle Ages

7 The century of war, plague and disorder

War with Scotland and France • The age of chivalry • The century of plagues • The poor in revolt • Heresy and orthodoxy

The fourteenth century was disastrous for Britain as well as most of Europe, because of the effect of wars and plagues. Probably one-third of Europe's population died of plague. Hardly anywhere escaped its effects.

Britain and France suffered, too, from the damages of war. In the 1330s England began a long struggle against the French Crown. In France villages were raided or destroyed by passing armies. France and England were exhausted economically by the cost of maintaining armies. England had the additional burden of fighting the Scots, and maintaining control of Ireland and Wales, both of which were trying to throw off English rule.

It is difficult to measure the effects of war and plague on fourteenth-century Britain, except in deaths. But undoubtedly one effect of both was an increasing challenge to authority. The heavy demands made by the king on gentry and merchants weakened the economic strength of town and countryside but increased the political strength of the merchants and gentry whenever they provided the king with money. The growth of an alliance between merchants and gentry at this time was of the greatest importance for later political developments, particularly for the strength of Parliament against the king in the seventeenth century, and also for the strength of society against the dangers of revolution at the end of the eighteenth century. Finally, the habit of war created a new class of armed men in the countryside, in place of the old feudal system of forty days' service. These gangs, in reality local private armies, damaged the local economy but increased the nobles' ability to challenge the authority of the Crown. Already in 1327 one king had been murdered by powerful nobles, and another one was murdered in 1399. These murders weakened respect for the Crown, and encouraged repeated struggles for it amongst the king's most powerful relations. In the following century a king, or a king's eldest son, was killed in 1461, 1471, 1483 and 1485. But in the end the nobles destroyed themselves and as a class they disappeared.

War with Scotland and France

England's wish to control Scotland had suffered a major setback at Bannockburn in 1314. Many of the English had been killed, and Edward II himself had been lucky to escape. After other unsuccessful attempts England gave up its claim to overlordship of Scotland in 1328. However, it was not long before the two countries were at war again, but this time because of England's war with France.

The repeated attempts of English kings to control Scotland had led the Scots to look for allies. After Edward I's attempt to take over Scotland in 1295, the Scots turned to the obvious ally, the king of France, for whom there were clear advantages in an alliance with Scotland. This "Auld [old] Alliance"

The Tower of London has been a fortress, palace and prison. One of its earliest prisoners was the French duke of Orleans, who was captured at the battle of Agincourt in 1415. He spent twenty-five years in English prisons before he was ransomed. He appears in this picture, seated in the Norman White Tower, guarded by English soldiers. The White Tower itself was built by William I with stone brought from Normandy. Behind the Tower is London Bridge, with houses built upon it.

43

lasted into the sixteenth century. France benefited more than Scotland from it, but both countries agreed that whenever England attacked one of them, the other would make trouble behind England's back. The alliance did not operate the whole time. There were long periods when it was not needed or used.

England's troubles with France resulted from the French king's growing authority in France, and his determination to control all his nobles, even the greatest of them. France had suffered for centuries from rebellious vassals, and the two most troublesome were the duke of Burgundy and the English king (who was still the king of France's vassal as duke of Aquitaine), both of whom refused to recognise the French king's overlordship.

To make his position stronger, the king of France began to interfere with England's trade. Part of Aquitaine, an area called Gascony, traded its fine wines for England's corn and woollen cloth. This trade was worth a lot of money to the English Crown. But in 1324 the French king seized part of Gascony. Burgundy was England's other major trading partner, because it was through Burgundy's province of Flanders (now Belgium) that almost all England's wool exports were made. Any French move to control these two areas was a direct threat to England's wealth. The king of France tried to make the duke of Burgundy accept his authority. To prevent this, England threatened Burgundy with economic collapse by stopping wool exports to Flanders. This forced the duke of Burgundy to make an alliance with England against France.

England went to war because it could not afford the destruction of its trade with Flanders. It was difficult to persuade merchants to pay for wars against the Scots or the Welsh, from which there was so little wealth to be gained. But the threat to their trade and wealth persuaded the rich merchant classes of England that war against France was absolutely necessary. The lords, knights and fighting men also looked forward to the possibility of winning riches and lands.

Edward III declared war on France in 1337. His excuse was a bold one: he claimed the right to the French Crown. It is unlikely that anyone, except for the English, took his claim very seriously, but it was a good enough reason for starting a war. The war Edward began, later called the Hundred Years War, did not finally end until 1453, with the English Crown losing all its possessions in France except for Calais, a northern French port.

At first the English were far more successful than the French on the battlefield. The English army was experienced through its wars in Wales and in Scotland. It had learnt the value of being lightly armed, and quick in movement. Its most important weapon was the Welsh longbow, used by most of the ordinary footsoldiers. It was very effective on the battlefield because of its quick rate of fire. An experienced man could fire a second arrow into the air before the first had reached its destination. Writers of the time talk of "clouds" of arrows darkening the sky. These arrows could go through most armour. The value of the longbow was proved in two victories, at Crécy in 1346 and at Poitiers in 1356, where the French king himself was taken prisoner. The English captured a huge quantity of treasure, and it was said that after the battle of Poitiers every woman in England had a French bracelet on her arm. The French king bought his freedom for £500,000, an enormous amount of money in those days.

By the treaty of Brétigny, in 1360, Edward III was happy to give up his claim to the French throne because he had re-established control over areas previously held by the English Crown. The French recognised his ownership of all Aquitaine, including Gascony; parts of Normandy and Brittany, and the newly captured port of Calais. But because the French king had only unwillingly accepted this situation the war did not end, and fighting soon began again. All this land, except for the valuable coastal ports of Calais, Cherbourg, Brest, Bordeaux and Bayonne, was taken back by French forces during the next fifteen years. It was a warning that winning battles was a good deal easier than winning wars.

True to the "Auld Alliance" the king of Scots had attacked England in 1346, but he was defeated and taken prisoner. English forces raided as far as Edinburgh, destroying and looting. However, Edward III allowed the French to ransom the Scots king David and, satisfied with his successes in France, Edward gave up trying to control the Scots Crown. For a while there was peace, but the struggle between the French and English kings over French territories was to continue into the fifteenth century.

The age of chivalry

Edward III and his eldest son, the Black Prince, were greatly admired in England for their courage on the battlefield and for their courtly manners. They became symbols of the "code of chivalry", the way in which a perfect knight should behave. During the reign of Edward interest grew in the legendary King Arthur. Arthur, if he ever existed, was probably a Celtic ruler who fought the Anglo-Saxons, but we know nothing more about him. The fourteenth-century legend created around Arthur included both the imagined magic and mystery of the Celts, and also the knightly values of the court of Edward III.

According to the code of chivalry, the perfect knight fought for his good name if insulted, served God and the king, and defended any lady in need. These ideas were expressed in the legend of the Round Table, around which King Arthur and his knights sat as equals in holy brotherhood.

Edward introduced the idea of chivalry into his court. Once, a lady at court accidentally dropped her garter and Edward III noticed some of his courtiers laughing at her. He picked up the garter and tied it to his own leg, saying in French, *"Honi soit qui mal y pense,"* which meant "Let him be ashamed who sees wrong in it." From this strange yet probably true story, the Order of the Garter was founded in 1348. Edward chose as members of the order twenty-four knights, the same number the legendary Arthur had chosen. They met once a year on St George's Day at Windsor Castle, where King Arthur's Round Table was supposed to have

Edward III receives his sword and shield from the mythical St George. This is a propaganda picture. As patron saint of England, and of the Order of the Garter which Edward III has founded, St George is used in this way to confirm Edward's position.

been. The custom is still followed, and *Honi Soit Qui Mal Y Pense* is still the motto of the royal family.

Chivalry was a useful way of persuading men to fight by creating the idea that war was a noble and glorious thing. War could also, of course, be profitable. But in fact cruelty, death, destruction and theft were the reality of war, as they are today. The Black Prince, who was the living example of chivalry in England, was feared in France for his cruelty.

Knights, according to the ideals of chivalry, would fight to defend a lady's honour. In peacetime knights fought one against another in tournaments. Here a knight prepares to fight, and is handed his helmet and shield by his wife and daughter. Other knights could recognise by the design on his shield and on his horse's coat that the rider was Sir Geoffrey Luttrell.

The century of plagues

The year 1348 brought an event of far greater importance than the creation of a new order of chivalry. This was the terrible plague, known as the Black Death, which reached almost every part of Britain during 1348–9. Probably more than one-third of the entire population of Britain died, and fewer than one person in ten who caught the plague managed to survive it. Whole villages disappeared, and some towns were almost completely deserted until the plague itself died out.

The Black Death was neither the first natural disaster of the fourteenth century, nor the last. Plagues had killed sheep and other animals earlier in the century. An agricultural crisis resulted from the growth in population and the need to produce more food. Land was no longer allowed to rest one year in three, which meant that it was over-used, resulting in years of famine when the harvest failed. This process had already begun to slow down population growth by 1300.

After the Black Death there were other plagues during the rest of the century which killed mostly the young and healthy. In 1300 the population of Britain had probably been over four million. By the end of the century it was probably hardly half that figure, and it only began to grow again in the second half of the fifteenth century. Even so, it took until the seventeenth century before the population reached four million again.

The dramatic fall in population, however, was not entirely a bad thing. At the end of the thirteenth century the sharp rise in prices had led an increasing number of landlords to stop paying workers for their labour, and to go back to serf labour in order to avoid losses. In return villagers were given land to farm, but this tenanted land was often the poorest land of the manorial estate. After the Black Death there were so few people to work on the land that the remaining workers could ask for more money for their labour. We know they did this because the king and Parliament tried again and again to control wage increases. We also know from these repeated efforts that they cannot have been successful. The poor found that they could demand more money and did so. This finally led to the end of serfdom.

Because of the shortage and expense of labour, landlords returned to the twelfth-century practice of letting out their land to energetic freeman farmers who bit by bit added to their own land. In the twelfth century, however, the practice of letting out farms had been a way of increasing the landlord's profits. Now it became a way of avoiding losses. Many "firma" agreements were for a whole life span, and some for several life spans. By the mid-fifteenth century few landlords had home farms at all. These smaller farmers who rented the manorial lands slowly became a new class, known as the "yeomen". They became an important part of the agricultural economy, and have always remained so.

Overall, agricultural land production shrank, but those who survived the disasters of the fourteenth century enjoyed a greater share of the agricultural economy. Even for peasants life became more comfortable. For the first time they had enough money to build more solid houses, in stone where it was available, in place of huts made of wood, mud and thatch.

There had been other economic changes during the fourteenth century. The most important of these was the replacement of wool by finished cloth as

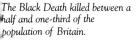
The Black Death killed between a half and one-third of the population of Britain.

England's main export. This change was the natural result of the very high prices at which English wool was sold in Flanders by the end of the thirteenth century. Merchants decided they could increase their profits further by buying wool in England at half the price for which it was sold in Flanders, and produce finished cloth for export. This process suddenly grew very rapidly after the Flemish cloth industry itself collapsed during the years 1320 to 1360. Hundreds of skilled Flemings came to England in search of work. They were encouraged to do so by Edward III because there was a clear benefit to England in exporting a finished product rather than a raw material. The surname "Fleming" has been a common one in England ever since, particularly in East Anglia, where many Flemings settled.

At the beginning of the century England had exported 30,000 sacks of raw wool but only 8,000 lengths of cloth each year. By the middle of the century it exported only 8,000 sacks of wool but 50,000 lengths of cloth, and by the end of the century this increased to well over 100,000. The wool export towns declined. They were replaced by towns and villages with fast-flowing rivers useful for the new process of cleaning and treating wool. Much of the clothmaking process, like spinning, was done in the workers' own homes. Indeed, so many young women spun wool that "spinster" became and has remained the word for an unmarried woman.

The West Country, Wales, and Yorkshire in the north all did well from the change in clothmaking. But London remained much larger and richer. By the late fourteenth century its 50,000 inhabitants were supported by trade with the outside world, especially the Baltic, Mediterranean and North Sea ports. Its nearest trade rival was Bristol.

The poor in revolt

It is surprising that the English never rebelled against Edward III. He was an expensive king at a time when many people were miserably poor and sick with plagues. At the time of the Black Death he was busy with expensive wars against France and Scotland. The demands he made on merchants and peasants were enormous, but Edward III handled these people with skill.

Edward's grandson, Richard, was less fortunate. He became king on his grandfather's death in 1377 because his father, the Black Prince, had died a few months earlier. Richard II inherited the problems of discontent but had neither the diplomatic skill of his grandfather, nor the popularity of his father. Added to this he became king when he was only eleven, and so others governed for him. In the year he became king, these advisers introduced a tax payment for every person over the age of fifteen. Two years later, this tax was enforced again. The people paid.

But in 1381 this tax was enforced for a third time and also increased to three times the previous amount. There was an immediate revolt in East Anglia and in Kent, two of the richer parts of the country. The poorer parts of the country, the north and northwest, did not rebel. This suggests that in the richer areas ordinary people had become more aware and confident of their rights and their power.

The new tax had led to revolt, but there were also other reasons for discontent. The landlords had been trying for some time to force the peasants back into serfdom, because serf labour was cheaper than paid labour. The leader of the revolt, Wat Tyler, was the first to call for fair treatment of England's poor people: "We are men formed in Christ's likeness," he claimed, "and we are kept like animals." The people sang a revolutionary rhyme suggesting that when God created man he had not made one man master over another:

> When Adam delved, and Eve span,
> Who was then the gentleman?

The idea that God had created all people equal called for an end to feudalism and respect for honest labour. But the Peasants' Revolt, as it was called, only lasted for four weeks. During that period the peasants took control of much of London. In fact the revolt was not only by peasants from the countryside: a number of poorer townspeople also revolted, suggesting that the discontent went beyond the question of feudal service. When Wat Tyler was killed, Richard II skilfully quietened the angry crowd. He promised to meet all the people's demands, including an end to serfdom, and the people peacefully went home.

As soon as they had gone, Richard's position changed. Although he did not try to enforce the tax, he refused to keep his promise to give the peasants their other demands. "Serfs you are," he said, "and serfs you shall remain." His officers hunted down other leading rebels and hanged them. But the danger of revolt by the angry poor was a warning to the king, the nobles and to the wealthy of the city of London.

Heresy and orthodoxy

The Peasants' Revolt was the first sign of growing discontent with the state. During the next century discontent with the Church also grew. There had already been a few attacks on Church property in towns controlled by the Church. In 1381 one rebel priest had called for the removal of all bishops and archbishops, as well as all the nobles.

The greed of the Church was one obvious reason for its unpopularity. The Church was a feudal power, and often treated its peasants and townspeople with as much cruelty as the nobles did. There was another reason why the people of England disliked paying taxes to the pope. Edward's wars in France were beginning to make the English conscious of their "Englishness" and the pope was a foreigner. To make matters worse the pope had been driven out of Rome, and was living in Avignon in France. It seemed obvious to the English that the pope must be on the French side, and that the taxes they paid to the Church were actually helping France against England. This was a matter on which the king and people in England agreed. The king reduced the amount of tax money

the pope could raise in Britain, and made sure that most of it found its way into his own treasury instead.

One might have expected the bishops and clergy to oppose the king. They did not, because almost all of them were English and came from noble families, and so shared the political views of the nobility. Most of them had been appointed by the king and some of them also acted as his officers. When the peasants stormed London in 1381 they executed the Archbishop of Canterbury, who was also the king's chancellor. It was unlikely that his killers saw much difference between the two offices. Archbishop or chancellor, he was part of an oppressive establishment.

Another threat to the Church during the fourteenth century was the spread of religious writings, which were popular with an increasingly literate population. These books were for use in private prayer and dealt with the death of Jesus Christ, the lives of the Saints and the Virgin Mary. The increase in private prayer was a direct threat to the authority of the Church over the religious life of the population. This was because these writings allowed people to pray and think independently of Church control. Private religious experience and the increase of knowledge encouraged people to challenge the Church's authority, and the way it used this to advance its political influence.

Most people were happy to accept the continued authority of the Church, but some were not. At the end of the fourteenth century new religious ideas appeared in England which were dangerous to Church authority, and were condemned as heresy. This heresy was known as "Lollardy", a word which probably came from a Latin word meaning "to say prayers". One of the leaders of Lollardy was John Wycliffe, an Oxford professor. He believed that everyone should be able to read the Bible in English, and to be guided by it in order to save their soul. He therefore translated it from Latin, finishing the work in 1396. He was not allowed to publish his new Bible in England, and was forced to leave Oxford. However, both he and the other Lollards were admired by those nobles and scholars who

The Peasants' Revolt ended when the Lord Mayor of London killed Wat Tyler at Smithfield. Perhaps he feared that Tyler would kill King Richard, to whom Tyler was talking. Richard II can be seen a second time, talking to the peasant army (right) and calming them with the words, "Sirs, will you shoot your king? I am your leader, follow me." In fact he sent them to their homes, and sent his officers to arrest and execute the leaders.

were critical of the Church, its wealth and the poor quality of its clergy.

If the Lollards had been supported by the king, the English Church might have become independent from the papacy in the early fifteenth century. But Richard's successor, Henry IV, was not sympathetic. He was deeply loyal to the Church, and in 1401 introduced into England for the first time the idea of executing the Lollards by burning. Lollardy was not well enough organised to resist. In the next few years it was driven underground, and its spirit was not seen again for a century.

8　The crisis of kings and nobles

The crisis of kingship · Wales in revolt · The struggle in France · The Wars of the Roses · Scotland

Richard II. This is probably the earliest portrait of a sovereign painted from life to have survived to this day. This is a copy of the original in Westminster Abbey.

The crisis of kingship

During the fourteenth century, towards the end of the Middle Ages, there was a continuous struggle between the king and his nobles. The first crisis came in 1327 when Edward II was deposed and cruelly murdered. His eleven-year-old son, Edward III, became king, and as soon as he could, he punished those responsible. But the principle that kings were neither to be killed nor deposed was broken.

Towards the end of the fourteenth century Richard II was the second king to be killed by ambitious lords. He had made himself extremely unpopular by his choice of advisers. This was always a difficult matter, because the king's advisers became powerful, and those not chosen lost influence and wealth. Some of Richard's strongest critics had been the most powerful men in the kingdom.

Richard was young and proud. He quarrelled with these nobles in 1388, and used his authority to humble them. He imprisoned his uncle, John of Gaunt, the third son of Edward III, who was the most powerful and wealthy noble of his time. John of Gaunt died in prison. Other nobles, including John of Gaunt's son, Henry duke of Lancaster, did not forget or forgive. In 1399, when Richard II was busy trying to establish royal authority again in Ireland, they rebelled. Henry of Lancaster, who had left England, returned and raised an army. Richard was deposed.

Unlike Edward II, however, Richard II had no children. There were two possible successors. One was the earl of March, the seven-year-old grandson of Edward III's second son. The other was Henry of Lancaster, son of John of Gaunt. It was difficult to

51

say which had the better claim to the throne. But Henry was stronger. He won the support of other powerful nobles and took the crown by force. Richard died mysteriously soon after.

Henry IV spent the rest of his reign establishing his royal authority. But although he passed the crown to his son peacefully, he had sown the seeds of civil war. Half a century later the nobility would be divided between those who supported his family, the "Lancastrians", and those who supported the family of the earl of March, the "Yorkists".

Wales in revolt

Edward I had conquered Wales in the 1280s, and colonised it. He brought English people to enlarge small towns. Pembrokeshire, in the far southwest, even became known as "the little England beyond Wales". Edward's officers drove many of the Welsh into the hills, and gave their land to English farmers. Many Welsh were forced to join the English army, not because they wanted to serve the English but because they had lost their land and needed to live. They fought in Scotland and in France, and taught the English their skill with the longbow.

A century later the Welsh found a man who was ready to rebel against the English king, and whom they were willing to follow. Owain Glyndwr was the first and only Welsh prince to have wide and popular support in every part of Wales. In fact it was he who created the idea of a Welsh nation. He was descended from two royal families which had ruled in different parts of Wales before the Normans came.

Owain Glyndwr's rebellion did not start as a national revolt. At first he joined the revolt of Norman–Welsh border lords who had always tried to be free of royal control. But after ten years of war Owain Glyndwr's border rebellion had developed into a national war, and in 1400 he was proclaimed Prince of Wales by his supporters. This was far more popular with the Welsh people than Edward I's trick with his newborn son at Caernarfon in 1284. However, Glyndwr was not strong enough to

defeat the English armies sent against him. He continued to fight a successful guerrilla war which made the control of Wales an extremely expensive problem for the English. But after 1410 Glyndwr lost almost all his support as Welsh people realised that however hard they fought they would never be free of the English. Owain Glyndwr was never captured. He did for Wales what William Wallace had done for Scotland a century earlier. He created a feeling of national identity.

Cilgerran Castle, near Cardigan in southwest Wales, was captured by Owain Glyndwr in 1405. Although it had been built two hundred years earlier, it was clearly strong and must have been difficult to capture.

The struggle in France

By the end of the fourteenth century, the long war with France, known as the Hundred Years War, had already been going on for over fifty years. But there had been long periods without actual fighting.

When Henry IV died in 1413 he passed on to his son Henry V a kingdom that was peaceful and united. Henry V was a brave and intelligent man, and like Richard I, he became one of England's favourite kings.

Since the situation was peaceful at home Henry V felt able to begin fighting the French again. His French war was as popular as Edward III's had been. Henry had a great advantage because the king of France was mad, and his nobles were quarrelsome. The war began again in 1415 when Henry renewed Edward III's claim to the throne of France. Burgundy again supported England, and the English army was able to prove once more that it was far better in battle than the French army. At Agincourt the same year the English defeated a French army three times its own size. The English were more skilful, and had better weapons.

Between 1417 and 1420 Henry managed to capture most of Normandy and the nearby areas. By the treaty of Troyes in 1420 Henry was recognised as heir to the mad king, and he married Katherine of Valois, the king's daughter. But Henry V never became king of France because he died a few months before the French king in 1422. His nine-month-old baby son, Henry VI, inherited the thrones of England and France.

As with Scotland and Wales, England found it was easier to invade and conquer France than to keep it. At first Henry V's brother, John duke of Bedford, continued to enlarge the area under English control. But soon the French began to fight back. Foreign invasion had created for the first time strong French national feeling. The English army was twice defeated by the French, who were inspired by a mysterious peasant girl called Joan of Arc, who claimed to hear heavenly voices. Joan of Arc was captured by the Burgundians, and given to

Henry V is remembered as possibly the most heroic of English kings because of his brilliant campaigns in France. His death in 1422 brought to an end the English kings' hopes of ruling France.

the English. The English gave her to the Church in Rouen which burnt her as a witch in 1431.

England was now beginning to lose an extremely costly war. In 1435 England's best general, John of Bedford, died. Then England's Breton and Burgundian allies lost confidence in the value of the English alliance. With the loss of Gascony in 1453, the Hundred Years War was over. England had lost everything except the port of Calais.

The battle of Agincourt in 1415 was Henry V's most famous victory against
the French. The English army with the royal standard attacks (left). The
French royal standard is to be seen on the ground (bottom right) as French
soldiers die. Although the English were outnumbered by more than three to
one, Henry's archers destroyed the French feudal cavalry.

The Wars of the Roses

Henry VI, who had become king as a baby, grew up to be simple-minded and book-loving. He hated the warlike nobles, and was an unsuitable king for such a violent society. But he was a civilised and gentle man. He founded two places of learning that still exist, Eton College not far from London, and King's College in Cambridge. He could happily have spent his life in such places of learning. But Henry's simple-mindedness gave way to periods of mental illness.

England had lost a war and was ruled by a mentally ill king who was bad at choosing advisers. It was perhaps natural that the nobles began to ask questions about who should be ruling the country. They remembered that Henry's grandfather Henry of Lancaster had taken the throne when Richard II was deposed.

There were not more than sixty noble families controlling England at this time. Most of them were related to each other through marriage. Some of the nobles were extremely powerful. Many of them continued to keep their own private armies after returning from the war in France, and used them to frighten local people into obeying them. Some of these armies were large. For example, by 1450 the duke of Buckingham had 2,000 men in his private army.

The discontented nobility were divided between those who remained loyal to Henry VI, the "Lancastrians", and those who supported the duke of York, the "Yorkists". The duke of York was the son of the earl of March, who had lost the competition for the throne when Richard II was deposed in 1399. In 1460 the duke of York claimed the throne for himself. After his death in battle, his son Edward took up the struggle and won the throne in 1461.

Edward IV put Henry into the Tower of London, but nine years later a new Lancastrian army rescued Henry and chased Edward out of the country. Like the Lancastrians, Edward was able to raise another army. Edward had the advantage of his popularity with the merchants of London and the southeast of England. This was because the Yorkists had strongly encouraged profitable trade, particularly with Burgundy. Edward returned to England in 1471 and defeated the Lancastrians. At last Edward IV was safe on the throne. Henry VI died in the Tower of London soon after, almost certainly murdered.

The war between York and Lancaster would probably have stopped then if Edward's son had been old enough to rule, and if Edward's brother, Richard of Gloucester, had not been so ambitious. But when Edward IV died in 1483, his own two sons, the twelve-year-old Edward V and his younger brother, were put in the Tower by Richard of Gloucester. Richard took the Crown and became King Richard III. A month later the two princes were murdered. William Shakespeare's play *Richard III*, written a century later, accuses Richard of murder and almost everyone believed it. Richard III had a better reason than most to wish his two nephews dead, but his guilt has never been proved.

Richard III was not popular. Lancastrians and Yorkists both disliked him. In 1485 a challenger with a very distant claim to royal blood through John of Gaunt landed in England with Breton soldiers to claim the throne. Many discontented lords, both Lancastrians and Yorkists, joined him. His name was Henry Tudor, duke of Richmond, and he was half Welsh. He met Richard III at Bosworth. Half of Richard's army changed sides, and the battle quickly ended in his defeat and death. Henry Tudor was crowned king immediately, on the battlefield.

The war had finally ended, though this could not have been clear at the time. Much later, in the nineteenth century, the novelist Walter Scott named these wars the "Wars of the Roses", because York's symbol was a white rose, and Lancaster's a red one.

The Wars of the Roses nearly destroyed the English idea of kingship for ever. After 1460 there had been little respect for anything except the power to take the Crown. Tudor historians made much of these wars and made it seem as if much of England had been destroyed. This was not true. Fighting took place for only a total of fifteen months out of the whole twenty-five year period. Only the nobles and their armies were involved.

It is true, however, that the wars were a disaster for the nobility. For the first time there had been no purpose in taking prisoners, because no one was interested in payment of ransom. Everyone was interested in destroying the opposing nobility. Those captured in battle were usually killed immediately. By the time of the battle of Bosworth in 1485, the old nobility had nearly destroyed itself. Almost half the lords of the sixty noble families had died in the wars. It was this fact which made it possible for the Tudors to build a new nation state.

Scotland

Scotland experienced many of the disasters that affected England at this time. The Scots did not escape the Black Death or the other plagues, and they also suffered from repeated wars.

Scotland paid heavily for its "Auld Alliance" with France. Because it supported France during the Hundred Years War, the English repeatedly invaded the Scottish Lowlands, from which most of the Scots king's wealth came. England renewed its claim to overlordship of Scotland, and Edward IV's army occupied Edinburgh in 1482.

Like the English kings, the Scottish kings were involved in long struggles with their nobles. Support for France turned attention away from establishing a strong state at home. And, as in England, several kings died early. James I was murdered in 1437, James II died in an accident before he was thirty in 1460, and James III was murdered in 1488. The early death of so many Scots kings left government in the hands of powerful nobles until the dead king's son was old enough to rule. Naturally these nobles took the chance to make their own position more powerful.

As in England, the nobles kept private armies, instead of using serfs for military service as they had done earlier. This new system fitted well with the Celtic tribal loyalties of the Highlands. The Gaelic word for such tribes, "clan", means "children", in other words members of one family. But from the

fourteenth century, a "clan" began to mean groups of people occupying an area of land and following a particular chief. Not all the members of a clan were related to each other. Some groups joined a clan for protection, or because they were forced to choose between doing so or leaving the area. The most powerful of the Highland clans by the fifteenth century was Clan Donald. The clan chiefs were almost completely independent.

By the end of the Middle Ages, however, Scotland had developed as a nation in a number of ways. From 1399 the Scots demanded that a parliament should meet once a year, and kings often gathered together leading citizens to discuss matters of government. As in England, towns grew in importance, mainly because of the wool trade which grew thanks to the help of Flemish settlers. There was a large export trade in wool, leather and fish, mostly to the Netherlands.

Scotland's alliance with France brought some benefits. At a time when much of the farmland was repeatedly destroyed by English armies, many Scotsmen found work as soldiers for the French king. Far more importantly, the connection with France helped develop education in Scotland. Following the example of Paris, universities were founded in Scotland at St Andrews in 1412, Glasgow in 1451 and at Aberdeen in 1495. Scotland could rightly claim to be equal with England in learning. By the end of the fifteenth century it was obvious that Scotland was a separate country from England. Nobody, either in England or in Scotland, believed in the English king's claim to be overlord of Scotland.

9 Government and society

Government and society · The condition of women · Language and culture

Government and society

The year 1485 has usually been taken to mark the end of the Middle Ages in England. Of course, nobody at the time would have seen it as such. There was no reason to think that the new King Henry VII would rule over a country any different from the one ruled over by Richard III. Before looking at the changes in England under the House of Tudor it might be worth looking back at some of the main social developments that had taken place in the late Middle Ages.

Society was still based upon rank. At the top were dukes, earls and other lords, although there were far fewer as a result of war. Below these great lords were knights. Most knights, even by Edward I's time, were no longer heavily armed fighters on horses. They were "gentlemen farmers" or "landed gentry" who had increased the size of their landholdings, and improved their farming methods. This class had grown in numbers. Edward I had ordered that all those with an income of £20 a year must be made knights. This meant that even some

Sir Geoffrey Luttrell with his family and retainers at dinner. Food was eaten without forks, at a simple table. However, young men in particular had to remember their manners. "Don't sit down until you are told to and keep your hands and feet still," they were told. "Cut your bread with your knife and do not tear it. Don't lean on the table and make a mess on the cloth or drink with a full mouth. Don't take so much in your mouth that you cannot answer when someone speaks to you." Several people shared the same cup, so a final piece of advice was "wipe your mouth and hands clean with a cloth, so that you do not dirty the cup and make your friends unwilling to drink with you."

Great Chalfield manor, rebuilt in 1480, is a fine example of a late Middle Ages manor house. It was owned by a local landowner and lawyer who, like many of the gentry class, profited greatly from the destruction of the nobility in the Wars of the Roses. The front of the house is almost exactly as it was in 1480, but the building on the right is much later. The great hall is immediately inside the main entrance, a typical arrangement for this period.

of the yeoman farmers became part of the "landed gentry", while many "esquires", who had served knights in earlier times, now became knights themselves. The word "esquire" became common in written addresses, and is only now slowly beginning to be used less.

Next to the gentlemen were the ordinary freemen of the towns. By the end of the Middle Ages, it was possible for a serf from the countryside to work for seven years in a town craft guild, and to become a "freeman" of the town where he lived. The freemen controlled the life of a town. Towns offered to poor men the chance to become rich and successful through trade. The most famous example of this was Dick Whittington. The story tells how he arrived in London as a poor boy from the

countryside, and became a successful merchant and Lord Mayor of London three times. Whittington was, actually, the son of a knight. He was probably an example of the growing practice of the landed families of sending younger sons to town to join a merchant or craft guild. At the same time, many successful merchant families were doing the opposite thing, and obtaining farmland in the countryside. These two classes, the landed gentry and the town merchants, were beginning to overlap.

In the beginning the guilds had been formed to protect the production or trade of a whole town. Later, they had come to protect those already enjoying membership, or who could afford to buy it, from the poorer classes in the same town. As

A leading citizen of Bristol is made mayor, 1479. The appointment of the mayor and alderman of a city was usually controlled by senior members of a city's merchant and craft guilds.

they did not have the money or family connections to become members of the guilds, the poorer skilled workers tried to join together to protect their own interests. These were the first efforts to form a trade union. Several times in the fourteenth century skilled workers tried unsuccessfully to protect themselves against the power of the guilds. The lives of skilled workers were hard, but they did not suffer as much as the unskilled, who lived in poor and dirty conditions. However, even the condition of the poorest workers in both town and country was better than it had been a century earlier.

In fact, the guilds were declining in importance because of a new force in the national economy. During the fourteenth century a number of English merchants established trading stations, "factories", in different places in Europe. The merchant organisations necessary to operate these factories became important at a national level, and began to replace the old town guilds as the most powerful trading institutions. However, they copied the aims and methods of the guilds, making sure English merchants could only export through their factories, and making sure that prices and quality were maintained.

All women, from the highest, as in this picture, to the lowest in the land were expected to know how to prepare, spin and weave wool. From Saxon times onwards English women were famous for their embroidery skills. Women were expected to spend their time in embroidery or in making garments right up to the end of the nineteenth century.

One of the most important of these factories was the "Company of the Staple" in Calais. The "staple" was an international term used by merchants and governments meaning that certain goods could only be sold in particular places. Calais became the "staple" for all English wool at the end of the fourteenth century when it defeated rival English factories in other foreign cities. The staple was an arrangement which suited the established merchants, as it prevented competition, and it also suited the Crown, which could tax exports more easily. The other important company was called the "Merchant Adventurers". During the fourteenth century there had been several Merchant Adventurers' factories in a number of foreign towns. But all of them, except for the Merchant Adventurers in Antwerp, Flanders, closed during the fifteenth century. The Antwerp Merchant Adventurers' factory survived because of its sole control of cloth exports, a fact recognised by royal charter.

Wages for farmworkers and for skilled townspeople rose faster than the price of goods in the fifteenth century. There was plenty of meat and cereal prices were low. But there were warning signs of problems ahead. More and more good land was being used for sheep instead of food crops. Rich and powerful sheep farmers started to fence in land which had always been used by other villagers. In the sixteenth century this led to social and economic crisis.

Meanwhile, in the towns, a new middle class was developing. By the fifteenth century most merchants were well educated, and considered themselves to be the equals of the esquires and gentlemen of the countryside. The lawyers were another class of city people. In London they were considered equal in importance to the big merchants and cloth manufacturers. When law schools were first established, student lawyers lived in inns on the western side of the City of London while they studied. Slowly these inns became part of the law schools, just as the student accommodation halls of Oxford and Cambridge eventually became the colleges of these two universities.

By the end of the Middle Ages the more successful of these lawyers, merchants, cloth manufacturers, exporters, esquires, gentlemen and yeoman farmers were increasingly forming a single class of people with interests in both town and country. This was also true in Wales and Scotland. A number of Welsh landowners came to England; some studied at Oxford, and some traded, or practised law in London. Fewer Scots came to England, because they had their own universities, and their own trade centres of Edinburgh, Glasgow and Aberdeen.

The growth of this new middle class, educated and skilled in law, administration and trade, created a new atmosphere in Britain. This was partly because of the increase in literacy. Indeed, the middle class could be described as the "literate class". This literate class questioned the way in which the Church and the state were organised, for both religious and practical reasons. On the religious side support for Wycliffe came mainly from members of this new middle class, who believed it was their right to read the Bible in the English language. They disliked serfdom partly because it was now increasingly viewed as unchristian, but also for the practical reason that it was not economic. The middle class also questioned the value of the feudal system because it did not create wealth.

The development of Parliament at this time showed the beginnings of a new relationship between the middle class and the king. Edward I had invited knights from the country and merchants from the towns to his parliament because he wanted money and they, more than any other group, could provide it. But when Edward III asked for money from his parliament, they asked to see the royal accounts. It was an important development because for the first time the king allowed himself to be "accountable" to Parliament. Merchants and country gentlemen were very anxious to influence the king's policies both at home and abroad. They wanted to protect their interests. When France threatened the wool trade with Flanders, for example, they supported Edward III in his war.

During the time of Edward III's reign Parliament became organised in two parts: the Lords, and the Commons, which represented the middle class. Only those commoners with an income of forty shillings or more a year could qualify to be members of Parliament. This meant that the poor had no way of being heard except by rebellion. The poor had no voice of their own in Parliament until the middle of the nineteenth century.

The alliance between esquires and merchants made Parliament more powerful, and separated the Commons more and more from the Lords. Many European countries had the same kind of parliaments at this time, but in most cases these disappeared when feudalism died out. In England, however, the death of feudalism helped strengthen the House of Commons in Parliament.

There was another important change that had taken place in the country. Kings had been taking law cases away from local lords' courts since the twelfth century, and by the middle of the fourteenth century the courts of local lords no longer existed. But the king's courts could not deal with all the work. In 1363 Edward III appointed "justices of the peace" to deal with smaller crimes and offences, and to hold court four times a year.

These JPs, as they became known, were usually less important lords or members of the landed gentry. They were, and still are, chosen for their fairness

and honesty. The appointment of landed gentry as
JPs made the middle classes, that class of people
who were neither nobles nor peasants, still
stronger. Through the system of JPs the landed
gentry took the place of the nobility as the local
authority. During the Wars of the Roses the nobles
used their private armies to force JPs and judges to
do what they wanted. But this was the last time the
nobility in Britain tried to destroy the authority of
the king. The JPs remained the only form of local
government in the countryside until 1888. They
still exist to deal with small offences.

The condition of women

Little is known about the life of women in the
Middle Ages, but without doubt it was hard. The
Church taught that women should obey their
husbands. It also spread two very different ideas
about women: that they should be pure and holy
like the Virgin Mary; and that, like Eve, they could
not be trusted and were a moral danger to men.
Such religious teaching led men both to worship
and also to look down on women, and led women
to give in to men's authority.

Marriage was usually the single most important
event in the lives of men and women. But the
decision itself was made by the family, not the
couple themselves. This was because by marriage a
family could improve its wealth and social position.
Everyone, both rich and poor, married for mainly
financial reasons. Once married, a woman had to
accept her husband as her master. A disobedient
wife was usually beaten. It is unlikely that love
played much of a part in most marriages.

The first duty of every wife was to give her husband
children, preferably sons. Because so many children
died as babies, and because there was little that
could be done if a birth went wrong, producing
children was dangerous and exhausting. Yet this
was the future for every wife from twenty or
younger until she was forty.

The wife of a noble had other responsibilities.
When her lord was away, she was in charge of the
manor and the village lands, all the servants and

*Women defending their castle. Throughout the Middle Ages, if a castle or
manor was attacked while its lord was away, it was the duty of his wife, the
"chatelaine" (or "castlekeeper"), to defend it. A lady had to know
everything about administering her lord's manor and lands, for she was
responsible when he was away. One lady who did not completely trust her
lord's ability to manage while she was away, wrote to him, "Keep all well
about you till I come home, and treat not [do not enter into business
arrangements] without me, and then all things shall be well."*

villagers, the harvest and the animals. She also had
to defend the manor if it was attacked. She had to
run the household, welcome visitors, and store
enough food, including salted meat, for winter. She
was expected to have enough knowledge of herbs
and plants to make suitable medicines for those in
the village who were sick. She probably visited the
poor and the sick in the village, showing that the

Bay Leaf Farm, a fifteenth-century Kent farmhouse, a timber-frame building with walls made of "wattle and daub", basically sticks and mud. This was a very effective type of building, but required skilled carpenters to make a strong frame. One man who did not like this new method called these houses little more than "paper work". But examples are still lived in as ordinary homes in many parts of England.

rulers "cared" for them. She had little time for her own children, who in any case were often sent away at the age of eight to another manor, the boys to "be made into men".

Most women, of course, were peasants, busy making food, making cloth and making clothes from the cloth. They worked in the fields, looked after the children, the geese, the pigs and the sheep, made the cheese and grew the vegetables. The animals probably shared the family shelter at night. The family home was dark and smelly.

A woman's position improved if her husband died. She could get control of the money her family had given the husband at the time of marriage, usually about one-third of his total land and wealth. But she might have to marry again: men wanted her land, and it was difficult to look after it without the help of a man.

Language and culture

With the spread of literacy, cultural life in Britain naturally developed also. In the cities, plays were performed at important religious festivals. They were called "mystery plays" because of the mysterious nature of events in the Bible, and they were a popular form of culture. In the larger cities some guilds made themselves responsible for particular plays, which became traditional yearly events.

The language itself was changing. French had been used less and less by the Norman rulers during the thirteenth century. In the fourteenth century Edward III had actually forbidden the speaking of French in his army. It was a way of making the whole army aware of its Englishness.

After the Norman Conquest English (the old Anglo-Saxon language) continued to be spoken by ordinary people but was no longer written. By the end of the fourteenth century, however, English was once again a written language, because it was being used instead of French by the ruling, literate class. But "Middle English", the language of the fourteenth and fifteenth centuries, was very different from Anglo-Saxon. This was partly because it had not been written for three hundred years, and partly because it had borrowed so much from Norman French.

Two writers, above all others, helped in the rebirth of English literature. One was William Langland, a mid-fourteenth century priest, whose poem *Piers Plowman* gives a powerful description of the times in which he lived. The other, Geoffrey Chaucer, has become much more famous. He lived at about the same time as Langland. His most famous work was *The Canterbury Tales*, written at the end of the fourteenth century.

The Canterbury Tales describe a group of pilgrims travelling from London to the tomb of Thomas Becket at Canterbury, a common religious act in England in the Middle Ages. During the journey each character tells a story. Collections of stories were popular at this time because almost all literature, unlike today, was written to be read out aloud. The stories themselves are not Chaucer's own. He used old stories, but rewrote them in an interesting and amusing way. The first chapter, in which he describes his characters, is the result of Chaucer's own deep understanding of human nature. It remains astonishingly fresh even after six hundred years. It is a unique description of a nation: young and old, knight and peasant, priest and merchant, good and bad, townsman and countryman. Here is part of Chaucer's description (in a modernised version) of the knight, and his son, the squire:

There was a *knight*, a most distinguished man,
Who from the day on which he first began
To ride abroad had followed chivalry,
Truth, honour, generousness and courtesy . . .
He had his son with him, a fine young *squire*,
A lover and cadet, a lad of fire
With locks as curly as if they had been pressed.
He was some twenty years of age, I guessed . . .
He was embroidered like a meadow bright
And full of freshest flowers, red and white.
Singing he was, or fluting all the day;
He was as fresh as is the month of May.
Short was his gown, the sleeves were long and
    wide;
He knew the way to sit a horse and ride.
He could make songs and poems and recite,
Knew how to joust and dance, to draw and write.
He loved so hotly that till dawn grew pale
He slept as little as a nightingale.

By the end of the Middle Ages, English as well as Latin was being used in legal writing, and also in elementary schools. Education developed enormously during the fifteenth century, and many schools were founded by powerful men. One of these was William of Wykeham, Bishop of Winchester and Lord Chancellor of England, who founded both Winchester School, in 1382, and New College, Oxford. Like Henry VI's later foundations at Eton and Cambridge they have remained famous for their high quality. Many other schools were also opened at this time, because there was a growing need for educated people who could administer the government, the Church, the law and trade. Clerks started grammar schools where students could learn the skills of reading and writing. These schools offered their pupils a future in the Church or the civil service, or at the universities of Oxford and Cambridge. The universities themselves continued to grow as colleges and halls where the students could both live and be taught were built. The college system remains the basis of organisation in these two universities.

The Middle Ages ended with a major technical development: William Caxton's first English printing press, set up in 1476. Caxton had learnt the skill of printing in Germany. At first he printed popular books, such as Chaucer's *Canterbury Tales* and Malory's *Morte d'Arthur*. This long poem described the adventures of the legendary King Arthur, including Arthur's last battle, his death, and the death of other knights of the Round Table. Almost certainly Malory had in mind the destruction of the English nobility in the Wars of the Roses, which were taking place as he wrote.

Caxton's printing press was as dramatic for his age as radio, television and the technological revolution are for our own. Books suddenly became cheaper and more plentiful, as the quicker printing process replaced slow and expensive copywriting by hand. Printing began to standardise spelling and grammar, though this process was a long one. More important, just as radio brought information and ideas to the illiterate people of the twentieth century, Caxton's press provided books for the newly educated people of the fifteenth century, and encouraged literacy. Caxton avoided printing any dangerous literature. But the children and grandchildren of these literate people were to use printing as a powerful weapon to change the world in which they lived.

The chapel of King's College, Cambridge, with its fan-vaulted roof and large areas of glass and delicate stone work, marks the highest point of Gothic architecture in England. It was finished at the end of the fifteenth century, and the wooden organ screen across the centre of the chapel is of Tudor design.

The Tudors

10   The birth of the nation state

The new monarchy · The Reformation · The Protestant–Catholic struggle

The century of Tudor rule (1485–1603) is often thought of as a most glorious period in English history. Henry VII built the foundations of a wealthy nation state and a powerful monarchy. His son, Henry VIII, kept a magnificent court, and made the Church in England truly English by breaking away from the Roman Catholic Church. Finally, his daughter Elizabeth brought glory to the new state by defeating the powerful navy of Spain, the greatest European power of the time. During the Tudor age England experienced one of the greatest artistic periods in its history.

There is, however, a less glorious view of the Tudor century. Henry VIII wasted the wealth saved by his father. Elizabeth weakened the quality of government by selling official posts. She did this to avoid asking Parliament for money. And although her government tried to deal with the problem of poor and homeless people at a time when prices rose much faster than wages, its laws and actions were often cruel in effect.

The new monarchy

Henry VII is less well known than either Henry VIII or Elizabeth I. But he was far more important in establishing the new monarchy than either of

them. He had the same ideas and opinions as the growing classes of merchants and gentleman farmers, and he based royal power on good business sense.

Henry VII firmly believed that war and glory were bad for business, and that business was good for the state. He therefore avoided quarrels either with Scotland in the north, or France in the south.

Left: *The defeat of the Spanish Armada in 1588 was the most glorious event of Elizabeth I's reign. It marked the arrival of England as a great European sea power, leading the way to the development of the empire over the next two centuries. It also marked the limit of Spain's ability to recapture Protestant countries for the Catholic Church.*

Right: *Henry VII was clever with people and careful with money. He holds a red Lancastrian rose in his hand, but he brought unity to the Houses of York and Lancaster. His successors symbolised this unity by use of a red rose with white outer petals, the "Tudor" rose.*

During the fifteenth century, but particularly during the Wars of the Roses, England's trading position had been badly damaged. The strong German Hanseatic League, a closed trading society, had destroyed English trade with the Baltic and northern Europe. Trade with Italy and France had also been reduced after England's defeat in France in the mid-fifteenth century. The Low Countries (the Netherlands and Belgium) alone offered a way in for trade in Europe. Only a year after his victory at Bosworth in 1485, Henry VII made an important trade agreement with the Netherlands which allowed English trade to grow again.

Henry was fortunate. Many of the old nobility had died or been defeated in the recent wars, and their

Henry VIII, by the great court painter Hans Holbein. Henry was hard, cruel, ambitious and calculating. Few survived his anger. He executed two of his wives, Anne Boleyn and Catherine Howard, and several of his ministers and leading churchmen. Best known among these were his Lord Chancellor, Thomas More, and his assistant in carrying out the Reformation, Thomas Cromwell.

lands had gone to the king. This meant that Henry had more power and more money than earlier kings. In order to establish his authority beyond question, he forbade anyone, except himself, to keep armed men.

The authority of the law had been almost completely destroyed by the lawless behaviour of nobles and their armed men. Henry used the "Court of Star Chamber", traditionally the king's council chamber, to deal with lawless nobles. Local justice that had broken down during the wars slowly began to operate again. Henry encouraged the use of heavy fines as punishment because this gave the Crown money.

Henry's aim was to make the Crown financially independent, and the lands and the fines he took from the old nobility helped him do this. Henry also raised taxes for wars which he then did not fight. He never spent money unless he had to. One might expect Henry to have been unpopular, but he was careful to keep the friendship of the merchant and lesser gentry classes. Like him they wanted peace and prosperity. He created a new nobility from among them, and men unknown before now became Henry's statesmen. But they all knew that their rise to importance was completely dependent on the Crown.

When Henry died in 1509 he left behind the huge total of £2 million, about fifteen years' worth of income. The only thing on which he was happy to spend money freely was the building of ships for a merchant fleet. Henry understood earlier than most people that England's future wealth would depend on international trade. And in order to trade, Henry realised that England must have its own fleet of merchant ships.

Henry VIII was quite unlike his father. He was cruel, wasteful with money, and interested in pleasing himself. He wanted to become an important influence in European politics. But much had happened in Europe since England had given up its efforts to defeat France in the Hundred Years War. France was now more powerful than England, and Spain was even more powerful, because it was united with the Holy Roman Empire (which included much of central Europe). Henry VIII wanted England to hold the balance of power between these two giants. He first unsuccessfully allied himself with Spain, and when he was not rewarded he changed sides. When friendship with France did not bring him anything, Henry started talking again to Charles V of Spain.

Henry's failure to gain an important position in European politics was a bitter disappointment. He spent so much on maintaining a magnificent court, and on wars from which England had little to gain, that his father's carefully saved money was soon gone. Gold and silver from newly discovered America added to economic inflation. In this serious financial crisis, Henry needed money. One way of doing this was by reducing the amount of silver used in coins. But although this gave Henry immediate profits, it rapidly led to a rise in prices. It was therefore a damaging policy, and the English coinage was reduced to a seventh of its value within twenty-five years.

The Reformation

Henry VIII was always looking for new sources of money. His father had become powerful by taking over the nobles' land, but the lands owned by the Church and the monasteries had not been touched. The Church was a huge landowner, and the monasteries were no longer important to economic and social growth in the way they had been two hundred years earlier. In fact they were unpopular because many monks no longer led a good religious life but lived in wealth and comfort.

Henry disliked the power of the Church in England because, since it was an international organisation, he could not completely control it. If Henry had been powerful enough in Europe to influence the pope it might have been different. But there were two far more powerful states, France, and Spain, with the Holy Roman Empire, lying between him and Rome. The power of the Catholic Church in England could therefore work against his own authority, and the taxes paid to the Church

reduced his own income. Henry was not the only European king with a wish to "centralise" state authority. Many others were doing the same thing. But Henry had another reason for standing up to the authority of the Church.

In 1510 Henry had married Catherine of Aragon, the widow of his elder brother Arthur. But by 1526 she had still not had a son who survived infancy and was now unlikely to do so. Henry tried to persuade the pope to allow him to divorce Catherine. Normally, Henry need not have expected any difficulty. His chief minister, Cardinal Wolsey, had already been skilful in advising on Henry's foreign and home policy. Wolsey hoped that his skills, and his important position in the Church, would be successful in persuading the pope. But the pope was controlled by Charles V, who was Holy Roman Emperor and king of Spain, and also Catherine's nephew. For both political and family reasons he wanted Henry to stay married to Catherine. The pope did not wish to anger either Charles or Henry, but eventually he was forced to do as Charles V wanted. He forbade Henry's divorce.

Henry was extremely angry and the first person to feel his anger was his own minister, Cardinal Wolsey. Wolsey only escaped execution by dying of natural causes on his way to the king's court, and after Wolsey no priest ever again became an important minister of the king. In 1531 Henry persuaded the bishops to make him head of the Church in England, and this became law after Parliament passed the Act of Supremacy in 1534. It was a popular decision. Henry was now free to divorce Catherine and marry his new love, Anne Boleyn. He hoped Anne would give him a son to follow him on the throne.

Henry's break with Rome was purely political. He had simply wanted to control the Church and to keep its wealth in his own kingdom. He did not approve of the new ideas of Reformation Protestantism introduced by Martin Luther in Germany and John Calvin in Geneva. He still believed in the Catholic faith. Indeed, Henry had earlier written a book criticising Luther's teaching and the pope had rewarded him with the title *Fidei Defensor*, Defender of the Faith. The pope must have regretted his action. The letters "F.D." are still to be found on every British coin.

Like his father, Henry VIII governed England through his close advisers, men who were completely dependent on him for their position. But when he broke with Rome, he used Parliament to make the break legal. Through several Acts of Parliament between 1532 and 1536, England became politically a Protestant country, even though the popular religion was still Catholic.

Once England had accepted the separation from Rome Henry took the English Reformation a step further. Wolsey's place as the king's chief minister was taken by one of his assistants, Thomas Cromwell. Henry and Cromwell made a careful survey of Church property, the first properly organised tax survey since the Domesday Book 450 years earlier. Between 1536 and 1539 they closed 560 monasteries and other religious houses. Henry did this in order to make money, but he also wanted to be popular with the rising classes of landowners and merchants. He therefore gave or sold much of the monasteries' lands to them. Many smaller landowners made their fortunes. Most knocked down the old monastery buildings and used the stone to create magnificent new houses for themselves. Other buildings were just left to fall down.

Meanwhile the monks and nuns were thrown out. Some were given small sums of money, but many were unable to find work and became wandering beggars. The dissolution of the monasteries was probably the greatest act of official destruction in the history of Britain.

Henry proved that his break with Rome was neither a religious nor a diplomatic disaster. He remained loyal to Catholic religious teaching, and executed Protestants who refused to accept it. He even made an alliance with Charles V of Spain against France. For political reasons both of them were willing to forget the quarrel over Catherine of Aragon, and also England's break with Rome.

Henry died in 1547, leaving behind his sixth wife, Catherine Parr, and his three children. Mary, the eldest, was the daughter of Catherine of Aragon. Elizabeth was the daughter of his second wife, Anne Boleyn, whom he had executed because she was unfaithful. Nine-year-old Edward was the son of Jane Seymour, the only wife whom Henry had really loved, but who had died giving birth to his only son.

The ruins of Fountains Abbey in Yorkshire, one of the greatest and wealthiest English monasteries. If finally surrendered to Henry's reformation in 1539. The stained glass and lead window frames and roofing were removed immediately. But it was not until 1611 that some of the stone was taken to build Fountains Hall, nearby. Even so, the abbey was so huge that most of the stone was never taken and the abbey survived as a ruin.

The Protestant—Catholic struggle

Edward VI, Henry VIII's son, was only a child when he became king, so the country was ruled by a council. All the members of this council were from the new nobility created by the Tudors. They were keen Protestant reformers because they had benefited from the sale of monastery lands. Indeed, all the new landowners knew that they could only be sure of keeping their new lands if they made England truly Protestant.

Most English people still believed in the old Catholic religion. Less than half the English were Protestant by belief, but these people were allowed to take a lead in religious matters. In 1552 a new prayer book was introduced to make sure that all churches followed the new Protestant religion. Most people were not very happy with the new religion. They had been glad to see the end of some of the Church's bad practices like the selling of "pardons" for the forgiveness of sins. But they did not like the changes in belief, and in some places there was trouble.

Mary, the Catholic daughter of Catherine of Aragon, became queen when Edward, aged sixteen, died in 1553. A group of nobles tried to put Lady Jane Grey, a Protestant, on the throne. But Mary succeeded in entering London and took control of the kingdom. She was supported by the ordinary people, who were angered by the greed of the Protestant nobles.

However, Mary was unwise and unbending in her policy and her beliefs. She was the first queen of England since Matilda, 400 years earlier. At that time women were considered to be inferior to men. The marriage of a queen was therefore a difficult matter. If Mary married an Englishman she would be under the control of a man of lesser importance. If she married a foreigner it might place England under foreign control.

Mary, for political, religious and family reasons, chose to marry King Philip of Spain. It was an unfortunate choice. The ordinary people disliked the marriage, as Philip's Spanish friends in England were quick to notice. Popular feeling was so strong that a rebellion in Kent actually reached London before ending in failure. Mary dealt cruelly with the rebel leader, Wyatt, but she took the unusual step of asking Parliament for its opinion about her marriage plan. Parliament unwillingly agreed to Mary's marriage, and it only accepted Philip as king of England for Mary's lifetime.

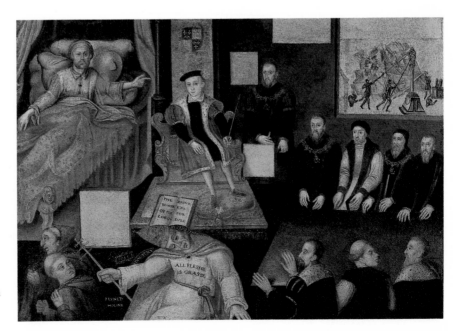

A Protestant propaganda picture of Edward VI being told by his dying father, Henry VIII, to uphold the true Protestant religion. At Edward's feet the pope collapses defeated. Under Edward England became far more Protestant than before, and more Protestant, probably, than his father intended. The young king was assisted by men who had profited from Church lands and property after the break with Rome.

Mary's marriage to Philip was the first mistake of her unfortunate reign. She then began burning Protestants. Three hundred people died in this way during her five-year reign, and the burnings began to sicken people. At the same time, the thought of becoming a junior ally of Spain was very unpopular. Only the knowledge that Mary herself was dying prevented a popular rebellion.

Elizabeth, Mary's half sister, was lucky to become queen when Mary died in 1558. Mary had considered killing her, because she was an obvious leader for Protestant revolt. Elizabeth had been wise enough to say nothing, do nothing, and to express neither Catholic nor Protestant views while Mary lived. And Philip persuaded Mary to leave Elizabeth unharmed.

When she became queen in 1558, Elizabeth I wanted to find a peaceful answer to the problems of the English Reformation. She wanted to bring together again those parts of English society which were in religious disagreement. And she wanted to make England prosperous. In some ways the kind of Protestantism finally agreed in 1559 remained closer to the Catholic religion than to other Protestant groups. But Elizabeth made sure that the Church was still under her authority, unlike politically dangerous forms of Protestantism in Europe. In a way, she made the Church part of the state machine.

The "parish", the area served by one church, usually the same size as a village, became the unit of state administration. People had to go to church on Sundays by law and they were fined if they stayed away. This meant that the parish priest, the "parson" or "vicar", became almost as powerful as the village squire. Elizabeth also arranged for a book of sermons to be used in church. Although most of the sermons consisted of Bible teaching, this book also taught the people that rebellion against the Crown was a sin against God.

The struggle between Catholics and Protestants continued to endanger Elizabeth's position for the next thirty years. Both France and Spain were Catholic. Elizabeth and her advisers wanted to avoid open quarrels with both of them. This was not easy, because both the French and Spanish kings wanted to marry Elizabeth and so join England to their own country. Elizabeth and her advisers knew how much damage Mary had done and that it was important that she should avoid such a marriage. At the same time, however, there was a danger that the pope would persuade Catholic countries to attack England. Finally, there was a danger from those Catholic nobles still in England who wished to remove Elizabeth and replace her with the queen of Scotland, who was a Catholic.

Mary, the Scottish queen, usually called "Queen of Scots", was the heir to the English throne because she was Elizabeth's closest living relative, and because Elizabeth had not married. Mary's mother had been French, and Mary had spent her childhood in France, and was a strong Catholic. When she returned to rule Scotland as queen, Mary soon made enemies of some of her nobles, and to avoid them she finally escaped to the safety of England. Elizabeth, however, kept Mary as a prisoner for almost twenty years. During that time Elizabeth discovered several secret Catholic plots, some of which clearly aimed at making Mary queen of England.

It was difficult for Elizabeth to decide what to do with Mary. She knew that France was unlikely to attack England in support of Mary. But she was afraid that Spain might do so. Mary's close connection with France, however, was a discouragement to Philip. He would not wish to defeat Elizabeth only to put Mary on the throne. It would be giving England to the French. So for a long time Elizabeth just kept Mary as a prisoner.

When Elizabeth finally agreed to Mary's execution in 1587, it was partly because Mary had named Philip as her heir to the throne of England, and because with this claim Philip of Spain had decided to invade England. Elizabeth no longer had a reason to keep Mary alive. In England Mary's execution was popular. The Catholic plots and the dangers of a foreign Catholic invasion had changed people's feelings. By 1585 most English people believed that to be a Catholic was to be an enemy of England. This hatred of everything Catholic became an important political force.

11 England and her neighbours

*The new foreign policy · The new trading empire · Wales · Ireland ·
Scotland and England · Mary Queen of Scots and the Scottish
Reformation · A Scottish king for England*

The new foreign policy

During the Tudor period, from 1485 until 1603, English foreign policy changed several times. But by the end of the period England had established some basic principles. Henry VII had been careful to remain friendly with neighbouring countries. His son, Henry VIII, had been more ambitious, hoping to play an important part in European politics. He was unsuccessful. Mary allied England to Spain by her marriage. This was not only unpopular but was politically unwise: England had nothing to gain from being allied to a more powerful country. Elizabeth and her advisers considered trade the most important foreign policy matter, as Henry VII had done. For them whichever country was England's greatest trade rival was also its greatest enemy. This idea remained the basis of England's foreign policy until the nineteenth century.

Elizabeth's grandfather, Henry VII, had recognised the importance of trade and had built a large fleet of merchant ships. His son, Henry VIII, had spent money on warships and guns, making English guns the best in Europe.

Elizabeth's foreign policy carried Henry VII's work much further, encouraging merchant expansion. She correctly recognised Spain as her main trade rival and enemy. Spain at that time ruled the Netherlands, although many of the people were Protestant and were fighting for their independence from Catholic Spanish rule. Because Spain and France were rivals, Spanish soldiers could only reach the Netherlands from Spain by sea. This

meant sailing up the English Channel. Elizabeth helped the Dutch Protestants by allowing their ships to use English harbours from which they could attack Spanish ships, often with the help of the English. When it looked as if the Dutch rebels might be defeated, after they lost the city of Antwerp in 1585, Elizabeth agreed to help them with money and soldiers. It was almost an open declaration of war on Spain.

English ships had already been attacking Spanish ships as they returned from America loaded with silver and gold. This had been going on since about 1570, and was the result of Spain's refusal to allow England to trade freely with Spanish American colonies. Although these English ships were privately owned "privateers", the treasure was shared with the queen. Elizabeth apologised to Spain but kept her share of what had been taken from Spanish ships. Philip knew quite well that Elizabeth was encouraging the "sea dogs", as they were known. These seamen were traders as well as pirates and adventurers. The most famous of them were John Hawkins, Francis Drake and Martin Frobisher, but there were many others who were also trying to build English sea trade and to interrupt Spain's.

Philip decided to conquer England in 1587 because he believed this had to be done before he would be able to defeat the Dutch rebels in the Netherlands. He hoped that enough Catholics in England would be willing to help him. Philip's large army was already in the Netherlands. He built a great fleet of ships, an "Armada", to move his army across the

Elizabeth triumphant. The famous "Armada portrait" shows the Spanish Armada in full sail (left) and wrecked upon Ireland's shores (right). Under Elizabeth's right hand lies the world, a reference to Francis Drake's successful voyage around the world, the expeditions of other explorers, and England's growing seapower. Elizabeth enjoyed glory, and her great vanity shows in this portrait.

English Channel from the Netherlands. But in 1587 Francis Drake attacked and destroyed part of this fleet in Cadiz harbour.

Philip started again, and built the largest fleet that had ever gone to sea. But most of the ships were designed to carry soldiers, and the few fighting ships were not as good as the English ones. English ships were longer and narrower, so that they were faster, and their guns could also shoot further than the Spanish ones.

When news of this Armada reached England in summer 1588, Elizabeth called her soldiers together. She won their hearts with well-chosen words: "I am come . . . to live or die amongst you all, to lay down for my God, and for my kingdom, and for my people, my honour and my blood even in the dust. I know I have the body of a weak and feeble woman, but I have the heart and stomach of a king, and of a king of England too."

The Spanish Armada was defeated more by bad weather than by English guns. Some Spanish ships were sunk, but most were blown northwards by the wind, many being wrecked on the rocky coasts of Scotland and Ireland. For England it was a glorious moment, but it did not lead to an end of the war with Spain, and England found itself

having to spend more than ever on England's defence. Peace was only made with Spain once Elizabeth was dead.

The new trading empire

Both before and after the Armada, Elizabeth followed two policies. She encouraged English sailors like John Hawkins and Francis Drake to continue to attack and destroy Spanish ships bringing gold, silver and other treasures back from the newly discovered continent of America. She also encouraged English traders to settle abroad and to create colonies. This second policy led directly to Britain's colonial empire of the seventeenth and eighteenth centuries.

The first English colonists sailed to America towards the end of the century. One of the best known was Sir Walter Raleigh, who brought tobacco back to England. The settlers tried without success to start profitable colonies in Virginia, which was named after Elizabeth, the "virgin" or unmarried queen. But these were only beginnings.

England also began selling West African slaves to work for the Spanish in America. John Hawkins carried his first slave cargo in 1562. By 1650 slavery had become an important trade, bringing wealth

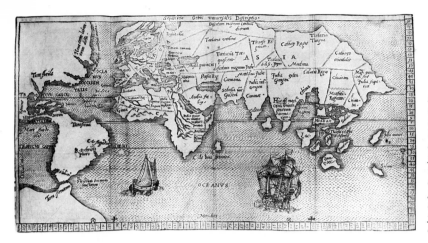

A map of the world drawn in the early years of the sixteenth century shows geographical knowledge decreasing with distance from Europe. Australia, for example, is still completely unknown. Even so, this map was a great improvement on geographical knowledge a century earlier. By the end of the century far more accurate maps were appearing.

particularly to Bristol in southwest England. It took until the end of the eighteenth century for this trade to be ended.

This growth of trade abroad was not entirely new. The Merchant Adventurers Company had already been established with royal support before the end of the fifteenth century. During Elizabeth's reign more "chartered" companies, as they were known, were established. A "charter" gave a company the right to all the business in its particular trade or region. In return for this important advantage the chartered company gave some of its profits to the Crown. A number of these companies were established during Elizabeth's reign: the Eastland Company to trade with Scandinavia and the Baltic in 1579; the Levant Company to trade with the Ottoman Empire in 1581; the Africa Company to trade in slaves, in 1588; and the East India Company to trade with India in 1600.

The East India Company was established mainly because the Dutch controlled the entire spice trade with the East Indies (Indonesia). Spices were extremely important for making the winter salted meat tastier. The English were determined to have a share in this rich trade, but were unsuccessful. However, the East India Company did begin to operate in India, Persia and even in Japan, where it had a trading station from 1613–23. The quarrel over spices was England's first difficulty with the Dutch. Before the end of the seventeenth century trading competition with the Dutch had led to three wars.

Wales

Closer to home, the Tudors did their best to bring Wales, Ireland and Scotland under English control.

Henry VII was half Welsh. At the battle of Bosworth in 1485 Henry's flag was the red dragon of Wales. It had been the badge of the legendary last British (Welsh) king to fight against the Saxons. At the time, Caxton was printing Malory's poem *Morte d'Arthur*. Henry cleverly made the most of popular "Arthurian" interest to suggest that he was somehow connected with the ancient British king, and named his eldest son Arthur. He also brought many Welshmen to his court.

Arthur, Prince of Wales, died early and Henry's second son became Henry VIII. But he did not share his father's love of Wales. His interest was in power and authority, through direct control. He wanted the Welsh to become English.

One example of the changes Henry VIII made was in the matter of names. At that time the Welsh did not have family names. They used their own first name with those of their father and grandfather, using *ap*, which meant "son of". Names were long, and the English, who had been using family names for about three hundred years, found them difficult. From 1535 the English put pressure on the Welsh to use an English system of names by preventing Welsh names being used in law courts and on official papers. By 1750 the use of Welsh names had almost disappeared, although not before one Welshman had made a final and humorous protest.

He signed his name "Sion ap William ap Sion ap William ap Sion ap Dafydd ap Ithel Fychan as Cynrig ap Robert ap Iowerth ap Rhyrid ap Iowerth ap Madoc ap Ednawain Bendew, called after the English fashion John Jones." Many Welsh people accepted wrong English ways of pronouncing their names. Others took their fathers' first names and ap Richard, ap Robert, ap Hywel, ap Hugh soon became Pritchard, Probert, Powell and Pugh. Others who had not used "ap" were known as Williams, Thomas, Davies, Hughes and so on.

Between 1536 and 1543 Wales became joined to England under one administration. English law was now the only law for Wales. Local Welshmen were appointed as JPs, so that the Welsh gentry became part of the ruling English establishment. Those parts of Wales which had not been "shired" were now organised like English counties. Welshmen entered the English parliament. English became the only official language, and Welsh was soon only spoken in the hills. Although Welsh was not allowed as an official language, Henry VIII gave permission for a Welsh Bible to be printed, which became the basis on which the Welsh language survived.

Although most people gave up speaking Welsh, poets and singers continued to use it. The spoken word had remained the most important part of Welsh culture since the Saxon invasion. The introduction of schools, using English, almost destroyed this last fortress of Welsh culture. The gatherings of poets and singers, known as *eisteddfods*, which had been going on since 1170 suddenly stopped. But at the end of the eighteenth century, there were still a few who could speak Welsh. *Eisteddfods* began again, bringing back a tradition which still continues today.

Ireland

Henry VIII wanted to bring Ireland under his authority, as he had done with Wales. Earlier kings had allowed the powerful Anglo-Irish noble families to rule, but Henry destroyed their power. He persuaded the Irish parliament to recognise him as king of Ireland.

However, Henry also tried to make the Irish accept his English Church Reformation. But in Ireland, unlike England, the monasteries and the Church were still an important part of economic and social life. And the Irish nobility and gentry, unlike the English, felt it was too dangerous to take monastic land. They refused to touch it. When an Anglo-Irish noble rebelled against Henry VIII, he did so in the name of Catholicism. Henry VIII failed to get what he wanted in Ireland. In fact he made things worse by bringing Irish nationalism and Catholicism together against English rule.

It is possible that, without the danger of foreign invasion, the Tudors might have given up trying to control the Irish. But Ireland tempted Catholic Europe as a place from which to attack the English. In 1580, during Elizabeth I's reign, many Irish rebelled, encouraged by the arrival of a few Spanish and French soldiers.

Queen Elizabeth's soldiers saw the rebellious Irish population as wild and primitive people and treated them with great cruelty. Edmund Spenser, a famous Elizabethan poet, was secretary to the English commander. After the rebellion was defeated he wrote, "Out of every corner of the woods . . . they [the Irish rebels] came creeping forth upon their hands, for their legs would not bear them. They looked like . . . death. They spoke like ghosts crying out of their graves. They did eat the dead . . . happy where they could find them."

The Tudors fought four wars during the period to make the Irish accept their authority and their religion. In the end they destroyed the old Gaelic way of life and introduced English government.

Ireland became England's first important colony. The effect of English rule was greatest in the north, in Ulster, where the Irish tribes had fought longest. Here, after the Tudor conquest, lands were taken and sold to English and Scottish merchants. The native Irish were forced to leave or to work for these settlers.

The Protestant settlers took most of the good land in Ulster. Even today most good land in Ulster is owned by Protestants, and most poor land by Catholics. The county of Derry in Ulster was taken over by a group of London merchants and divided among the twelve main London guilds. The town of Derry was renamed Londonderry, after its new merchant owners. This colonisation did not make England richer, but it destroyed much of Ireland's society and economy. It also laid the foundations for war between Protestants and Catholics in Ulster in the second half of the twentieth century.

Scotland and England

The Scottish monarchs tried to introduce the same kind of centralised monarchy that the Tudors had so successfully developed in England. But it was much harder, because the Scottish economy was weaker, and Scottish society more lawless. However, James IV, James V, Mary who was executed by her cousin Elizabeth of England, and her son James VI made important steps forward. They tried to control the lawless border country with England, and the disobedient Highland clans in the north. For the Scottish kings there was always a problem. The most disobedient were often the best fighters, and no king wanted to make enemies of those who might help him in battle against the English.

Knowing how weak they were, the Scottish kings usually avoided war with England. They made a peace treaty with Henry VII, the first with an English king since 1328, and James IV married Henry's daughter Margaret. But Henry VIII still wanted Scotland to accept his authority. In 1513 his army destroyed the Scottish army at Flodden. It was the worst defeat the Scots ever experienced. James himself was killed, and with him over twenty Scottish nobles.

The battle of Flodden increased the disagreement between those Scottish nobles who felt that Scotland should move towards a closer friendship with England and those who wanted to remain loyal to the Auld Alliance with France. The Scottish monarch had to find a balance between these two, to keep both his nobles and his neighbours happy. The Protestant Reformation in Europe, and particularly in England, also increased the uncertainty and danger. There was talk of a

Catholic invasion of England by France and Spain. Many Scots wanted to stay on the side of Catholic Europe in the hope of sharing the fruits of a Catholic invasion of England.

But Henry VIII reminded the Scots that it was dangerous to work against him. He sent another army into Scotland to make the Scottish James V accept his authority. James's army was badly defeated and James himself died shortly after. Henry hoped to marry his son Edward to the baby Queen of Scots, Mary, and in this way join the two countries together under an English king. An agreement was reached in 1543.

Ordinary Scots were most unhappy at the idea of being ruled by England. In spite of their fear of the powerful English armies, a new Scottish parliament, aware of popular feeling, turned down the marriage agreement. For the next two years English soldiers punished them by burning and destroying the houses of southern Scotland. Rather than give little Mary to the English, the Scots sent her to France, where she married the French king's son in 1558.

Mary Queen of Scots and the Scottish Reformation

Mary was troubled by bad luck and wrong decisions. She returned to Scotland as both queen and widow in 1561. She was Catholic, but during her time in France Scotland had become officially and popularly Protestant.

The Scottish nobles who supported friendship with England had welcomed Protestantism for both political and economic reasons. The new religion brought Scotland closer to England than France. Financially, the Scottish monarch could take over the great wealth of the Church in Scotland and this would almost certainly mean awards of land to the nobles. The yearly income of the Church in Scotland had been twice that of the monarch.

Unlike the English, however, the Scots were careful not to give the monarch authority over the new Protestant Scottish "Kirk", as the Church in Scotland was called. This was possible because the Reformation took place while the queen, Mary, was not in Scotland, and unable to interfere. The new Kirk was a far more democratic organisation than the English Church, because it had no bishops and was governed by a General Assembly. The Kirk taught the importance of personal belief and the study of the Bible, and this led quickly to the idea that education was important for everyone in Scotland. As a result most Scots remained better educated than other Europeans, including the English, until the end of the nineteenth century.

Protestantism had spread quickly through the Scottish universities, which were closely connected to those in Germany and Scandinavia. The new Kirk in Scotland disliked Mary and her French Catholicism. Mary was careful not to give the Kirk any reason for actually opposing her. She made it clear she would not try to bring back Catholicism.

Mary was soon married again, to Lord Darnley, an English Catholic. But when she tired of him, she allowed herself to agree to his murder and married the murderer, Bothwell. Scottish society, in spite of its lawlessness, was shocked. The English government did not look forward to the possibility of Mary succeeding Elizabeth as queen. In addition to her Catholicism and her strong French culture, she had shown very poor judgement. By her behaviour Mary probably destroyed her chance of inheriting the English throne. She found herself at war with her Scottish opponents, and was soon captured and imprisoned. However, in 1568 she escaped to England, where she was held by Elizabeth for nineteen years before she was finally executed.

A Scottish king for England

Mary's son, James VI, started to rule at the age of twelve in 1578. He showed great skill from an early age. He knew that if he behaved correctly he could expect to inherit the English throne after Elizabeth's death, as he was her closest relative. He also knew that a Catholic alliance between Spain and France might lead to an invasion of England so he knew he had to remain friendly with them too. He managed to "face both ways", while remaining publicly the Protestant ally of England.

Mary Queen of Scots had poor judgement, but she was a beauty. Neither of these qualities helped her in her relations with her cousin Elizabeth I, and an act of foolishness finally lost her her head.

James VI is remembered as a weak man and a bad decision-maker. But this was not true while he was king only in Scotland. Early in his reign, in the last years of the sixteenth century, he rebuilt the authority of the Scottish Crown after the disasters which had happened to his mother, grandfather and great-grandfather. He brought the Catholic and Protestant nobles and also the Kirk more or less under royal control. These were the successes of an extremely clever diplomat. Like the Tudors, he was a firm believer in the authority of the Crown, and like them he worked with small councils of ministers, rather than Parliament. But he did not have the money or military power of the Tudors.

James VI's greatest success was in gaining the English throne when Elizabeth died in 1603 at the unusually old age of 70. If Elizabeth's advisers had had serious doubts about James as a suitable Protestant ruler, they would probably have tried to find another successor to Elizabeth. Few in England could have liked the idea of a new king coming from Scotland, their wild northern neighbour. The fact that England accepted him suggests that its leading statesmen had confidence in James's skills.

12   Government and society

Tudor parliaments · Rich and poor in town and country · Domestic life · Language and culture

During the Tudor period the changes in government, society and the economy of England were more far-reaching than they had been for centuries. But most far-reaching of all were the changes in ideas, partly as a result of the rebirth of intellectual attitudes known as the Renaissance, which had spread slowly northwards from its beginnings in Italy. In England the nature of the Renaissance was also affected by the Protestant Reformation and the economic changes that followed from it.

Tudor parliaments

The Tudor monarchs did not like governing through Parliament. Henry VII had used Parliament only for law making. He seldom called it together, and then only when he had a particular job for it. Henry VIII had used it first to raise money for his military adventures, and then for his struggle with Rome. His aim was to make sure that the powerful members from the shires and towns supported him, because they had a great deal of control over popular feeling. He also wanted to frighten the priests and bishops into obeying him, and to frighten the pope into giving in to his demands.

Perhaps Henry himself did not realise that by inviting Parliament to make new laws for the Reformation he was giving it a level of authority it never had before. Tudor monarchs were certainly not more democratic than earlier kings, but by using Parliament to strengthen their policy, they actually increased Parliament's authority.

Parliament strengthened its position again during Edward VI's reign by ordering the new prayer book to be used in all churches, and forbidding the Catholic mass. When the Catholic Queen Mary came to the throne she succeeded in making Parliament cancel all the new Reformation laws, and agree to her marriage to Philip of Spain. But she could not persuade Parliament to accept him as king of England after her death.

Only two things persuaded Tudor monarchs not to get rid of Parliament altogether: they needed money and they needed the support of the merchants and landowners. In 1566 Queen Elizabeth told the French ambassador that the three parliaments she had already held were enough for any reign and she would have no more. Today Parliament must meet every year and remain "in session" for three-quarters of it. This was not at all the case in the sixteenth century.

In the early sixteenth century Parliament only met when the monarch ordered it. Sometimes it met twice in one year, but then it might not meet again for six years. In the first forty-four years of Tudor rule Parliament met only twenty times. Henry VIII assembled Parliament a little more often to make the laws for Church reformation. But Elizabeth, like her grandfather Henry VII, tried not to use Parliament after her Reformation Settlement of 1559, and in forty-four years she only let Parliament meet thirteen times.

During the century power moved from the House of Lords to the House of Commons. The reason for this was simple. The Members of Parliament (MPs) in the Commons represented richer and more influential classes than the Lords. In fact, the idea of getting rid of the House of Lords, still a real question in British politics today, was first suggested in the sixteenth century.

The old system of representation in the Commons, with two men from each county and two from each "borough", or town, remained the rule. However, during the sixteenth century the size of the Commons nearly doubled, as a result of the inclusion of Welsh boroughs and counties and the inclusion of more English boroughs.

But Parliament did not really represent the people. Few MPs followed the rule of living in the area they represented, and the monarchy used its influence to make sure that many MPs would support royal policy, rather than the wishes of their electors.

In order to control discussion in Parliament, the Crown appointed a "Speaker". Even today the Speaker is responsible for good behaviour during debates in the House of Commons. His job in Tudor times was to make sure that Parliament discussed what the monarch wanted Parliament to discuss, and that it made the decision which he or she wanted.

Until the end of the Tudor period Parliament was supposed to do three things: agree to the taxes needed; make the laws which the Crown suggested; and advise the Crown, but only when asked to do so. In order for Parliament to be able to do these things, MPs were given important rights: freedom of speech (that is freedom to speak their thoughts freely without fear), freedom from fear of arrest, and freedom to meet and speak to the monarch.

The Tudor monarchs realised that by asking Parliament for money they were giving it power in the running of the kingdom. All the Tudor monarchs tried to get money in other ways. By 1600 Elizabeth had found ways to raise money that were extremely unwise. She sold "monopolies", which gave a particular person or company total control over a trade. In 1601, the last parliament of Elizabeth's reign complained to her about the bad effect on free trade that these monopolies had.

Elizabeth and her advisers used other methods. She and her chief adviser, Lord Burghley, sold official positions in government. Burghley was paid about £860 a year, but he actually made at least £4,000 by selling official positions. He kept this secret from Parliament. Elizabeth's methods of raising money would today be considered dishonest as well as foolish.

In their old age Elizabeth and Burghley noticed less and became more careless and slower at making decisions. They allowed the tax system to become less effective, and failed to keep information on how much money people should be paying. England needed tax reform, which could only be carried out with the agreement of Parliament. Parliament wanted to avoid the matter of tax, and so did local government because the JPs who were responsible for collecting taxes were also landlords who would have to pay them. As JPs were not paid, they saw no reason for collecting unpopular taxes. Elizabeth left her successors to deal with the problem.

Elizabeth avoided open discussion on money matters with Parliament. There was clearly an unanswered question about the limits of Parliament's power. Who should decide what Parliament could discuss: the Crown or Parliament itself? Both the Tudor monarchs and their MPs would have agreed that it was the Crown that decided. However, during the sixteenth century the Tudors asked Parliament to discuss, law-make and advise on almost every subject.

Parliament naturally began to think it had a *right* to discuss these questions. By the end of the sixteenth century it was beginning to show new confidence, and in the seventeenth century, when the gentry and merchant classes were far more aware of their own strength, it was obvious that Parliament would challenge the Crown. Eventually this resulted in war.

Rich and poor in town and country

Even in 1485 much of the countryside was still untouched. There were still great forests of oak trees, and unused land in between. There were still

Hardwick Hall in Derbyshire, built in the 1580s, astonished local people by the daring use of so much glass. Never had domestic buildings been so light inside. The owner, Elizabeth of Shrewsbury, was newly wealthy and anxious to be remembered. So she had the initials "E.S." placed in the stonework. In Tudor times furniture became better. Chairs replaced benches and stools, feather mattresses replaced straw mattresses. By 1600 the chests used to store clothes were larger, with a drawer in the bottom. It was the beginning of the chest of drawers.

wild animals, wild pigs, wild cattle, and even a few wolves. Scattered across this countryside were "islands" of human settlement, villages and towns. Few towns had more than 3,000 people, the size of a large village today. Most towns, anyway, were no more than large villages, with their own fields and farms. Even London, a large city of over 60,000 by 1500, had fields farmed by its citizens.

In the sixteenth century, however, this picture began to change rapidly. The population increased, the unused land was cleared for sheep, and large areas of forest were cut down to provide wood for the growing shipbuilding industry. England was beginning to experience greater social and economic problems than ever before.

The price of food and other goods rose steeply during the sixteenth and early seventeenth centuries. This inflation was without equal until the twentieth century. The price of wheat and barley, necessary for bread and beer, increased over five times between 1510 and 1650. While most other prices increased by five times between 1500 and 1600, real wages fell by half. The government tried to deal with the problem of rising costs by making coins which contained up to 50 per cent less precious metal. This only reduced the value of money, helping to push prices up.

People thought that inflation was caused by silver and gold pouring into Europe from Spanish America. But a greater problem was the sudden increase in population. In England and Wales the population almost doubled from 2.2 million in 1525 to four million in 1603. Twice the number of people needed twice the amount of food. It was not produced. Living conditions got worse as the population rose. It is not surprising that fewer people married than ever before.

In the countryside the people who did best in this situation were the yeoman farmers who had at least 100 acres of land. They produced food to sell, and employed men to work on their land. They worked as farmers during the week, but were "gentlemen" on Sundays. They were able to go on increasing their prices because there was not enough food in the markets.

Most people, however, had only twenty acres of land or less. They had to pay rent for the land, and often found it difficult to pay when the rent increased. Because of the growing population it was harder for a man to find work, or to produce enough food for his family.

Many landowners found they could make more money from sheep farming than from growing crops. They could sell the wool for a good price to the rapidly growing cloth industry. In order to keep sheep they fenced off land that had always belonged to the whole village. Enclosing land in this way was

A wedding feast in the village Bermondsey, now a London suburb. Merry-making is just beginning, and the view gives a good idea of village life. The Tower of London can be seen across the river in the background.

often against the law, but because JPs were themselves landlords, few peasants could prevent it. As a result many poor people lost the land they farmed as well as the common land where they kept animals, and the total amount of land used for growing food was reduced.

There was a clear connection between the damage caused by enclosures and the growth of the cloth trade As one man watching the problem wrote in 1583, "these enclosures be the causes why rich men eat up poor men as beasts do eat grass." All through the century the government tried to control enclosures but without much success. Many people became unemployed.

There were warning signs that the problem was growing. In 1536 large numbers of people from the north marched to London to show their anger at the dissolution of the monasteries. Their reasons were only partly religious. As life had become harder, the monasteries had given employment to many and provided food for the very poor. This "Pilgrimage of Grace", as it was known, was cruelly

put down, and its leaders were executed. Without work to do, many people stole food in order to eat. It is thought that about 7,000 thieves were hanged during Henry VIII's reign.

Efforts were made by government to keep order in a situation of rising unemployment. In 1547 Parliament gave magistrates the power to take any person who was without work and give him for two years to any local farmer who wanted to use him. Any person found homeless and unemployed a second time could be executed. It did not solve the crime problem. As one foreign visitor reported, "There are incredible numbers of robbers here, they go about in bands of twenty . . ."

In 1563 Parliament made JPs responsible for deciding on fair wages and working hours. A worker was expected to start at five o'clock in the morning and work until seven or eight at night with two and a half hours allowed for meals. In order to control the growing problem of wandering homeless people, workers were not allowed to move from the parish where they had been born without permission. But

A wealthy family in the 1560s. The grisl in the centre are twins, but the family likeness of the others is evident. Children wore the same style of clothing as their parents. The dinner tables of the great and wealthy had become a good deal more orderly since the days of Sir Geoffrey Luttrell (see page 57). Parents often placed their children at the age of eight or nine in households of higher social standing. This offered the chance of an advantageous marriage later, and a rise in status and wealth.

already there were probably over 10,000 homeless people on the roads.

Good harvests through most of the century probably saved England from disaster, but there were bad ones between 1594 and 1597, making the problem of the poor worse again. In 1601 Parliament passed the first Poor Law. This made local people responsible for the poor in their own area. It gave power to JPs to raise money in the parish to provide food, housing and work for the poor and homeless of the same parish.

Many of the poor moved to towns, where there was a danger they would join together to fight against and destroy their rulers. The government had good reason to be afraid. In 1596, during the period of bad harvests, peasants in Oxfordshire rioted against the enclosures of common land. Apprentices in London rioted against the city authorities. The Elizabethan Poor Law was as much a symbol of authority as an act of kindness. It remained in operation until 1834.

The pattern of employment was changing. The production of finished cloth, the most important of England's products, reached its greatest importance during the sixteenth century. Clothmakers and merchants bought raw wool, gave it to spinners, who were mostly women and children in cottages, collected it and passed it on to weavers and other clothworkers. Then they sold it.

The successful men of this new capitalist class showed off their success by building magnificent houses and churches in the villages where they worked. England destroyed the Flemish cloth-making industry, but took advantage of the special skills of Flemish craftsmen who came to England.

The lives of rich and poor were very different. The rich ate good quality bread made from wheat, while the poor ate rough bread made from rye and barley. When there was not enough food the poor made their bread from beans, peas, or oats. The rich showed off their wealth in silk, woollen or linen clothing, while the poor wore simple clothes of leather or wool.

By using coal instead of wood fires, Tudor England learnt how to make greatly improved steel, necessary for modern weapons. Henry VIII replaced the longbow with the musket, an early kind of hand-held gun. Muskets were not as effective as longbows, but gunpowder and bullets were cheaper than arrows, and the men cheaper to train. Improved steel was used for making knives and forks, clocks, watches, nails and pins. Birmingham, by using coal fires to make steel, grew in the sixteenth century from a village into an important industrial city. In both Birmingham and Manchester ambitious members of the working and trading classes could now develop new industries, free from the controls placed on workers by the trade guilds in London and in many other older towns.

Coal was unpopular, but it burnt better than wood and became the most commonly used fuel, especially in London, the rapidly growing capital. In Henry VIII's reign London had roughly 60,000 inhabitants. By the end of the century this number had grown to almost 200,000. In 1560 London used 33,000 tons of coal from Newcastle, but by 1600 it used five times as much, and the smoke darkened the sky over London. A foreign ambassador wrote that the city stank, and was "the filthiest in the world".

Domestic life

Foreign visitors were surprised that women in England had greater freedom than anywhere else in Europe. Although they had to obey their husbands, they had self-confidence and were not kept hidden in their homes as women were in Spain and other countries. They were allowed free and easy ways with strangers. As one foreigner delightedly noticed, "You are received with a kiss by all, when you leave you are sent with a kiss. You return and kisses are repeated."

However, there was a dark side to married life. Most women bore between eight and fifteen children, and many women died in childbirth. Those who did not saw half their children die at a young age. No one dared hope for a long married life because the dangers to life were too great. For this reason, and because marriage was often an economic arrangement, deep emotional ties often seem to have been absent. When a wife died, a husband looked for another.

Both rich and poor lived in small family groups. Brothers and sisters usually did not live with each other or with their parents once they had grown up. They tried to find a place of their own. Over half the population was under twenty-five, while few were over sixty. Queen Elizabeth reached the age of seventy, but this was unusual. People expected to work hard and to die young. Poor children started work at the age of six or seven.

An Italian visitor to England gives an interesting view of English society in Tudor times: "The English are great lovers of themselves, and of everything belonging to them; they think that there are no other men than themselves, and no other world but England: and whenever they see a handsome foreigner, they say that 'he looks like an Englishman'." The English did not love their children, he thought, for "having kept them at home till they arrive at the age of seven or nine years at the most, they put them out, boys and girls, to hard service in the houses of other people, holding them to seven or eight years' hard service. They say they do it in order that their children might learn better manners. But I believe that they do it because they are better served by strangers than they would be by their own children."

In spite of the hard conditions of life, most people had a larger and better home to live in than ever before. Chimneys, which before had only been found in the homes of the rich, were now built in every house. This technical development made cooking and heating easier and more comfortable. For the first time more than one room could be used in winter.

Between 1530 and 1600 almost everyone doubled their living space. After 1570 the wealthy yeoman's family had eight or more rooms and workers' families had three rooms instead of one, and more furniture was used than ever before.

One group of people suffered particularly badly during the Tudor period. These were the unmarried women. Before the Reformation many of these women could become nuns, and be assured that in the religious life they would be safe and respected. After the dissolution of the monasteries, thousands became beggars on the roads of England. In future an unmarried woman could only hope to be a servant in someone else's house, or to be kept by her own family. She had little choice in life.

Language and culture

At the beginning of the Tudor period English was still spoken in a number of different ways. There were still reminders of the Saxon, Angle, Jute and Viking invasions in the different forms of language spoken in different parts of the country. Since the time of Chaucer, in the mid-fourteenth century, London English, itself a mixture of south Midland and southeastern English, had become accepted as standard English. Printing made this standard English more widely accepted amongst the literate population. For the first time, people started to think of London pronunciation as "correct" pronunciation. One educator in Henry VIII's time spoke of the need to teach children to speak English "which is clean, polite, [and] perfectly . . . pronounced." Until Tudor times the local forms of speech had been spoken by lord and peasant alike. From Tudor times onwards the way people spoke began to show the difference between them. Educated people began to speak "correct" English, and uneducated people continued to speak the local dialect.

Literacy increased greatly during the mid-sixteenth century, even though the religious houses, which had always provided traditional education, had closed. In fact, by the seventeenth century about half the population could read and write.

Nothing, however, showed England's new confidence more than its artistic flowering during the Renaissance. England felt the effects of the Renaissance later than much of Europe because it was an island. In the early years of the sixteenth century English thinkers had become interested in the work of the Dutch philosopher Erasmus. One of them, Thomas More, wrote a study of the ideal nation, called *Utopia*, which became extremely popular throughout Europe.

The Renaissance also influenced religion, encouraging the Protestant Reformation, as well as a freer approach to ways of thinking within the Catholic Church. In music England enjoyed its most fruitful period ever. There was also considerable interest in the new painters in Europe, and England developed its own special kind of painting, the miniature portrait.

Literature, however, was England's greatest art form. Playwrights like Christopher Marlowe, Ben Jonson, and William Shakespeare filled the theatres with their exciting new plays.

Shakespeare was born in Stratford-upon-Avon, and went to the local grammar school. His education was typical of the Tudor age, because at this time the "grammar" schools, which tried to teach "correct" English, became the commonest form of education. His plays were popular with both educated and uneducated people. Many of his plays were about English history, but he changed fact to suit public opinion.

Nothing shows the adventurous spirit of the age better than the "soldier poets". These were true Renaissance men who were both brave and cruel in war, but also highly educated. Sir Edmund Spenser, who fought with the army in Ireland, was one. Sir Philip Sidney, killed fighting the Spanish in the Netherlands, was another. A third was Sir Walter Raleigh, adventurer and poet. While imprisoned in the Tower of London waiting to be executed, he wrote a poem which describes how time takes away youth and gives back only old age and dust. It was found in his Bible after his execution:

> Even such is time, that takes in trust
> Our youth, our joys, our all we have,
> And pays us but with earth and dust.
> Who, in the dark and silent grave,
> When we have wandered all our ways,
> Shuts up the story of our days.
> But from this earth, this grave, this dust,
> My God shall raise me up, I trust.

The Stuarts

13 Crown and Parliament
Parliament against the Crown · Religious disagreement · Civil war

The Stuart monarchs, from James I onwards, were less successful than the Tudors. They quarrelled with Parliament and this resulted in civil war. The only king of England ever to be tried and executed was a Stuart. The republic that followed was even more unsuccessful, and by popular demand the dead king's son was called back to the throne. Another Stuart king was driven from his throne by his own daughter and her Dutch husband, William of Orange. William became king by Parliament's election, not by right of birth. When the last Stuart, Queen Anne, died in 1714, the monarchy was no longer absolutely powerful as it had been when James VI rode south from Scotland in 1603. It had become a "parliamentary monarchy" controlled by a constitution.

These important changes did not take place simply because the Stuarts were bad rulers. They resulted from a basic change in society. During the seventeenth century economic power moved even faster into the hands of the merchant and landowning farmer classes. The Crown could no longer raise money or govern without their co-operation. These groups were represented by the House of Commons. In return for money the Commons demanded political power. The victory of the Commons and the classes it represented was unavoidable.

It would be interesting to know how the Tudors would have dealt with the growing power of the House of Commons. They had been lucky not to have this problem. But they had also been more

James I was a disappointment to the English. As James VI in Scotland he had acted skilfully to survive the plots of his nobles. In England he was better known for his lack of skill in dealing with Parliament and with his ministers.

Charles I on horseback, painted in 1633 by the great court painter Anthony Van Dyck. This picture announces the triumph of kingship. At the time Charles was at the height of his power. He had no need of Parliament and it seemed that the king could rule alone, as the king of France was doing. Charles was fatally wrong. It was Parliament that triumphed during the seventeenth century. By the end of the century the powers of the sovereign were limited by the will of Parliament. In the bottom left corner are the Stuart arms, combining for the first time the English "quarters" with the Scottish Lion Rampant and the Irish Harp.

willing to give up their beliefs in order that their policies would succeed. The Stuarts, on the other hand, held onto their beliefs however much it cost them, even when it was foolish to do so.

The political developments of the period also resulted from basic changes in thinking in the seventeenth century. By 1700 a ruler like Henry VIII or Elizabeth I would have been quite unthinkable. By the time Queen Anne died, a new age of reason and science had arrived.

Parliament against the Crown

The first signs of trouble between Crown and Parliament came in 1601, when the Commons were angry over Elizabeth's policy of selling monopolies. But Parliament did not demand any changes. It did not wish to upset the ageing queen whom it feared and respected.

Like Elizabeth, James I tried to rule without Parliament as much as possible. He was afraid it would interfere, and he preferred to rule with a small council.

James was clever and well educated. As a child in Scotland he had been kidnapped by groups of nobles, and had been forced to give in to the Kirk. Because of these experiences he had developed strong beliefs and opinions. The most important of these was his belief in the divine right of kings. He believed that the king was chosen by God and therefore only God could judge him. James's ideas were not different from those of earlier monarchs, or other monarchs in Europe.

He expressed these opinions openly, however, and this led to trouble with Parliament. James had an unfortunate habit of saying something true or clever at the wrong moment. The French king described James as "the wisest fool in Christendom". It was unkind, but true. James, for all his cleverness, seemed to have lost the commonsense which had helped him in Scotland.

When Elizabeth died she left James with a huge debt, larger than the total yearly income of the Crown. James had to ask Parliament to raise a tax to pay the debt. Parliament agreed, but in return insisted on the right to discuss James's home and foreign policy. James, however, insisted that he alone had the "divine right" to make these decisions. Parliament disagreed, and it was supported by the law.

James had made the mistake of appointing Elizabeth's minister, Sir Edward Coke, as Chief Justice. Coke made decisions based on the law which limited the king's power. He judged that the king was not above the law, and even more important, that the king and his council could not make new laws. Laws could only be made by Act of Parliament. James removed Coke from the position of Chief Justice, but as an MP Coke continued to make trouble. He reminded Parliament of Magna Carta, interpreting it as the great charter of English freedom. Although this was not really true, his claim was politically useful to Parliament. This was the first quarrel between James and Parliament, and it started the bad feeling which lasted during his entire reign, and that of his son Charles.

James was successful in ruling without Parliament between 1611 and 1621, but it was only possible because Britain remained at peace. James could not afford the cost of an army. In 1618, at the beginning of the Thirty Years War in Europe, Parliament wished to go to war against the Catholics. James would not agree. Until his death in 1625 James was always quarrelling with Parliament over money and over its desire to play a part in his foreign policy.

Charles I found himself quarrelling even more bitterly with the Commons than his father had done, mainly over money. Finally he said, "Parliaments are altogether in my power . . . As I find the fruits of them good or evil, they are to continue or not to be." Charles dissolved Parliament.

Charles's need for money, however, forced him to recall Parliament, but each time he did so, he quarrelled with it. When he tried raising money without Parliament, by borrowing from merchants, bankers and landowning gentry, Parliament decided to make Charles agree to certain "parliamentary rights". It hoped Charles could not raise enough money without its help, and in 1628 this happened. In return for the money he badly needed, Charles promised that he would only raise money by Act of Parliament, and that he would not imprison anyone without lawful reason.

These rights, known as the Petition of Right, established an important rule of government by Parliament, because the king had now agreed that Parliament controlled both state money, the "national budget", and the law. Charles realised that the Petition made nonsense of a king's "divine right". He decided to prevent it being used by dissolving Parliament the following year.

Charles surprised everyone by being able to rule successfully without Parliament. He got rid of much dishonesty that had begun in the Tudor period and continued during his father's reign. He was able to balance his budgets and make administration efficient. Charles saw no reason to explain his policy or method of government to anyone. By 1637 he was at the height of his power. His authority seemed to be more completely accepted than the authority of an English king had been for centuries. It also seemed that Parliament might never meet again.

Religious disagreement

In 1637, however, Charles began to make serious mistakes. These resulted from the religious situation in Britain. His father, James, had been pleased that the Anglican Church had bishops. They willingly supported him as head of the English Church. And he disliked the Presbyterian Kirk in Scotland because it had no bishops. It was a more democratic institution and this gave political as well as religious power to the literate classes in Scotland. They had given him a difficult time before he became king of England in 1603.

There were also people in England, known as Puritans, who, like the Scottish Presbyterians, wanted a democratic Church. Queen Elizabeth had been careful to prevent them from gaining power in the Anglican Church. She even executed a few of them for printing books against the bishops. In

1604, Puritans met James to ask him to remove the Anglican bishops to make the English Church more like the Kirk, but he saw only danger for the Crown. "A Scottish Presbytery agrees as well with monarchy as God with the Devil," he remarked, and sent them away with the words, "No bishop, no king."

Charles shared his father's dislike of Puritans. He had married a French Catholic, and the marriage was unpopular in Protestant Britain. Many MPs were either Puritans or sympathised with them, and many of the wealth-creating classes were Puritan. But Charles took no notice of popular feeling, and he appointed an enemy of the Puritans, William Laud, as Archbishop of Canterbury.

Archbishop Laud brought back into the Anglican Church many Catholic practices. They were extremely unpopular. Anti-Catholic feeling had been increased by an event over thirty years earlier, in 1605. A small group of Catholics had been caught trying to blow up the Houses of Parliament with King James inside. One of these men, Guy Fawkes, was captured in the cellar under the House. The escape of king and Parliament caught people's imagination, and 5 November, the anniversary, became an occasion for celebration with fireworks and bonfires.

Archbishop Laud tried to make the Scottish Kirk accept the same organisation as the Church in England. James I would have realised how dangerous this was, but his son, Charles, did not because he had never lived in Scotland. When Laud tried to introduce the new prayer book in Scotland in 1637 the result was national resistance to the introduction of bishops and what Scots thought of as Catholicism.

In spring 1638 Charles faced a rebel Scottish army. Without the help of Parliament he was only able to put together an inexperienced army. It marched north and found that the Scots had crossed the border. Charles knew his army was unlikely to win against the Scots. So he agreed to respect all Scottish political and religious freedoms, and also to pay a large sum of money to persuade the Scots to return home.

It was impossible for Charles to find this money except through Parliament. This gave it the chance to end eleven years of absolute rule by Charles, and to force him to rule under parliamentary control. In return for its help, Parliament made Charles accept a new law which stated that Parliament had to meet at least once every three years. However, as the months went by, it became increasingly clear that Charles was not willing to keep his agreements with Parliament. Ruling by "divine right", Charles felt no need to accept its decisions.

Civil war

Events in Scotland made Charles depend on Parliament, but events in Ireland resulted in civil war. James I had continued Elizabeth's policy and had colonised Ulster, the northern part of Ireland, mainly with farmers from the Scottish Lowlands. The Catholic Irish were sent off the land, and even those who had worked for Protestant settlers were now replaced by Protestant workers from Scotland and England.

In 1641, at a moment when Charles badly needed a period of quiet, Ireland exploded in rebellion against the Protestant English and Scottish settlers. As many as 3,000 people, men, women and children, were killed, most of them in Ulster. In London, Charles and Parliament quarrelled over who should control an army to defeat the rebels. Many believed that Charles only wanted to raise an army in order to dissolve Parliament by force and to rule alone again. Charles's friendship towards the Catholic Church increased Protestant fears. Already some of the Irish rebels claimed to be rebelling against the English Protestant Parliament,

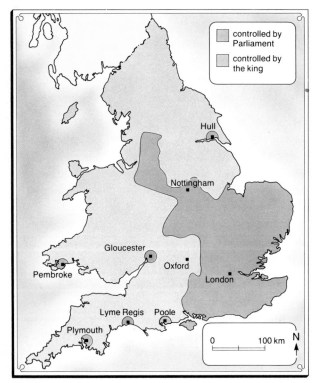

The areas controlled by Parliament and the king halfway through the Civil War, 1642–1645.

Parliament met at Westminster in 1640, determined to limit Charles I's freedom and to ensure that Parliament would meet regularly in future. Because of rebellions in Scotland and in Ireland, Charles had to give in to Parliament's wish to oversee government.

The battle of Naseby in 1645 marked the final defeat of Charles I by Parliament. Charles can be seen in front of his army. General Fairfax commanded the Parliamentarians, and his second-in-command, Oliver Cromwell, commanded the right wing of the army.

but not against the king. In 1642 Charles tried to arrest five MPs in Parliament. Although he was unsuccessful, it convinced Parliament and its supporters all over England that they had good reason to fear.

London locked its gates against the king, and Charles moved to Nottingham, where he gathered an army to defeat those MPs who opposed him. The Civil War had started. Most people, both in the country and in the towns, did not wish to be on one side or the other. In fact, no more than 10 per cent of the population became involved. But most of the House of Lords and a few from the Commons supported Charles. The Royalists, known as "Cavaliers", controlled most of the north and west. But Parliament controlled East Anglia and the southeast, including London. Its army at first consisted of armed groups of London apprentices. Their short hair gave the Parliamentarian soldiers their popular name of "Roundheads".

Unless the Royalists could win quickly it was certain that Parliament would win in the end. Parliament was supported by the navy, by most of the merchants and by the population of London. It therefore controlled the most important national and international sources of wealth. The Royalists, on the other hand, had no way of raising money. By 1645 the Royalist army was unpaid, and as a result soldiers either ran away, or stole from local villages and farms. In the end they lost their courage for the fight against the Parliamentarians, and at Naseby in 1645 the Royalist army was finally defeated.

Most people were happy that the war had ended. Trade had been interrupted, and Parliament had introduced new taxes to pay for the war. In many places people had told both armies to stay away from their areas. They had had enough of uncontrolled soldiers and of paying the cost of the war.

14 Republican and Restoration Britain

Republican Britain · Catholicism, the Crown and the new constitutional monarchy · Scotland and Ireland · Foreign relations

Republican Britain

Several MPs had commanded the Parliamentarian army. Of these, the strongest was an East Anglian gentleman farmer named Oliver Cromwell. He had created a new "model" army, the first regular force from which the British army of today developed. Instead of country people or gentry, Cromwell invited into his army educated men who wanted to fight for their beliefs.

Cromwell and his advisers had captured the king in 1645, but they did not know what to do with him. This was an entirely new situation in English history. Charles himself continued to encourage rebellion against Parliament even after he had surrendered and had been imprisoned. He was able to encourage the Scots to rebel against the Parliamentarian army. After the Scots were defeated some Puritan officers of the Parliamentarian army demanded the king's death for treason.

The Parliamentarian leaders now had a problem. They could either bring Charles back to the throne and allow him to rule, or remove him and create a new political system. By this time most people in both Houses of Parliament and probably in the country wanted the king back. They feared the Parliamentarians and they feared the dangerous behaviour of the army. But some army commanders were determined to get rid of the king. These men were Puritans who believed they could build God's kingdom in England.

Two-thirds of the MPs did not want to put the king on trial. They were removed from Parliament by

It is said that Oliver Cromwell, with Puritan humility, told his painter, Samuel Cooper, to include the warts on his face. But as well as humility Cromwell also had a soldier's belief in authority. As a result he was unpopular as Lord Protector. He failed to persuade the English that republican government was better than monarchy, mainly because people had less freedom under his authoritarian rule than they had under Charles I.

the army, and the remaining fifty-three judged him and found him guilty of making "war against his kingdom and the Parliament". On 31 January 1649 King Charles was executed. It was a cold day and he wore two shirts so that the crowd who came to watch would not see him shiver and think him frightened.

King Charles died bravely. As his head was cut from his body the large crowd groaned. Perhaps the execution was Charles's own greatest victory, because most people now realised that they did not want Parliamentary rule, and were sorry that Charles was not still king.

From 1649–1660 Britain was a republic, but the republic was not a success. Cromwell and his friends created a government far more severe than Charles's had been. They had got rid of the monarchy, and they now got rid of the House of Lords and the Anglican Church.

The Scots were shocked by Charles's execution. They invited his son, whom they recognised as King Charles II, to join them and fight against the English Parliamentary army. But they were defeated, and young Charles himself was lucky to escape to France. Scotland was brought under English republican rule.

Cromwell took an army to Ireland to punish the Irish for the killing of Protestants in 1641, and for the continued Royalist rebellion there. He captured two towns, Drogheda and Wexford. His soldiers killed the inhabitants of both, about 6,000 people in all. These killings were probably no worse than the killings of Protestants in 1641, but they remained powerful symbols of English cruelty to the Irish.

The army remained the most powerful force in the land. Disagreements between the army and Parliament resulted in Parliament's dissolution in 1653. It was the behaviour of the army and the dissolution of Parliament that destroyed Cromwell's hopes. Many in the army held what were thought to be strange beliefs. A group called "Levellers" wanted a new equality among all men. They wanted Parliament to meet every two years, and for most men over the age of twenty-one to have the right to elect MPs to it. They also wanted complete religious freedom, which would have allowed the many new Puritan groups to follow their religion in the way they wished.

Two hundred years later, such demands were thought of as basic citizens' rights. But in the middle of the seventeenth century they had little popular support. Levellers in the army rebelled, but their rebellion was defeated.

From 1653 Britain was governed by Cromwell alone. He became "Lord Protector", with far greater powers than King Charles had had. His efforts to govern the country through the army were extremely unpopular, and the idea of using the army to maintain law and order in the kingdom has remained unpopular ever since. Cromwell's government was unpopular for other reasons. For example, people were forbidden to celebrate Christmas and Easter, or to play games on a Sunday.

When Cromwell died in 1658, the Protectorate, as his republican administration was called, collapsed. Cromwell had hoped that his son, rather than Parliament, would take over when he died. But Richard Cromwell was not a good leader and the army commanders soon started to quarrel among themselves. One of these decided to act. In 1660 he marched to London, arranged for free elections and invited Charles II to return to his kingdom. The republic was over.

When Charles II returned to England as the publicly accepted king, the laws and Acts of Cromwell's government were automatically cancelled.

Charles managed his return with skill. Although Parliament was once more as weak as it had been in the time of James I and Charles I, the new king was careful to make peace with his father's enemies. Only those who had been responsible for his father's execution were punished. Many Parliamentarians were given positions of authority or responsibility in the new monarchy. But Parliament itself remained generally weak. Charles shared his father's belief in divine right. And he greatly admired the magnificent, all-powerful, absolute ruler of France, Louis XIV.

Charles II, who "never said a foolish thing, nor ever did a wise one," was a welcome change from Cromwellian rule. Charles II believed as strongly as his father and grandfather in the divine right of kings, but had the good sense to avoid an open break with Parliament. His reign was carefree and relaxed, as this portrait suggests, quite different from the mood suggested in Van Dyck's portrait of his father (page 86).

Catholicism, the Crown and the new constitutional monarchy

Charles hoped to make peace between the different religious groups. He wanted to allow Puritans and Catholics who disliked the Anglican Church to

meet freely. But Parliament was strongly Anglican, and would not allow this. Before the Civil War, Puritans looked to Parliament for protection against the king. Now they hoped that the king would protect them against Parliament.

Charles himself was attracted to the Catholic Church. Parliament knew this and was always afraid that Charles would become a Catholic. For this reason Parliament passed the Test Act in 1673, which prevented any Catholic from holding public office. Fear of Charles's interest in the Catholic Church and of the monarchy becoming too powerful also resulted in the first political parties in Britain.

One of these parties was a group of MPs who became known as "Whigs", a rude name for cattle drivers. The Whigs were afraid of an absolute monarchy, and of the Catholic faith with which they connected it. They also wanted to have no regular or "standing" army. In spite of their fear of a Catholic king, the Whigs believed strongly in allowing religious freedom. Because Charles and his wife had no children, the Whigs feared that the Crown would go to Charles's Catholic brother, James. They wanted to prevent this, but they were undecided over who they did want as king.

The Whigs were opposed by another group, nicknamed "Tories", an Irish name for thieves. It is difficult to give a simple definition of each party, because they were loosely formed groups. Generally speaking, however, the Tories upheld the authority of the Crown and the Church, and were natural inheritors of the "Royalist" position. The Whigs were not against the Crown, but they believed that its authority depended upon the consent of Parliament. As natural inheritors of the "Parliamentarian" values of twenty years earlier, they felt tolerant towards the new Protestant sects which the Anglican Church so disliked. These two parties, the Whigs and the Tories, became the basis of Britain's two-party parliamentary system of government.

The struggle over Catholicism and the Crown became a crisis when news was heard of a Catholic plot to murder Charles and put his brother James on the throne. In fact the plan did not exist. The story had been spread as a clever trick to frighten people and to make sure that James and the Catholics did not come to power. The trick worked. Parliament passed an Act forbidding any Catholic to be a member of either the Commons or the Lords. It was not successful, however, in preventing James from inheriting the crown. Charles would not allow any interference with his brother's divine right to be king. Stuarts might give in on matters of policy, but never on matters of principle.

James II became king after his brother's death in 1685. The Tories and Anglicans were delighted, but not for long. James had already shown his dislike of Protestants while he had been Charles's governor in Scotland. His soldiers had killed many Presbyterian men, women and children. This period is still remembered in some parts of Scotland as the "killing times".

James then tried to remove the laws which stopped Catholics from taking positions in government and Parliament. He also tried to bring back the Catholic Church, and allow it to exist beside the Anglican Church. James almost certainly believed sincerely that this would result in many returning to the Catholic Church. But Parliament was very angry, particularly the Tories and Anglicans who had supported him against the Whigs.

James tried to get rid of the Tory gentry who most strongly opposed him. He removed three-quarters of all JPs and replaced them with men of lower social class. He tried to bring together the Catholics and the Puritans, now usually called "Nonconformists" because they would not agree with or "conform" to the Anglican Church.

In spite of their anger, Tories, Whigs and Anglicans did nothing because they could look forward to the succession of James's daughter, Mary. Mary was Protestant and married to the Protestant ruler of Holland, William of Orange. But this hope was destroyed with the news in June 1688 that James's son had been born. The Tories and Anglicans now joined the Whigs in looking for a Protestant rescue.

They invited William of Orange to invade Britain. It was a dangerous thing for William to do, but he was already at war with France and he needed the help of Britain's wealth and armed forces. At this important moment James's determination failed him. It seems he actually had some kind of mental breakdown.

William entered London, but the crown was offered only to Mary. William said he would leave Britain unless he also became king. Parliament had no choice but to offer the crown to both William and Mary.

However, while William had obtained the crown, Parliament had also won an important point. After he had fled from England, Parliament had decided that James II had lost his right to the crown. It gave as its reason that he had tried to undermine "the constitution of the kingdom by breaking the original contract between King and People." This idea of a contract between ruler and ruled was not entirely new. Since the restoration of Charles II in 1660 there had been a number of theories about the nature of government. In the 1680s two of the more important theorists, Algernon Sidney and John Locke, had argued that government was based upon the consent of the people, and that the powers of the king must be strictly limited. The logical conclusion of such ideas was that the "consent of the people" was represented by Parliament, and as a result Parliament, not the king, should be the overall power in the state. In 1688 these theories were fulfilled.

Like the Civil War of 1642, the Glorious Revolution, as the political results of the events of 1688 were called, was completely unplanned and unprepared for. It was hardly a revolution, more a *coup d'etat* by the ruling class. But the fact that Parliament made William king, not by inheritance but by their choice, was revolutionary. Parliament was now beyond question more powerful than the king, and would remain so. Its power over the monarch was written into the Bill of Rights in 1689. The king was now unable to raise taxes or keep an army without the agreement of Parliament, or to act against any MP for what he said or did in Parliament.

In 1701 Parliament finally passed the Act of Settlement, to make sure only a Protestant could inherit the crown. It stated that if Mary had no children the crown would pass to her sister Anne. If she also died without children, it would go to a granddaughter of James I, who had married the German elector of Hanover, and her children. The Act of Settlement was important, and has remained in force ever since, although the Stuarts tried three times to regain the crown. Even today, if a son or daughter of the monarch becomes a Catholic, he or she cannot inherit the throne.

Scotland and Ireland

Neither Scotland,nor Ireland accepted the English removal of James peacefully. In Scotland supporters of the Stuarts rebelled, but although they successfully defeated a government army, their rebellion ended after the death of their leader. Most of the rebels were Highlanders, many of them still Catholic.

Scotland was still a separate kingdom, although it shared a king with England (James II had been James VII of Scotland). The English wanted Scotland and England to be united. But the English Act of Settlement was not law in Scotland. While Scotland remained legally free to choose its own king there was a danger that this might be used to put a Stuart back on the throne. Scotland might renew its Auld Alliance with France, which was now England's most dangerous European enemy.

On·the other hand, Scotland needed to remove the limits on trade with England from which it suffered economically. The English Parliament offered to remove these limits if the Scots agreed to union with England. The Scots knew that if they did not agree there was a real danger that an English army would once again march into Scotland. In 1707 the union of Scotland and England was completed by Act of Parliament. From that moment both countries no longer had separate parliaments, and a new parliament of Great Britain, the new name of the state, met for the first time. Scotland, however, kept its own separate legal and judicial system, and its own separate Church.

"No surrender", the motto of the Londonderry Protestants under siege in 1690 by the Catholic Irish, has remained the motto of the Ulster Protestants to this day. This Protestant home displays the crossed flags of the Union of Great Britain and Northern Ireland and of Ulster.

In Ireland the Catholicism of James II had raised the hopes of those who had lost their lands to the Protestant settlers. When he lost his throne in England, James naturally thought that Ireland would make a strong base from which to take back his throne. In 1689 he landed in Ireland, with French support.

In Dublin a Catholic parliament immediately passed an Act taking away all the property of Protestants in Ireland. But it was not so easy to carry this out. Thirty thousand Protestants locked themselves in the city of Londonderry (or "Derry" as the Catholics continued to call it). James encircled the city but the defenders refused to surrender. After fifteen weeks, English ships arrived bringing fresh supplies and the struggle for Londonderry was over. The battlecry of the Protestants of Londonderry "No Surrender!" has remained to this day the cry of Ulster Protestantism.

King William landed in Ireland in 1690, and defeated James's army at the River Boyne. James left Ireland for France a few days later, and never returned to any of his kingdoms. With the battle of the Boyne the Protestant victory was complete.

Foreign relations

During the seventeenth century Britain's main enemies were Spain, Holland and France. War with Holland resulted from competition in trade. After three wars in the middle of the century, when Britain had achieved the trade position it wanted, peace was agreed, and Holland and Britain co-operated against France.

At the end of the century Britain went to war against France. This was partly because William of Orange brought Britain into the Dutch struggle with the French. But Britain also wanted to limit French power, which had been growing under Louis XIV. Under the duke of Marlborough, the British army won several important victories over the French at Blenheim (on the Danube), Ramillies, Oudenarde and Malplaquet (in the Netherlands).

By the treaty of Utrecht in 1713 France accepted limits on its expansion, as well as a political settlement for Europe. It accepted Queen Anne instead of James II's son as the true monarch of Britain. In the war Britain had also won the rock of Gibraltar, and could now control the entrance to the Mediterranean.

The capture of foreign land was important for Europe's economic development. At this stage Britain had a smaller empire abroad than either Spain or Holland. But it had greater variety. On the east coast of America, Britain controlled about twelve colonies. Of far greater interest were the new possessions in the West Indies, where sugar was grown. Sugar became a craze from which Britain has not yet recovered.

The growing sugar economy of the West Indies increased the demand for slaves. By 1645, for example, there were 40,000 white settlers and 6,000 negro slaves in Barbados. By 1685 the balance had changed, with only 20,000 white settlers but 46,000 slaves. The sugar importers used their great influence to make sure that the government did not stop slavery.

During this time Britain also established its first trading settlements in India, on both the west and east coasts. The East India Company did not interfere in Indian politics. Its interest was only in trade. A hundred years later, however, competition with France resulted in direct efforts to control Indian politics, either by alliance or by the conquest of Indian princely states.

15 Life and thought

The revolution in thought · Life and work in the Stuart age · Family life

The political revolution during the Stuart age could not have happened if there had not been a revolution in thought. This influenced not only politics, but also religion and science. By 1714 people's ideas and beliefs had changed enormously. The real Protestant revolution did not, in fact, happen until the seventeenth century, when several new religious groups appeared. But there were also exciting new scientific ideas, quite separate from these new beliefs. For the first time it was reasonable to argue that everything in the universe had a natural explanation, and this led to a new self-confidence.

Another reason for this self-confidence was the change in Britain's international position during the century. In 1603, in spite of the Armada victory of 1588 and in spite of the union of England and Scotland under one sovereign, Britain was still considered less important than France, Spain and the Holy Roman Empire. But by 1714 the success of its armies against France had made Britain a leading European power. At the same time Britain had so many new colonies that it was now in competition with earlier colonial nations, Spain, Portugal and the Netherlands.

The revolution in thought

The influence of Puritanism increased greatly during the seventeenth century, particularly among the merchant class and lesser gentry. It was the Puritans who persuaded James I to permit a new official ("authorised") translation of the Bible. It was published in 1611. This beautiful translation

A Quaker meeting addressed by a woman. Quakers had a number of striking ideas, for example, that all men and women were equal. The Quaker movement began during the Civil War, and in 1661 it adopted the "peace principle", the idea that all war was wrong. Since then Quakers have been pacifist.

was a great work of English literature, and it encouraged Bible reading among all those who could read. Although the Bible was read most by merchants and lesser gentry, many literate labourers began to read it too. Some of them understood the Bible in a new and revolutionary way. As a result, by the middle years of the seventeenth century Puritanism had led to the formation of a large number of small new religious groups, or "sects", including the "Levellers".

Most of these Nonconformist sects lasted only a few years, but two are important, the Baptists and the Quakers. In spite of opposition in the seventeenth century, both sects have survived and have had an important effect on the life of the nation. The Quakers became particularly famous for their reforming social work in the eighteenth century. These sects brought hope to many of the poor and the powerless. Social reform and the later growth of trade unionism both owed much to Nonconformism. In spite of their good work, however, the Nonconformists continued to be disliked by the ruling class until the end of the nineteenth century.

The Anglican Church, unlike the Nonconformist churches, was strong politically, but it became weaker intellectually. The great religious writers of the period, John Bunyan, who wrote *The Pilgrim's Progress*, and John Milton, who wrote *Paradise Lost*, were both Puritan.

For some Nonconformists, the opposition to their beliefs was too great to bear. They left Britain to live a free life in the new found land of America. In 1620, the "Pilgrim Fathers" sailed in a ship called the *Mayflower* to Massachusetts. Catholic families settled in Maryland for the same reasons. But most of the 400,000 or so who left England were young men without families, who did so for economic and not religious reasons. They wanted the chance to start a new life. At the same time there were other people coming in from abroad to live in Britain. Cromwell allowed Jews to settle again, the first Jews since the earlier community had been expelled 350 years earlier. And after 1685 many French Protestants, known as Huguenots, escaped from Louis XIV's persecution and settled in Britain.

The revolution in religious thinking was happening at the same time as a revolution in scientific thinking. Careful study of the natural world led to important new discoveries.

It was not the first time that the people of Britain had taken a lead in scientific matters. Almost a thousand years earlier, the English monk and historian, Bede, had argued that the earth stood still, fixed in space, and was surrounded by seven heavens. This, of course, was not correct, but no one doubted him for centuries. In the twelfth century, during the reign of Henry I, another English scientist had gained European fame. He was Adelard of Bath, and he played a large part in the revolution in scientific thinking at the time. He knew that the Church considered his ideas dangerous. "I do not want to claim," he wrote, "that God is less than all-powerful. But nature has its own patterns and order, and we should listen to those who have learnt something of it."

In the thirteenth and early fourteenth centuries English scientists, most of them at the University of Oxford, had led Europe. Friar Roger Bacon, one of the more famous of them, had experimented with light, heat and magnetism. Another, William of Ockham, had studied falling objects. Another, William Marlee, had been one of the first to keep a careful record of the weather. Chaucer himself wrote a book to teach his son how to use an astrolabe. At the same time, the practical effects of such curiosity were seen in new machinery, water mills, geared wheels and lathes.

But the seventeenth century saw the development of scientific thinking on an entirely new scale. The new mood had been established at the very beginning of the century by a remarkable man, Francis Bacon. He became James I's Lord Chancellor, but he was better known for his work on scientific method. Every scientific idea, he argued, must be tested by experiment. With idea and experiment following one after the other, eventually the whole natural world would be understood. In the rest of the century British scientists put these ideas into practice. The British have remained at the front of experiment and research ever since.

In 1628 William Harvey discovered the circulation of blood and this led to great advances in medicine and in the study of the human body. The scientists Robert Boyle and Robert Hooke used Harvey's methods when they made discoveries in the chemistry and mechanics of breathing.

These scientific studies were encouraged by the Stuarts. The Royal Society, founded by the Stuart monarchy, became an important centre where thinkers could meet, argue, enquire and share information. Charles II, a strong supporter of its work, gave the Royal Society firm direction "to examine all systems, theories, principles ... elements, histories and experiments of things natural, mathematical and mechanical".

In 1666 the Cambridge Professor of Mathematics, Sir Isaac Newton, began to study gravity, publishing his important discovery in 1684. In 1687 he published *Principia*, on "the mathematical principles of natural philosophy", perhaps the greatest book in the history of science. Newton's work remained the basis of physics until Einstein's discoveries in the twentieth century. Newton's importance as a "founding father" of modern science was recognised in his own time, and Alexander Pope, a leading poet of the day, summed it up neatly:

Nature, and Nature's laws lay hid in night: God said, *Let Newton be!* and all was light.

Newton had been encouraged and financed by his friend, Edmund Halley, who is mostly remembered for tracking a comet (Halley's Comet) in 1682. There was at that time a great deal of interest in astronomy. The discovery of the geometric movement of stars and planets destroyed old beliefs in astrology and magic. Everything, it seemed, had a natural explanation.

It was no accident that the greatest British architect of the time, Christopher Wren, was also Professor of Astronomy at Oxford. In 1666, following a year of terrible plague, a fire destroyed most of the city of London. Eighty-seven churches, including the great medieval cathedral of St Paul, were destroyed. Wren was ordered to rebuild them in the modern style, which he did with skill.

The Royal Observatory at Greenwich was founded by Charles II, who had a great interest in scientific matters. On the left a quadrant is being used, larger but similar to those used for navigation on ocean-going ships. On the right an extremely long telescope is being used to observe the heavenly bodies.

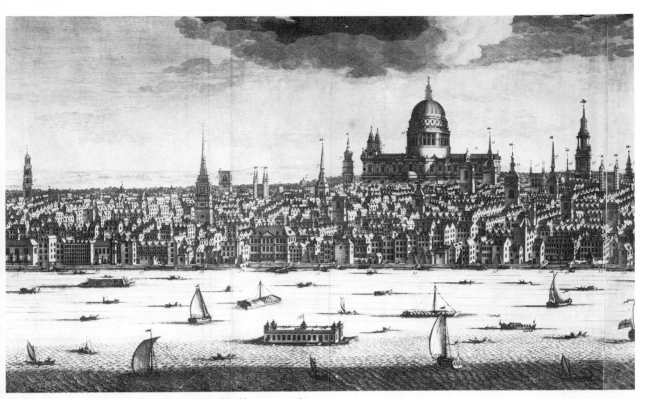

When London was rebuilt, a new law made sure that all buildings were made of brick or stone. The jewel of the new city was the new cathedral, designed by Sir Christopher Wren. Almost every church in the new city was also designed by Wren, or by his able assistant, Nicholas Hawksmoor. Although some buildings were pulled down and others built during the next 250 years, the city only changed significantly in the rebuilding that followed the Second World War.

As a result of the rapid spread of literacy and the improvement in printing techniques, the first newspapers appeared in the seventeenth century. They were a new way of spreading all kinds of ideas, scientific, religious and literary. Many of them included advertisements. In 1660 Charles II advertised for his lost dog.

Life and work in the Stuart age

The situation for the poor improved in the second half of the seventeenth century. Prices fell compared with wages, and fewer people asked for help from the parish. But it was the middle groups who continued to do well. Many who started life as yeoman farmers or traders became minor gentry or merchants. Part of their success resulted from a strong interest in farming improvements, which could now be studied in the many new books on the subject.

By the middle of the century the government had already begun to control the trade in cereals to make sure that merchants did not export these while Britain still needed them. However, by 1670 Britain was able to export cereals to Europe, where living conditions, particularly for the poor, were much worse than in Britain. This was partly the result of the Thirty Years War, 1618–48, which had badly damaged European agriculture.

Trade within Britain itself changed enormously in the seventeenth century. The different regions became less economically separate from each other. No place in Britain was more than seventy-five miles from the sea, and by 1690 few places were more than twenty miles from a river or canal. These waterways became important means of transport, allowing each region to develop its own special produce. Kent, for example, grew more fruit and vegetables to export to other regions, and became known as "the garden of England".

Improved transport resulted in a change in buying and selling. Most towns did not have shops before the seventeenth century. They had market days when farmers and manufacturers sold their produce in the town square or marketplace. By 1690, however, most towns also had proper shops. Shopkeepers travelled around the country to buy goods for their shops, which were new and exciting and drew people from the country to see them. Towns which had shops grew larger, while smaller towns without shops remained no more than villages.

London remained far larger than any other town, with more than 500,000 people by 1650. It controlled almost all the sea trade with other countries. The next largest cities, Norwich, Newcastle and Bristol, had only 25,000 each. (London's great plague of 1665 killed 68,000 people in only six months, almost equal to the total population of these three cities.) After the fire of 1666, the richer citizens for the first time had water supplied to their houses, through specially made wooden pipes. The city streets had traffic jams just as bad as today's, and the noise was probably far worse, with the sound of iron-tyred wheels and the hammering of craftsmen.

In London there was a new class of rich "aristocrats", most of whom belonged to the nobility, but not all. Money could buy a high position in British society more easily than in Europe. After 1650 the rich began to meet in the new coffeehouses, which quickly became the meeting places for conversation and politics.

"The Tichborne Dole", a late seventeenth-century picture, shows a Hampshire landowner, his family, servants and farm tenants. It shows the way in which dress differed according to class and occupation. One of the servants on the left is black, while there is a Quaker woman (holding a baby) among the farming people on the right.

Coffeehouses became very popular at the end of the seventeenth century, and remained so for much of the eighteenth century. While coffeehouses were visited only by men, their wives increasingly held tea parties at home. Tea drinking, and the special utensils necessary for this, became very popular among the wealthy. At first tea was made in silver teapots and was drunk from bowls without handles. In the second half of the century china pots replaced silver ones, and teacups replaced bowls. These teacups sat in saucers, the little dishes that were normally used for holding sauces.

Some of the old nobility, however, did not accept the new rich as equals. While new Stuart yeomen wanted to be gentry, descendants of the older Tudor gentry started to call themselves "squires", the ruling class of the countryside. They did not wish to be confused with the new gentry.

The squires and JPs governed locally during Cromwell's Protectorate, and continued to do so afterwards. They had the power to tax for local purposes, to call out soldiers and to try most criminals. They had the same interests as the government, and were therefore usually willing to

pay taxes. As one gentleman said in 1625, "we must not give an example of disobedience to those beneath us".

While the rich of London visited the coffeehouses, the ordinary people went to the drinking houses, called "alehouses", in town and country. These soon became the centre of popular culture, where news and ideas could be passed on. By the end of the century the government had secret informers watching the alehouses and listening for rebellious talk.

Family life

After the rapid increase in population in the Tudor century, the number of births began to fall in the Stuart age. In 1600 Britain and Ireland had a total population of 6 million. Although it increased to 7.7 million by 1650, the rate then started to fall. No one is quite sure why the population either rose so rapidly in the Tudor age, or steadied during the seventeenth century.

One reason for the smaller number of births was that people married later than anywhere else in Europe. Most people married in their mid twenties, and by the end of the century the average age of first marriages was even older, at twenty-seven. This, of course, meant that women had fewer babies. Some women tried to control the size of their families by breast-feeding babies for as long as possible. It also seems that more men remained unmarried than before. But the pattern of population growth and human behaviour remains puzzling. A study of south Wales, for example, shows that one in three of all heads of gentry families remained unmarried at the end of the seventeenth century. A century earlier, hardly any heads of gentry families in the area had remained unmarried. There is uncertainty as to why this should have been.

By the end of the sixteenth century there were already signs that the authority of the husband was increasing. This resulted from the weakening of wider family ties. Furthermore, just as the power of the monarch became more absolute during the sixteenth and early seventeenth centuries, so also did that of the husband and father. But while the power of the monarchy was brought under control, the authority of the head of the family continued to grow.

This power partly resulted from the increasing authority of the Church following the Reformation. The Protestants believed that personal faith was important, and put extra responsibility on the head of the family for its spiritual welfare. The father always led daily family prayers and Bible reading. In some ways he had taken the place of the priest. As a result, his wife and children belonged to him, mind, body and soul. Absolute obedience was expected. Disobedience was considered an act against God as well as the head of the house.

One result of this increase in the father's authority was that from the early seventeenth century children were frequently beaten to break their "sinful" will. The child who was not beaten was unusual. William Penn, the Quaker who founded the colony of Pennsylvania in north America, advised parents to "love them [their children] with wisdom, correct them with affection, never strike in passion, and suit the corrections to their ages as well as their fault." It is unlikely his advice was accepted except among the Quaker sect, which rejected all violence. Another result was the loss of legal rights by women over whatever property they had brought into a marriage.

However, the Protestant religion also gave new importance to the individual, especially in Presbyterian Scotland. Many Scottish women were not afraid to stand up to both their husbands and the government on matters of personal belief. In fact many of those who chose to die for their beliefs during Scotland's "killing times" were women. This self-confidence was almost certainly a result of greater education and religious democracy in Scotland at this time.

The eighteenth century

16　The political world

Politics and finance · Wilkes and liberty · Radicalism and the loss of the American colonies · Ireland · Scotland

Well before the end of the eighteenth century Britain was as powerful as France. This resulted from the growth of its industries and from the wealth of its large new trading empire, part of which had been captured from the French. Britain now had the strongest navy in the world; the navy controlled Britain's own trade routes and endangered those of its enemies. It was the deliberate policy of the government to create this trading empire, and to protect it with a strong navy. This was made possible by the way in which government had developed during the eighteenth century.

For the first time, it was the king's ministers who were the real policy and decision-makers. Power now belonged to the groups from which the ministers came, and their supporters in Parliament. These ministers ruled over a country which had become wealthy through trade. This wealth, or "capital", made possible both an agricultural and an industrial revolution which made Britain the most advanced economy in the world.

However, there was an enormous price to pay, because while a few people became richer, many others lost their land, their homes and their way of life. Families were driven off the land in another period of enclosures. They became the working

"proletariat" of the cities that made Britain's trade and industrial empire of the nineteenth century possible. The invention of machinery destroyed the old "cottage industries" and created factories. The development of industry led to the sudden growth of cities like Birmingham, Glasgow, Manchester and Liverpool and other centres in the north Midlands.

None of this could have happened without great danger to the established order. In France the misery of the poor and the power of the trading classes led to revolution in 1789. The British government was afraid of dangerous revolutionary ideas spreading from France to the discontented in Britain. In fact, Britain ended the century fighting against the great French leader, Napoleon Bonaparte, and eventually defeating him. In this way, perhaps, many who might have been discontented were more concerned with the defeat of Napoleon. Revolution was still a possibility, but Britain was saved partly by the high level of local control of the ruling class in the countryside and partly by Methodism, a new religious movement which offered hope and self-respect to the new proletariat. Methodism was careful to deal only with heavenly matters. It did not question political or social injustices on earth.

Politics and finance

When Queen Anne, the last of the Stuarts, died in 1714, it was not entirely certain that the Protestant ruler of Hanover, George, would become king. There were some Tories who wanted the deposed

The port of Bristol in the eighteenth century. International trade became the basis of Britain's rise to world greatness during the century. Britain had the best ships and also the guns to force its will where trade alone did not succeed. Bristol became the second largest city after London early in the century, based on the triangular trade: British-made goods to West Africa, West African slaves to the New World, and New World sugar, cotton and tobacco to Britain.

James II's son to return to Britain as James III. If he had given up Catholicism and accepted the Anglican religion he probably would have been crowned James III. But like other members of his family, James was unwilling to change his mind, and he would not give up his religion. Nor would he give up his claim to the throne, so he tried to win it by force.

In 1715 he started a rebellion against George I, who had by this time arrived from Hanover. But the rebellion was a disaster, and George's army had little difficulty in defeating the English and Scottish "Jacobites", as Stuart supporters were known. Because of the Tory connection with the Jacobites, King George allowed the Whigs to form his government.

Government power was increased because the new king spoke only German, and did not seem very interested in his new kingdom. Among the king's ministers was Robert Walpole, who remained the greatest political leader for over twenty years. He is considered Britain's first Prime Minister.

Walpole came to power as a result of his financial ability. At the end of the seventeenth century the government had been forced to borrow money in order to pay for the war with France. There was nothing new about this, except that because of the war the government's borrowing increased enormously. In 1694, a group of financiers who lent to the government decided to establish a bank, and the government agreed to borrow from it alone. The new bank, called the Bank of England, had authority to raise money by printing "bank notes". This was not an entirely new idea. For hundreds of years bankers and money dealers had been able to give people "promisory notes" signed by themselves. These could be handed on as payment to a third or fourth person. This way of making trade easier had been made lawful during the reign of Henry I, six hundred years earlier. The cheques we use today developed from these promisory notes.

At a time when many people had money to invest, there was popular interest in financial matters. People wanted to invest money in some of the trading companies doing business in the West

Indies, the East Indies or in other newly developing areas. The possibility of high profits, and the excitement this possibility caused, made the cost of a share in these trading adventures expensive. In 1720 the South Sea Company offered to pay off the government's national debt if it was given monopoly rights to trading in the South Seas. It raised money by selling shares which quickly rose in value with the increasing excitement. When people's confidence in the South Sea Company suddenly fell, so did the price of shares, and thousands of people who had invested their money lost everything. Robert Walpole was able to bring back public confidence. He made sure that something like the "South Sea Bubble" could not happen again. This was the first step in making companies responsible to the public for the money which they borrowed by the sale of shares.

In the other countries of Europe kings and queens had absolute power. Britain was unusual, and Walpole was determined to keep the Crown under the firm control of Parliament. He knew that with the new German monarchy this was more possible than it had been before.

Walpole skilfully developed the idea that government ministers should work together in a small group, which was called the "Cabinet". He introduced the idea that any minister who disagreed deeply with other Cabinet ministers was expected to resign. From this basic idea grew another important rule in British politics: that all members of the Cabinet were together responsible for policy decisions. Walpole built on the political results of the Glorious Revolution of 1688. It was he who made sure that the power of the king would always be limited by the constitution.

The limits to monarchy were these: the king could not be a Catholic; the king could not remove or change laws; the king was dependent on Parliament for his financial income and for his army. The king was supposed to "choose" his ministers. Even today the government of Britain is "Her Majesty's Government". But in fact the ministers belonged as much to Parliament as they did to the king.

Walpole wanted to avoid war and to increase taxes so that the government could pay back everything it had borrowed, and get rid of the national debt. He put taxes on luxury goods, such as tea, coffee and chocolate, all of which were drunk by the rich, and were brought to Britain from its new colonies by wealthy traders. Tea had become a national drink by 1700, when 50,000 kg were already being imported each year. Walpole raised the government's income, but this had little effect on the national debt, and he became very unpopular.

The most important of Walpole's political enemies was William Pitt "the Elder", later Lord Chatham. Chatham wanted Britain to be economically strong in the world, and he agreed with Daniel Defoe, the author of *Robinson Crusoe*, who had written in 1728, "Trade is the wealth of the world. Trade makes the difference between rich and poor, between one nation and another." But trade also involved competition. Chatham had studied French trade and industry, and he was certain that Britain must beat France in the race for an overseas trade empire.

In 1733 France made an alliance with Spain. Chatham feared that this alliance would give France a trade advantage over Britain through freer trade possibilities with the Spanish Empire in South America and the Far East. England had been trying unsuccessfully to develop trade with the Spanish Empire since the days of Drake. Once Chatham was in the government, he decided to make the British navy stronger than that of France or any other nation. He also decided to take over as many as possible of France's trading posts abroad.

War with France broke out in 1756. Britain had already been involved in a war against France, from 1743 to 1748, concerning control of the Austrian Empire. However, this time Chatham left Britain's ally, Prussia, to do most of the fighting in Europe. He directed British effort at destroying French trade. The navy stopped French ships reaching or leaving French ports.

The war against France's trade went on all over the world. In Canada, the British took Quebec in 1759 and Montreal the following year. This gave the British control of the important fish, fur and wood trades. Meanwhile the French navy was destroyed in a battle near the coast of Spain. In India, the army of the British East India Company defeated French armies both in Bengal, and in the south near Madras, destroying French trade interests. Many Indian princes allied themselves with one side or the other. In defeating France, Britain eventually went on to control most of India by conquest or treaty with the princes. Many Britons started to go to India to make their fortune. Unlike previous British traders, they had little respect for Indian people or for their culture. So, while India became the "jewel in the Crown" of Britain's foreign possessions, British–Indian relations slowly went sour.

Meanwhile, in 1759, Britain was drunk with victory. "One is forced to ask every morning what victory there is for fear of missing one," an Englishman said at the time. British pride had already been noticed by a Swiss visitor in 1727. The British have a very high opinion of themselves, he wrote, and they "think nothing is as well done elsewhere as in their own country". British pride was expressed in a national song written in 1742: "Rule Britannia, Britannia rule the waves, Britons never never never shall be slaves."

But a new king, George III, came to the throne in 1760. He did not wish Chatham to continue an expensive war. In 1763 George III made peace with France. Britain did this without informing Prussia, which was left to fight France alone.

For the rest of the century, Britain's international trade increased rapidly. By the end of the century the West Indies were the most profitable part of Britain's new empire. They formed one corner of a profitable trade triangle. British-made knives, swords and cloth were taken to West Africa and exchanged for slaves. These were taken to the West Indies, and the ships returned to Britain carrying sugar which had been grown by slaves. Britain's colonies were an important marketplace in which the British sold the goods they produced, from the eighteenth century until the end of the empire in the twentieth century.

An East India Company official with his escort of locally recruited soldiers. In India the officials of the East India Company made public fortunes for Britain, and private fortunes for themselves. Many, however, did not survive the effects of heat and disease. On the whole Indian society accepted "John Company", as the East India Company was locally known, in both trade and warfare as just another element in a complicated cultural scene. India was used to invaders. It was only in the nineteenth century that Indians began to hate the way the British extended their control over all India and the way that the British treated them.

Wilkes and liberty

George III was the first Hanoverian to be born in Britain. Unlike his father and grandfather he had no interest in Hanover. He wanted to take a more active part in governing Britain, and in particular he wished to be free to choose his own ministers. As long as he worked with the small number of aristocrats from which the king's ministers were chosen, and who controlled Parliament, it did not seem as if he would have much difficulty.

Parliament still represented only a very small number of people. In the eighteenth century only house owners with a certain income had the right to vote. This was based on ownership of land worth forty shillings a year in the counties, but the amount varied from town to town. As a result, while the mid-century population of Britain was almost eight million, there were fewer than 250,000 voters, 160,000 of them in the counties and 85,000 in the towns or "boroughs". Only 55 of the 200 boroughs had more than 500 voters. The others were controlled by a small number of very rich property owners, sometimes acting together as a "borough corporation". Each county and each borough sent two representatives to Parliament.

This meant that bargains could be made between the two most powerful groups of people in each "constituency", allowing the chosen representative of each group to be returned to Parliament.

It was not difficult for rich and powerful people either in the boroughs or in the counties to make sure that the man they wanted was elected to Parliament. In the countryside, most ordinary landowners also held land as tenants from the greater landowners. At that time voting was not done in secret, and no tenant would vote against the wishes of his landlord in case he lost his land. Other voters were frightened into voting for the "right man", or persuaded by a gift of money. In this way the great landowning aristocrats were able to control those who sat in Parliament, and make sure that MPs did what they wanted. Politics was a matter only for a small number of the gentry who had close connections with this political aristocracy. No one could describe Parliament in those days as democratic.

However, there was one MP, John Wilkes, who saw things differently. Wilkes was a Whig, and did not like the new government of George III. Unlike almost every other MP, Wilkes also believed that olitics should be open to free discussion by veryone. Free speech, he believed, was the basic ight of every individual. When George III made eace with France in 1763 without telling his ally rederick of Prussia, Wilkes printed a strong attack n the government in his own newspaper, *The North Briton*. The king and his ministers were xtremely angry. They were unwilling to accept free peech of this kind. Wilkes was arrested and nprisoned in the Tower of London and all his rivate papers were taken from his home.

Wilkes fought back when he was tried in court. The government claimed it had arrested Wilkes "of tate necessity". The judge turned down this rgument with the famous judgement that "public olicy is not an argument in a court of law". Wilkes von his case and was released. His victory stablished principles of the greatest importance: hat the freedom of the individual is more nportant than the interests of the state, and that o one could be arrested without a proper reason. Government was not free to arrest whom it chose. Government, too, was under the law. Wilkes's ictory angered the king, but made Wilkes the most opular man in London.

The ruling class was not used to considering the pinions of ordinary people. Between 1750 and

1770 the number of newspapers had increased. These were read by the enormous number of literate people who could never hope to vote, but who were interested in the important matters of the times. They were mainly clerks, skilled workers and tradesmen. Improved roads meant that a newspaper printed in London could be reprinted in Liverpool two days later.

Newspapers in their turn increased the amount of political discussion. Even working people read the papers and discussed politics and the royal family, as foreign visitors noticed. "Conversation" clubs met in different towns to discuss questions like "Under what conditions is a man most free?", or whether secret voting was necessary for political freedom. The fact that ordinary people who had no part to play in politics asked and discussed such questions explains why John Wilkes was so popular. His struggle showed that public opinion was now a new and powerful influence on politics.

Wilkes's victory was important because he had shown that Parliament did not represent the ordinary people, and that their individual freedom was not assured. As a result of his victory people began to organise political activity outside Parliament in order to win their basic rights. Politics were no longer a monopoly of the

The battle of Culloden in early 1746 (see page 113) marked the end not only of Bonnie Prince Charlie's attempt to regain the throne for the Stuarts. It also marked the beginning of the destruction of the Highland clan system. David Morier, the painter, was able to use Highland prisoners taken at Culloden for this picture. It therefore shows the real dress of the Highlanders. Although all these men are from Clan Cameron, the variety in their dress and tartan shows it was not exactly a uniform. These prisoners were sent to work on plantations in the New World. The artist died as a debtor in Fleet prison.

The Boston Teaparty, 1773, was one of the famous events leading to open rebellion by the American colonists. It was a protest against British taxation and British monopolies on imports. American colonists, dressed as native Americans, threw a shipload of tea into the harbour rather than pay tax on it.

landowning gentry. Newspapers were allowed to send their own reporters to listen to Parliament and write about its discussions in the newspapers. The age of public opinion had arrived.

Radicalism and the loss of the American colonies

In 1764 there was a serious quarrel over taxation between the British government and its colonies in America. It was a perfect example of the kind of freedom for which Wilkes had been fighting. The British government continued to think of the colonists as British subjects. In 1700 there had been only 200,000 colonists, but by 1770 there were 2.5 million. Such large numbers needed to be dealt with carefully.

Some American colonists decided that it was not lawful for the British to tax them without their agreement. Political opinion in Britain was divided. Some felt that the tax was fair because the money would be used to pay for the defence of the American colonies against French attack. But several important politicians, including Wilkes and Chatham, agreed with the colonists that there should be "no taxation without representation".

In 1773 a group of colonists at the port of Boston threw a shipload of tea into the sea rather than pay tax on it. The event became known as "the Boston Teaparty". The British government answered by closing the port. But the colonists then decided to prevent British goods from entering America until the port was opened again. This was rebellion, and the government decided to defeat it by force. The American War of Independence had begun.

The war in America lasted from 1775 until 1783. The government had no respect for the politics of the colonists, and the British army had no respect for their fighting ability. The result was a disastrous defeat for the British government. It lost everything except for Canada.

Many British politicians openly supported the colonists. They were called "radicals". For the first time British politicians supported the rights of the king's subjects abroad to govern themselves and to fight for their rights against the king. The war in America gave strength to the new ideas of democracy and of independence.

Two of the more important radicals were Edmund Burke and Tom Paine. Paine was the first to suggest that the American colonists should become ndependent of Britain. Burke, who himself held a mixture of both radical and conservative views, argued that the king and his advisers were once again too powerful, and that Parliament needed to get back proper control of policy.

reland

ames II's defeat by William of Orange in 1690 had severe and long-term effects on the Irish people. Over the next half century the Protestant parliament in Dublin passed laws to prevent the Catholics from taking any part in national life. Catholics could not become members of the Dublin parliament, and could not vote in parliamentary elections. No Catholic could become a lawyer, go to university, join the navy or accept any public post. Catholics were not even allowed to own a horse worth more than £5. It was impossible for Catholics to have their children educated according to their religion, because Catholic schools were forbidden. Although there were still far more Catholics than Protestants, they had now become second-class citizens in their own land.

New laws were passed which divided Catholic families. The son of Catholic parents who became Protestant could take over his parents' property and use it as he wanted. These actions put the Irish Catholic population in the same position as other colonised peoples later on. Hatred between the ruling Protestant settlers and the ruled Catholic Irish was unavoidable.

By the 1770s, however, life had become easier and some of the worst laws against Catholics were removed. But not everyone wanted to give the Catholics more freedom. In Ulster, the northern part of Ireland, Protestants formed the first "Orange Lodges", societies which were against any freedom for the Catholics.

In order to increase British control Ireland was united with Britain in 1801, and the Dublin parliament closed. The United Kingdom of Great Britain and Ireland lasted for 120 years. Politicians had promised Irish leaders that when Ireland became part of Britain the Catholics would get

equal voting opportunities. But George III, supported by most Tories and by many Protestant Irish landlords, refused to let this happen.

Scotland

Scotland also suffered from the efforts of the Stuarts to win back the throne. The first "Jacobite" revolt to win the crown for James II's son, in 1715, had been unsuccessful. The Stuarts tried again in 1745, when James II's grandson, Prince Charles Edward Stuart, better known as "Bonny Prince Charlie", landed on the west coast of Scotland. He persuaded some clan chiefs to join him. Many of these chiefs had great difficulty persuading the men in their clans to join the revolt. Some were told their homes would be burnt if they did not fight. Most clans did not join the rebellion, and nor did the men of the Scottish Lowlands.

Bonny Prince Charlie was more successful at first than anyone could have imagined. His army of Highlanders entered Edinburgh and defeated an English army in a surprise attack. Then he marched south. Panic spread through England, because much of the British army was in Europe fighting the French. But success for Bonny Prince Charlie depended on Englishmen also joining his army. When the Highland army was over halfway to London, however, it was clear that few of the English would join him, and the Highlanders themselves were unhappy at being so far from home. The rebels moved back to Scotland. Early in 1746 they were defeated by the British army at Culloden, near Inverness. The rebellion was finished.

The English army behaved with cruelty. Many Highlanders were killed, even those who had not joined the rebellion. Others were sent to work in America. Their homes were destroyed, and their farm animals killed. The fear of the Highland danger was so great that a law was passed forbidding Highlanders to wear their traditional skirt, the kilt. The old patterns of the kilt, called tartans, and the Scottish musical instrument, the bagpipe, were also forbidden. Some did not obey this law, and were shot.

17 Life in town and country

Town life • The rich • The countryside • Family life

Town life

In 1700 England and Wales had a population of about 5.5 million. This had increased very little by 1750, but then grew quickly to about 8.8 million by the end of the century. Including Ireland and Scotland, the total population was about 13 million.

In 1700 England was still a land of small villages. In the northern areas of England, in Lancashire and West Yorkshire, and in the West Midlands, the large cities of the future were only just beginning to grow. By the middle of the century Liverpool, Manchester, Birmingham, Sheffield and Leeds were already large. But such new towns were still treated as villages and so had no representation in Parliament.

All the towns smelled bad. There were no drains. Streets were used as lavatories and the dirt was seldom removed. In fact people added to it, leaving in the streets the rubbish from the marketplace and from houses. The streets were muddy and narrow, some only two metres wide. Around London and other larger towns a few vegetable growers took the dirt from the streets to put on their fields.

The towns were centres of disease. As a result only one child in four in London lived to become an adult. It was the poor who died youngest. They were buried together in large holes dug in the ground. These were not covered with earth until they were full. It was hardly surprising that poor people found comfort in drinking alcohol and in trying to win money from card games. Quakers, shocked by the terrible effects of gin drinking, developed the beer industry in order to replace gin with a less damaging drink.

During the eighteenth century, efforts were made to make towns healthier. Streets were built wider, so that carriages drawn by horses could pass each other. From 1734, London had a street lighting system. After 1760 many towns asked Parliament to allow them to tax their citizens in order to provide social services, such as street cleaning and lighting. Each house owner had to pay a local tax, the amount or "rate" of which was decided by the local council or corporation.

Catholics and Jews were still not allowed into Parliament, and for Nonconformists it continued to be difficult, but they were all able to belong to the town councils that were now being set up. As these "local authorities" grew, they brought together the merchants and industrial leaders. These started to create a new administrative class to carry out the council's will. Soon London and the other towns were so clean and tidy that they became the wonder of Europe. Indeed London had so much to offer that the great literary figure of the day, Samuel Johnson, made the now famous remark, "When a man is tired of London, he is tired of life. For there is in London all that life can afford."

There were four main classes of people in eighteenth-century towns: the wealthy merchants; the ordinary merchants and traders; the skilled craftsmen; and the large number of workers who had no skill and who could not be sure of finding work from one day to another.

The rich

Social conditions were probably better than in any other country in Europe. British aristocrats had less power over the poor than European aristocrats had. In 1760 an English lord was actually hanged for

Hogarth's famous "Gin Lane" was one of a series of powerful pictures of the less pleasant aspects of English social life. This picture illustrates the evils of drink. In fact gin drinking led to so much death and criminality that a number of Quakers began brewing beer commercially as an alternative, less damaging, drink. The cellar entrance, bottom left, has the inscription "Drink for a Penny, dead drunk for Twopence, clean straw for Nothing." This is a later copy of Hogarth's original black and white print.

At the other end of the social scale, Thomas Gainsborough, perhaps England's finest portrait painter, painted for the rich and famous. "The Morning Walk" has a clam domesticity about it. There is also informality and deep affection in this picture, quite different from the formality of "The Tichborne Dole" (pages 102–103) or the Tudor family (page 83).

killing his servant. There were few places in Europe where that would have happened. To foreigners, used to the absolute power of the king and his nobles, English law seemed an example of perfect justice, even if it was not really so.

Foreigners noticed how easy it was for the British to move up and down the social "ladder". In London a man who dressed as a gentleman would be treated as one. It was difficult to see a clear difference between the aristocracy, the gentry and the middle class of merchants. Most classes mixed freely together.

However, the difference between rich and poor could be very great. The duke of Newcastle, for example, had an income of £100,000 each year.

The workers on his lands were lucky if they were paid more than £15 a year.

The comfortable life of the gentry must have been dull most of the time. The men went hunting and riding, and carried out "improvements" to their estates. During the eighteenth century these improvements included rebuilding many great houses in the classical style. It was also fashionable to arrange natural-looking gardens and parks to create a carefully made "view of nature" from the windows of the house. Some of the gentry became interested in collecting trees or plants from abroad.

Women's lives were more boring, although during the winter there were frequent visits to London, where dances and parties were held. But even the

Somersetshire Buildings in Milsom Street, Bath, 1788, were among the finest town houses built in the "Georgian" period. Bath has survived as England's best preserved Georgian city because was very fashionable during the eighteenth century, but suddenly ceased to be so at the beginning of the nineteenth century. As a result the economy of Bath, based upon tourism, collapsed and very few of the splendid Georgian buildings were replaced during the nineteenth or twentieth centuries.

richest women's lives were limited by the idea that they could not take a share in more serious matters. They were only allowed to amuse themselves. As one lord wrote: "Women are only children of larger growth ... A man of sense only plays with them ... he neither tells them about, nor trusts them, with serious matters."

During the eighteenth century, people believed that the natural spring waters in "spa" towns such as Bath were good for their health. These towns became fashionable places where most people went to meet other members of high society. Bath, which is still the best example of an eighteenth-century English city, was filled with people who wished to be "seen". In Scotland a "New Town" on the edge of the old city of Edinburgh was built by Scotland's great architect, Robert Adam. Like Bath, it represented the height of eighteenth-century British civilised life.

The countryside

The cultural life of Edinburgh was in total contrast with life in the Scottish Highlands. Because the kilt and tartan were forbidden, everyone born since 1746 had grown up wearing Lowland (English) clothes. The old way of colouring and making tartan patterns from local plants had long been forgotten. By the time the law forbidding the kilt and tartan was abolished in 1782, it was too late.

Highland dress and tartans became fancy dress, to be worn by Scottish soldiers and by lovers of the past, but not by the real Highlanders. Very few of the tartans that were worn after 1782 would have been recognised as "clan" tartans by the men who had fought at Culloden.

The real disaster in the Highlands, however, was economic. Towards the end of the eighteenth century, the clan chiefs began to realise that money could be made from sheep for the wool trade. They began to push the people off the clan lands, and to replace them with sheep, a process known as the clearances. The chiefs treated the clan lands as their personal property, and the law supported them, just as it supported the enclosure of common land in England. Between 1790 and 1850 hundreds of thousands of Highlanders lost their old way of life so that their chiefs could make a profit from the land. Many Highlanders, men, women and children, lived poor on the streets of Glasgow. Others went to begin a new life, mainly in Canada, where many settled with other members of their clan. A smaller number went to Australia in the nineteenth century. Clan society in the Highlands had gone for ever.

In England the countryside changed even more than the towns in the eighteenth century. Most farming at the beginning of the century was still done as it had been for centuries. Each village stood in the middle of three or four large fields, and the villagers together decided what to grow, although individuals continued to work on their own small strips of land.

During the eighteenth century most of this land was enclosed. The enclosed land was not used for sheep farming, as it had been in Tudor times, but for mixed animal and cereal farms. People with money and influence, such as the village squire, persuaded their MP to pass a law through Parliament allowing them to take over common land and to enclose it. The MP was willing to do this because the landowner was often able to help him at the next election with the votes of those who worked for him.

One main cause of these enclosures was that a number of the greater landlords, including the aristocracy, had a great deal of money to invest. This had come partly from profits made from increased trade, especially with the West Indies and with India. It also came from investment in coal mines and ironworks, both of which had a growing part of the economy. Finally, some aristocrats had purchased development sites on the edge of London, most notably the dukes of Bedford and Westminster.

Most of them wanted to invest their money on the land, and having improved their own land, and built fine country houses, they looked to other land. Their reason was that farming had become much more profitable. From the mid-seventeenth century there had been a number of improvements in farming, and a growth of interest in farming methods. Britain and Holland were better at farming than any other country in Europe. At the beginning of the eighteenth century a "seed drill", a machine for sowing corn seed in straight lines and at fixed intervals, was invented by Jethro Tull. This made fields easier to weed, and made it possible to produce a greater crop. Other farmers had started to understand how to improve soil. At the same time, root crops grown in Holland were introduced in Britain.

Traditionally the land had been allowed to rest every three years. But by growing root crops one

The eighteenth-century enclosures of village farmland changed much of England's landscape. In this aerial view of Padbury, Buckinghamshire, the old strip farming pattern can still be seen, as well as the new hedgerows marking the enclosures of the gentry farmers.

year, animal food the next, and wheat the third, farmers could now produce more. Growing animal food also made it possible to keep animals through the winter. This was an important new development. Before the mid-eighteenth century most animals were killed before winter because there was never enough food to keep them until the following spring. For the first time people could now eat fresh meat all the year round.

These improvements, however, were a good deal more difficult to introduce when most farmland was still organised by the whole village community as it had been for centuries. No strip farmer could afford the necessary machinery, and it was not worth buying machinery for such small amounts of land in three different areas around the village. Richer farmers wanted to change the system of farming, including the system of landholding. With one large area for each farm the new machinery and methods would work very well. They had the money to do this, and could expect the help of the village squire and their MP, who were also rich farmers with the same interests. They had a strong economic argument for introducing change because it was clear that the new methods would produce more food for each acre of land than the traditional methods. There was also another strong reason, though at the time people may not have realised it. The population had started to grow at a greatly increased rate.

The enclosures, and the farming improvements from which they resulted, made possible far greater and more efficient food production than could be found in almost any other country in Europe. The records of Britain's largest meat market, Smithfield in London, show the extraordinary improvement in animal farming. In 1710 the average weight of an ox was 168 kg, by 1795 it was 364 kg. During the same period the average weight of a sheep in Smithfield rose from 17 kg to 36 kg.

Improved use of land made it possible to grow wheat almost everywhere. For the first time everyone, including the poor, could eat white wheat bread. White bread was less healthy than brown, but the poor enjoyed the idea that they could afford the same bread as the rich. In spite of the greatly increased production of food, however, Britain could no longer feed itself by the end of the century. Imported food from abroad became necessary to feed the rapidly growing population.

But in social terms the enclosures were damaging. Villagers sometimes knew nothing about an enclosure until they were sent off the land. Some had built their homes on common land and these were destroyed. Over one thousand parliamentary Acts resulted in the enclosure of about four million acres in the second half of the century. Many of the poor thought this was no better than stealing:

> They hang the man and flog the woman,
> That steals the goose from off the common,
> But leave the greater criminal loose
> That steals the common from the goose.

The enclosures changed the look of much of the countryside. Instead of a few large fields there were now many smaller fields, each encircled with a hedge, many with trees growing in them.

The problem of the growing landless class was made very much worse by the rapid increase in population in the second half of the century. Some were able to work with the new farming class. Others were not able to find work. Many of these had to depend on the help of the Poor Laws, first introduced by Queen Elizabeth I.

Another problem was that there were several years of bad harvests which resulted in a sharp increase in wheat prices. Local magistrates could have fixed wages to make sure the poor could afford to eat. But in many places, they chose instead to help those whose wages were particularly low out of the local rates. The most famous example was in a village called Speenhamland, and the "Speenhamland Act" was copied in many parts of the country. It was a disastrous system, because employers were now able to employ people cheaply knowing that the parish would have to add to the low wages they paid. Some employers even lowered their wages after the Speenhamland Act. It is not surprising that as a result the national cost of helping the poor rose from £2 million in 1790 to £4 million in 1800.

Another effect of the Speenhamland Act was to increase the growth of the population. Help was given to a family according to the number of children. Before the enclosures farmers had smaller families because the land had to be divided among the children, and because young men would not marry until they had a farm of their own. The enclosures removed the need for these limits, and the Speenhamland Act encouraged larger families since this meant an increase in financial help.

Neighbouring parishes joined together to build a "parish workhouse" where most of the poor were fed and housed. Some parishes hired the workhouse and its population to a local businessman who wanted cheap workers. He provided food in return for work. This quickly led to a system little better than slavery, with children as well as adults being made to work long hours. These effects brought about the collapse of the old Poor Law and led to a new law in 1834.

Other people left their village and went to the towns to find work. They provided the energy that made possible an even greater revolution which was to change the face of Britain.

Family life

In the eighteenth century families began to express affection more openly than before. In addition it seems that for the first time children were no longer thought of as small adults, but as a distinct group of people with special needs. A century after the Quaker, Penn, there was a growing voice advising gentleness with children. One popular eighteenth-century handbook on the upbringing of children, itself a significant development, warned: "Severe and frequent whipping is, I think, a very bad practice." In 1798 another handbook told mothers that "The first object in the education of a child should be to acquire its affection, and the second to obtain its confidence. The most likely thing to expand a youthful mind is . . . praise."

Girls, however, continued to be victims of the parents' desire to make them match the popular idea of feminine beauty of slim bodies, tight waists and a pale appearance. To achieve this aim, and so improve the chances of a good marriage, parents forced their daughters into tightly waisted clothes, and gave them only little food to avoid an unfashionably healthy appearance. Undoubtedly this behaviour explains the idea and reality of frail feminine health which continued into the nineteenth century.

Parents still often decided on a suitable marriage for their children, but they increasingly sought their children's opinion. However, sons and daughters often had to marry against their wishes. One man, forced to give up the only woman he ever loved, wrote, "I sighed as a lover, but I obeyed as a son." But love and companionship were slowly becoming accepted reasons for marriage. As one husband wrote to his wife after fifteen years of marriage, "I have only time to say that I love you dearly, – best of women, best of wives, and best of friends." If such feelings described a sixteenth- or seventeenth-century marriage they were less openly stated, and perhaps less openly expected.

The increase in affection was partly because people could now expect a reasonably long life. This resulted mainly from improved diet and the greater cleanliness of cotton rather than woollen underclothing. However, it was also the result of a

Hogarth is best known for his realistic pictures of society's ills, but to make money he also painted wealthy people. "The Graham Children" gives a delightful view of a warm relaxed and jolly atmosphere. Play began to be recognised as good for children, but only for young ones. It was feared that if older children played they would become lazy adults. One lord wrote to his son on his ninth birthday, "Childish toys and playthings must be thrown aside, and your mind directed to serious objects."

growing idea of kindness. For perhaps the first time people started to believe that cruelty either to humans or animals was wrong. It did not prevent bad factory conditions, but it did help those trying to end slavery. At the root of this dislike of cruelty was the idea that every human was an individual.

This growing individualism showed itself in a desire for privacy. In the seventeenth century middle-class and wealthier families were served by servants, who listened to their conversation as they ate. They lived in rooms that led one to another, usually through wide double doors. Not even the bedrooms were private. But in the eighteenth century families began to eat alone, preferring to serve themselves than to have servants listening to everything they had to say. They also rebuilt the insides of their homes, putting in corridors, so that every person in the family had their own private bedroom.

Britain was ahead of the rest of Europe in this individualism. Almost certainly this was the result of the political as well as economic strength of the middle class, and the way in which the middle class mixed so easily with the gentry and aristocracy. Individualism was important to trade and industrial success.

The most successful in trade and industry were often Nonconformists, who were especially hardworking. They could be hard on their families, as Puritan fathers had been a century earlier. But they were also ambitious for their sons, sending them away to boarding school at a young age. Removed from family affection, this kind of education increased individualism. Starved of emotional life, many of these boys grew up to put all their energy into power, either helping to build the empire, or helping to build trade and industry.

Such individualism could not exist for the poorer classes. Where women and children could find work making cloth, a worker family might double its income, and do quite well. But a poor family in which only the father could find work lived on the edge of starvation.

The Speenhamland Act was not practised everywhere. An increasing number of families had no choice but to go to the parish workhouse. Some babies were even killed or left to die by desperate mothers. A poor woman expecting a baby was often sent out of the parish, so that feeding the mother and child became the responsibility of another parish workhouse.

The use of child labour in the workhouse and in the new factories increased towards the end of the century. This was hardly surprising. A rapidly growing population made a world of children. Children of the poor had always worked as soon as they could walk. Workhouse children were expected to learn a simple task from the age of three, and almost all would be working by the age of six or seven. They were particularly useful to factory owners because they were easy to discipline, unlike adults, and they were cheap.

Then, quite suddenly at the end of the century, child labour began to be seen as shameful. This resulted partly from the growing dislike of cruelty, and also from the fact that hard child labour became more visible and more systematic now that so many people worked in factories rather than in fields and cottages. A first blow had been struck some years earlier. Horrified by the suffering of children forced to sweep chimneys, two men campaigned for almost thirty years to persuade Parliament to pass a Regulating Act in 1788 to reduce the cruelty involved. In the nineteenth century the condition of poor children was to become a main area of social reform. This was a response not only to the fact that children were suffering more, but also that their sufferings were more public.

18 The years of revolution

Industrial revolution · Society and religion · Revolution in France and the Napoleonic Wars

Industrial revolution

Several influences came together at the same time to revolutionise Britain's industry: money, labour, a greater demand for goods, new power, and better transport.

By the end of the eighteenth century, some families had made huge private fortunes. Growing merchant banks helped put this money to use.

Increased food production made it possible to feed large populations in the new towns. These populations were made up of the people who had lost their land through enclosures and were looking for work. They now needed to buy things they had never needed before. In the old days people in the villages had grown their own food, made many of their own clothes and generally managed without having to buy very much. As landless workers these people had to buy food, clothing and everything else they needed. This created an opportunity to make and sell more goods than ever before. The same landless people who needed these things also became the workers who made them.

By the early eighteenth century simple machines had already been invented for basic jobs. They could make large quantities of simple goods quickly and cheaply so that "mass production" became possible for the first time. Each machine carried out one simple process, which introduced the idea of "division of labour" among workers. This was to become an important part of the industrial revolution.

By the 1740s the main problem holding back industrial growth was fuel. There was less wood, and in any case wood could not produce the heat necessary to make iron and steel either in large quantities or of high quality. But at this time the use of coal for changing iron ore into good quality iron or steel was perfected, and this made Britain the leading iron producer in Europe. This happened only just in time for the many wars in which Britain was to fight, mainly against France, for the rest of the century. The demand for coal grew very quickly. In 1800 Britain was producing four times as much coal as it had done in 1700, and eight times as much iron.

Increased iron production made it possible to manufacture new machinery for other industries. No one saw this more clearly than John Wilkinson, a man with a total belief in iron. He built the largest ironworks in the country. He built the world's first iron bridge, over the River Severn, in 1779. He saw the first iron boats made. He built an iron chapel for the new Methodist religious sect, and was himself buried in an iron coffin. Wilkinson was also quick to see the value of new inventions. When James Watt made a greatly improved steam engine in 1769, Wilkinson improved it further by making parts of the engine more accurately with his special skills in ironworking. In this way the skills of one craft helped the skills of another. Until then steam engines had only been used for pumping, usually in coal mines. But in 1781 Watt produced an engine with a turning motion, made of iron and steel. It was a vital development because people were now no longer dependent on natural power.

Spinners at work. People looked back at the age of cottage industry as a happy time compared with the bleak discipline of factory employment. The view was, perhaps, over-idealised. Conditions were dark and less pleasant than this picture suggests. Frequently it was only women's spinning that kept a family from starvation. But at least families worked together as an economic unit. All this was broken up by the new machinery. Button making was one of the few cottage industries to survive beyond 1850.

An early coal mine in the Midlands. The use of coal for almost all energy led to a huge amount of smoke which blackened buildings and created dark "smogs", mixtures of smoke and fog, in winter.

One invention led to another, and increased production in one area led to increased production in others. Other basic materials of the industrial revolution were cotton and woollen cloth, which were popular abroad. In the middle of the century other countries were buying British uniforms, equipment and weapons for their armies. To meet this increased demand, better methods of production had to be found, and new machinery was invented which replaced handwork. The production of cotton goods had been limited by the spinning process, which could not provide enough cotton thread for the weavers. In 1764 a spinning machine was invented which could do the work of several hand spinners, and other improved machines were made shortly after. With the far greater production of cotton thread, the slowest part of the cotton clothmaking industry became weaving. In 1785 a power machine for weaving revolutionised clothmaking. It allowed Britain to make cloth more cheaply than elsewhere, and Lancashire cotton cloths were sold in every continent. But this machinery put many people out of work. It also changed what had been a "cottage industry" done at home into a factory industry, where workers had to keep work hours and rules set down by factory owners.

In the Midlands, factories using locally found clay began to develop very quickly, and produced fine quality plates, cups and other china goods. These soon replaced the old metal plates and drinking cups that had been used. Soon large quantities of china were being exported. The most famous factory was one started by Josiah Wedgwood. His high quality bone china became very popular, as it still is.

The cost of such goods was made cheaper than ever by improved transport during the eighteenth century. New waterways were dug between towns, and transport by these canals was cheaper than transport by land. Roads, still used mainly by people rather than by goods, were also improved during the century. York, Manchester and Exeter were three days' travel from London in the 1720s, but by the 1780s they could be reached in little over twenty-four hours. Along these main roads, the coaches stopped for fresh horses in order to keep up their speed. They became known as "stage" coaches, a name that became famous in the "Wild West" of America. It was rapid road travel and cheap transport by canal that made possible the economic success of the industrial revolution.

Soon Britain was not only exporting cloth to Europe. It was also importing raw cotton from its colonies and exporting finished cotton cloth to sell to those same colonies.

The social effects of the industrial revolution were enormous. Workers tried to join together to protect themselves against powerful employers. They wanted fair wages and reasonable conditions in which to work. But the government quickly banned these "combinations", as the workers' societies were known. Riots occurred, led by the unemployed who had been replaced in factories by machines. In 1799 some of these rioters, known as Luddites, started to break up the machinery which had put them out of work. The government supported the factory owners, and made the breaking of machinery punishable by death. The government was afraid of a revolution like the one in France.

Society and religion

Britain avoided revolution partly because of a new religious movement. This did not come from the Church of England, which was slow to recognise change. Many new industrial towns in fact had no church or priests or any kind of organised religion. The Church of England did not recognise the problems of these towns, and many priests belonged to the gentry and shared the opinions of the government and ruling class.

The new movement which met the needs of the growing industrial working class was led by a remarkable man called John Wesley. He was an Anglican priest who travelled around the country preaching and teaching. In 1738 Wesley had had a mystical experience. "I felt my heart strangely warmed," he wrote afterwards, "I felt that I did

A Methodist meeting in 1777. The habit of preaching in the open air drew poorer people who usually did not go to church. The Methodist preachers went everywhere, riding from village to village with their good news that Christ had died for everyone. They even visited prisons, often to comfort those condemned to hang.

trust in Christ, Christ alone for my salvation; and an assurance was given that he had taken *my* sins, even *mine*, and saved me from sin and death." For fifty-three years John Wesley travelled 224,000 miles on horseback, preaching at every village he came to. Sometimes he preached in three different villages in one day. Very soon others joined in his work. John Wesley visited the new villages and industrial towns which had no parish church.

John Wesley's "Methodism" was above all a personal and emotional form of religion. It was organised in small groups, or "chapels", all over the country. At a time when the Church of England itself showed little interest in the social and

spiritual needs of the growing population, Methodism was able to give ordinary people a sense of purpose and dignity. The Church was nervous of this powerful new movement which it could not control, and in the end Wesley was forced to leave the Church of England and start a new Methodist Church.

By the end of the century there were over 360 Methodist chapels, most of them in industrial areas. These chapels were more democratic than the Church of England, partly because the members of each chapel had to find the money to pay for them. The Anglican Church, on the other hand, had a good income from the land it owned.

John Wesley was no friend of the ruling classes but he was deeply conservative, and had no time for radicalism. He disapproved of Wilkes and thought the French Revolution was the work of the devil. "The greater the share the people have in government," he wrote, "the less liberty, civil or religious, does a nation enjoy." He carefully avoided politics, and taught people to be hardworking and honest. As a result of his teaching, people accepted many of the injustices of the times without complaint. Some became wealthy through working hard and saving their money. As an old man, Wesley sadly noted how hard work led to wealth, and wealth to pride and that this threatened to destroy his work. "Although the form of religion remains," he wrote, "the spirit is swiftly vanishing away." However, Wesley probably saved Britain from revolution. He certainly brought many people back to Christianity.

The Methodists were not alone. Other Christians also joined what became known as "the evangelical revival", which was a return to a simple faith based on the Bible. It was almost a reawakening of Puritanism, but this time with a social rather than a political involvement. Some, especially the Quakers, became well known for social concern. One of the best known was Elizabeth Fry, who made public the terrible conditions in the prisons, and started to work for reform.

It was also a small group of Christians who were the first to act against the evils of the slave trade, from which Britain was making huge sums of money. Slaves did not expect to live long. Almost 20 per cent died on the voyage. Most of the others died young from cruel treatment in the West Indies. For example, between 1712 and 1768 200,000 slaves were sent to work in Barbados, but during this period the population of Barbados only increased by 26,000.

The first success against slavery came when a judge ruled that "no man could be a slave in Britain", and freed a slave who had landed in Bristol. This victory gave a new and unexpected meaning to the words of the national song, "Britons never shall be slaves." In fact, just as Britain had taken a lead in slavery and the slave trade, it also took the lead internationally in ending them. The slave trade was abolished by law in 1807. But it took until 1833 for slavery itself to be abolished in all British colonies.

Others, also mainly Christians, tried to limit the cruelty of employers who forced children to work long hours. In 1802, as a result of their efforts, Parliament passed the first Factory Act, limiting child labour to twelve hours each day. In 1819 a new law forbade the employment of children under the age of nine. Neither of these two Acts were obeyed everywhere, but they were the early examples of government action to protect the weak against the powerful.

The influence of these eighteenth-century religious movements continued. A century later, when workers started to organise themselves more effectively, many of those involved had been brought up in Methodist or other Nonconformist sects. This had a great influence on trade unionism and the labour movement in Britain.

Revolution in France and the Napoleonic Wars

France's neighbours only slowly realised that its revolution in 1789 could be dangerous for them. Military power and the authority of kingship were almost useless against revolutionary ideas.

In France the revolution had been made by the "bourgeoisie", or middle class, leading the peasants and urban working classes. In England the bourgeoisie and the gentry had acted together for centuries in the House of Commons, and had become the most powerful class in Britain in the seventeenth century. They had no sympathy with the French revolutionaries, and were frightened by the danger of "awakening" the working classes. They saw the danger of revolution in the British countryside, where the enclosures were happening, and in the towns, to which many of the landless were going in search of work. They also saw the political dangers which could develop from the great increase in population.

125

"Breaking the Line" at the battle of Trafalgar, 1805. The traditional tactic was to exchange "broadsides" of gunfire between opposing ships. Nelson took his ships in two lines across (from right to left), rather than alongside, the enemy formation (French fleet sailing from back left to front right of picture). His ships' guns were able to fire down the length of each French ship as it passed. This had two advantages. The bows and stern of a warship were the least defended parts, so the English ships suffered much less in the exchange of gunfire. Secondly, the gunshot travelled the whole length of the enemy decks, causing great damage to the ship and loss of life.

A cartoon of the time shows William Pitt and Napoleon Bonaparte carving up the world. Napoleon has sliced off most of Europe. Pitt has taken the Atlantic which, like almost every other sea or ocean, was controlled by Britain's navy.

Several radicals sympathised with the cause of the French revolutionaries, and called for reforms in Britain. In other countries in Europe such sympathy was seen as an attack on the aristocracy. But in England both the gentry and the bourgeoisie felt they were being attacked, and the radicals were accused of putting Britain in danger. Tory crowds attacked the homes of radicals in Birmingham and several other cities. The Whig Party was split. Most feared "Jacobinism", as sympathy with the revolutionaries was called, and joined William Pitt, "the Younger" (the son of Lord Chatham), while those who wanted reform stayed with the radical Whig leader, Charles James Fox. In spite of its small size, Fox's party formed the link between the Whigs of the eighteenth century and the Liberals of the nineteenth century.

Not all the radicals sympathised with the revolutionaries in France. In many ways Edmund Burke was a conservative, in spite of his support for the American colonists in 1776. He now quarrelled with other radicals, and wrote *Reflections on the Revolution in France*, which became a popular book. He feared that the established order of kings in Europe would fall. Tom Paine, who had also supported the American colonists, wrote in answer *The Rights of Man*, in which he defended the rights of the ordinary people against the power of the monarchy and the aristocrats. The ideas in this book were thought to be so dangerous that Paine had to escape to France. He never returned to Britain. But the book itself has remained an important work on the question of political freedom.

These matters were discussed almost entirely by the middle class and the gentry. Hardly any working-class voices were heard, but it should be noted that the first definitely working-class political organisation, the Corresponding Society, was established at this time. It did not last long, because the government closed it down in 1798, and it only had branches in London, Norwich, Sheffield, Nottingham and one or two other centres.

The French Revolution had created fear all over Europe. The British government was so afraid that revolution would spread to Britain that it imprisoned radical leaders. It was particularly frightened that the army would be influenced by these dangerous ideas. Until then, soldiers had always lived in inns and private homes. Now the government built army camps, where soldiers could live separated from the ordinary people. The government also brought together yeomen and gentry who supported the ruling establishment and trained them as soldiers. The government claimed that these "yeomanry" forces were created in case of a French attack. This may have been true, but they were probably useless against an enemy army, and they were used to prevent revolution by the poor and discontented.

As an island, Britain was in less danger, and as a result was slower than other European states to make war on the French Republic. But in 1793 Britain went to war after France had invaded the Low Countries (today, Belgium and Holland). One by one the European countries were defeated by Napoleon, and forced to ally themselves with him. Most of Europe fell under Napoleon's control.

Britain decided to fight France at sea because it had a stronger navy, and because its own survival depended on control of its trade routes. British policy was to damage French trade by preventing French ships, including their navy, from moving freely in and out of French seaports. The commander of the British fleet, Admiral Horatio Nelson, won brilliant victories over the French navy, near the coast of Egypt, at Copenhagen, and finally near Spain, at Trafalgar in 1805, where he destroyed the French–Spanish fleet. Nelson was himself killed at Trafalgar, but became one of Britain's greatest national heroes. His words to the fleet before the battle of Trafalgar, "England expects that every man will do his duty," have remained a reminder of patriotic duty in time of national danger.

In the same year as Trafalgar, in 1805, a British army landed in Portugal to fight the French. This army, with its Portuguese and Spanish allies, was eventually commanded by Wellington, a man who had fought in India. But fighting the French on land was an entirely different matter. Almost everyone in Europe believed the French army, and its generals, to be the best in the world. Wellington was one of the very few generals who did not. "I am not afraid of them," he wrote on his appointment as commander. "I suspect that all the Continental armies were more than half beaten before the battle was begun. I, at least, will not be frightened beforehand." Like Nelson he quickly proved to be a great commander. After several victories against the French in Spain he invaded France. Napoleon, weakened by his disastrous invasion of Russia, surrendered in 1814. But the following year he escaped and quickly assembled an army in France. Wellington, with the timely help of the Prussian army, finally defeated Napoleon at Waterloo in Belgium in June 1815.

The nineteenth century

19 The years of power and danger
The danger at home, 1815–32 · Reform · Workers revolt · Family life

Britain in the nineteenth century was at its most powerful and self-confident. After the industrial revolution, nineteenth-century Britain was the "workshop" of the world. Until the last quarter of the century British factories were producing more than any other country in the world.

By the end of the century, Britain's empire was political rather than commercial. Britain used this empire to control large areas of the world. The empire gave the British a feeling of their own importance which was difficult to forget when Britain lost its power in the twentieth century. This belief of the British in their own importance was at its height in the middle of the nineteenth century, among the new middle class, which had grown with industrialisation. The novelist Charles Dickens nicely described this national pride. One of his characters, Mr Podsnap, believed that Britain had been specially chosen by God and "considered other countries a mistake".

The rapid growth of the middle class was part of the enormous rise in the population. In 1815 the population was 13 million, but this had doubled by 1871, and was over 40 million by 1914. This growth and the movement of people to towns from the countryside forced a change in the political balance, and by the end of the century most men had the right to vote. Politics and government during the nineteenth century became increasingly the property of the middle class. The aristocracy and the Crown had little power left by 1914.

William Bell Scott's "Iron and Coal", painted 1864–67, has a quite new atmosphere of pride in labour and industry. Such pride was the mark of Britain in the nineteenth century. One can feel the enormous energy of industrial revolution in this painting.

However, the working class, the large number of people who had left their villages to become factory workers, had not yet found a proper voice.

Britain enjoyed a strong place in European councils after the defeat of Napoleon. Its strength was not in a larger population, as this was half that of France and Austria, and only a little greater than that of Prussia. It lay instead in industry and trade, and the navy which protected this trade.

Britain wanted two main things in Europe: a "balance of power" which would prevent any single nation from becoming too strong, and a free market in which its own industrial and trade superiority would give Britain a clear advantage. It succeeded in the first aim by encouraging the recovery of France, to balance the power of Austria. Further east, it was glad that Russia's influence in Europe was limited by Prussia and the empires of Austria and Turkey. These all shared a border with Russia.

Outside Europe, Britain wished its trading position to be stronger than anyone else's. It defended its interests by keeping ships of its navy in almost every ocean of the world. This was possible because it had taken over and occupied a number of places during the war against Napoleon. These included Mauritius (in the Indian Ocean), the Ionian Islands (in the eastern Mediterranean), Sierra Leone (west Africa), Cape Colony (south Africa), Ceylon, and Singapore.

After 1815 the British government did not only try to develop its trading stations. Its policy now was to control world traffic and world markets to Britain's advantage. Britain did not, however, wish to colonise everywhere. There were many areas in which it had no interest. But there were other areas, usually close to its own possessions or on important trade routes, which it wished everyone else to leave alone. It was as a result of defending these interests that Britain took over more and more land. Britain's main anxiety in its foreign policy was that Russia would try to expand southwards, by taking over the Slavic parts of Turkey's Balkan possessions, and might reach the Mediterranean. For most of the century, therefore, Britain did its best to support Turkey against Russian expansion. In spite of its power, Britain also felt increasingly anxious about growing competition from France and Germany in the last part of the century. Most of the colonies established in the nineteenth century were more to do with political control than with trading for profit.

The concerns in Europe and the protection of trade routes in the rest of the world guided Britain's foreign policy for a hundred years. It was to keep the balance in Europe in 1838 that Britain promised to protect Belgium against stronger neighbours. In spite of political and economic troubles in Europe, this policy kept Britain from war in Europe for a century from 1815. In fact it was in defence of Belgium in 1914 that Britain finally went to war against Germany.

The danger at home, 1815–32

Until about 1850, Britain was in greater danger at home than abroad. The Napoleonic Wars had turned the nation from thoughts of revolution to the need to defeat the French. They had also hidden the social effects of the industrial revolution. Britain had sold clothes, guns, and other necessary war supplies to its allies' armies as well as its own. At the same time, corn had been imported to keep the nation and its army fed.

All this changed when peace came in 1815. Suddenly there was no longer such a need for factory-made goods, and many lost their jobs. Unemployment was made worse by 300,000 men from Britain's army and navy who were now looking for work. At the same time, the landowning farmers' own income had suffered

because of cheaper imported corn. These farmers persuaded the government to introduce laws to protect locally grown corn and the price at which it was sold. The cost of bread rose quickly, and this led to increases in the price of almost everything. While prices doubled, wages remained the same. New methods of farming also reduced the number of workers on the land.

The general misery began to cause trouble. In 1830, for example, starving farmworkers in the south of England rioted for increased wages. People tried to add to their food supply by catching wild birds and animals. But almost all the woods had been enclosed by the local landlord and new laws were made to stop people hunting animals for food. Many had to choose between watching their family go hungry and risking the severe punishment of those who were caught. A man found with nets in his home could be transported to the new "penal" colony in Australia for seven years. A man caught hunting with a gun or a knife might be hanged, and until 1823 thieves caught entering houses and stealing were also hanged. These laws showed how much the rich feared the poor, and although they were slowly softened, the fear remained.

There were good reasons for this fear. A new poor law in 1834 was intended to improve the help given to the needy. But central government did not provide the necessary money and many people received even less help than before. Now, only those who actually lived in the workhouse were given any help at all. The workhouses were feared and hated. They were crowded and dirty, with barely enough food to keep people alive. The inhabitants had to work from early morning till late at night. The sexes were separated, so families were divided. Charles Dickens wrote about the workhouse in his novels. His descriptions of the life of crime and misery into which poor people were forced shocked the richer classes, and conditions slowly improved.

In order to avoid the workhouse, many looked for a better life in the towns. Between 1815 and 1835 Britain changed from being a nation of country people to a nation mainly of townspeople. In the first thirty years of the nineteenth century, cities

Above: *Sheffield was little more than a large village in the early eighteenth century. By 1858 it was one of the fastest growing towns of the industrial revolution, with hundreds of factory chimneys creating a new skyline.*

Below: *England's population distribution. Even by 1801, the drift to the towns in the Midlands and northwest of England was considerable, and this movement increased during the first half of the nineteenth century.*

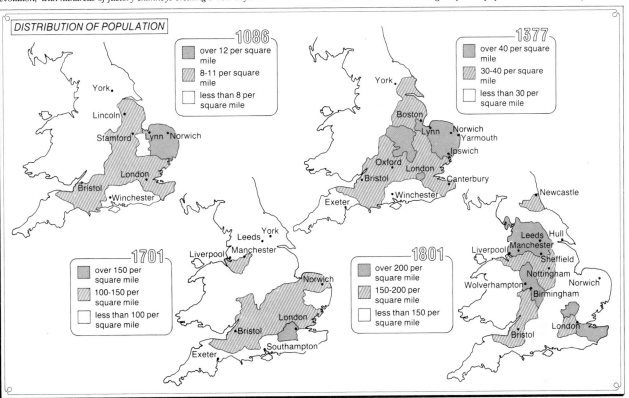

DISTRIBUTION OF POPULATION

1086
- over 12 per square mile
- 8-11 per square mile
- less than 8 per square mile

York
Lincoln
Stamford Lynn Norwich
London
Bristol
Winchester

1377
- over 40 per square mile
- 30-40 per square mile
- less than 30 per square mile

York
Boston
Lynn Norwich
Yarmouth
Oxford Ipswich
Bristol London
Exeter Canterbury
Winchester

1701
- over 150 per square mile
- 100-150 per square mile
- less than 100 per square mile

Leeds York
Liverpool Manchester
Norwich
London
Bristol
Exeter Southampton

1801
- over 200 per square mile
- 150-200 per square mile
- less than 150 per square mile

Newcastle
Leeds Hull
Liverpool Manchester
Sheffield
Nottingham
Wolverhampton Norwich
Birmingham
London
Bristol

like Birmingham and Sheffield doubled in size, while Manchester, Glasgow and Leeds more than doubled. Several towns close together grew into huge cities with no countryside left in between. The main city areas were northwest England, where the new cotton industry was based, the north Midlands, the area around Glasgow, and south Wales. But although these cities grew fast, London remained the largest. In 1820 London was home for 1.25 million, out of a total British population of about 15 million.

If the rich feared the poor in the countryside, they feared even more those in the fast-growing towns. These were harder to control. If they had been organised, a revolution like that in France might have happened. But they were not organised, and had no leaders. Only a few radical politicians spoke for the poor, but they failed to work in close co-operation with the workers who could have supported them.

Several riots did, however, take place, and the government reacted nervously. In 1819, for example, a large crowd of working people and their families gathered in Manchester to protest against their conditions and to listen to a radical speech in favour of change. Suddenly they were attacked by soldiers on horses. Eleven people were killed and more than one hundred wounded. The struggle between the government, frightened of revolution, and those who wanted change became greater.

Reform

The Whigs understood better than the Tories the need to reform the law in order to improve social conditions. Like the Tories they feared revolution, but unlike the Tories they believed it could only be avoided by reform. Indeed, the idea of reform to make the parliamentary system fairer had begun in the eighteenth century. It had been started by early radicals, and encouraged by the American War of Independence, and by the French Revolution.

The Tories believed that Parliament should represent "property" and the property owners, an idea that is still associated by some with today's Tory Party. The radicals believed that Parliament should represent the people. The Whigs, or Liberals as they later became known, were in the middle, wanting enough change to avoid revolution but little more.

The Tories hoped that the House of Lords would protect the interests of the property owners. When the Commons agreed on reform in 1830 it was turned down by the House of Lords. But the Tories fell from power the same year, and Lord Grey formed a Whig government. Grey himself had supported the call for reform as a radical in 1792. In 1832 the Lords accepted the Reform Bill, but more because they were frightened by the riots in the streets outside than because they now accepted the idea of reform. They feared that the collapse of political and civil order might lead to revolution.

At first sight the Reform Bill itself seemed almost a political revolution. Scotland's voters increased from 5,000 to 65,000. Forty-one English towns, including the large cities of Manchester, Birmingham and Bradford, were represented in Parliament for the very first time. But there were limits to the progress made. The total number of voters increased by only 50 per cent. The 349 electors of the small town of Buckingham still had as many MPs to represent them as the 4,192 electors of the city of Leeds. And England, with only 54 per cent of the British population, continued to have over 70 per cent of MPs as it had done before. However, in spite of its shortcomings, the 1832 Reform Bill was a political recognition that Britain had become an urban society.

Workers revolt

Since 1824 workers had been allowed to join together in unions. Most of these unions were small and weak. Although one of their aims was to make sure employers paid reasonable wages, they also tried to prevent other people from working in their particular trade. As a result the working classes still found it difficult to act together. Determined employers could still quite easily defeat strikers who refused to work until their pay was improved, and often did so with cruelty and violence. Soldiers

The Penny Black stamp introduced cheap postage in 1840, ensuring cheap communications for everyone. The Royal Mail prided itself on efficient service. Over the years it has remained one of the best postal services in the world.

The Chartist rally on Kennington Common, south London, marked the end of the movement. It failed to change much by constitutional means, and its leaders feared the results of trying to change society by unconstitutional methods. This rally, like previous ones, was attended mostly by men. Very few women can be seen.

were sometimes used to force people back to work or break up meetings.

In 1834, there was an event of great importance in trade union history. Six farmworkers in the Dorset village of Tolpuddle joined together, promising to be loyal to their "union". Their employer managed to find a law by which they could be punished. A judge had been specially appointed by the government to find the six men guilty, and this he did. In London 30,000 workers and radicals gathered to ask the government to pardon the "Tolpuddle Martyrs". The government, afraid of seeming weak, did not do so until the "martyrs" had completed part of their punishment. It was a bad mistake. Tolpuddle became a symbol of employers' cruelty, and of the working classes' need to defend themselves through trade union strength.

The radicals and workers were greatly helped in their efforts by the introduction of a cheap postage system in 1840. This enabled them to organise themselves across the country far better than before. For one penny a letter could be sent to anyone, anywhere in Britain.

Working together for the first time, unions, workers and radicals put forward a People's Charter in 1838. The Charter demanded rights that are now accepted by everyone: the vote for all adults; the right for a man without property of his own to be an MP; voting in secret (so that people could not be forced to vote for their landlord or his party); payment for MPs, and an election every year (which everyone today recognises as impractical). All of these demands were refused by the House of Commons.

The "Chartists" were not united for long. They were divided between those ready to use violence and those who believed in change by lawful means only. Many did not like the idea of women also getting the vote, partly because they believed it would make it harder to obtain voting rights for all men, and this demand, which had been included in the wording to the very first Charter, was quietly forgotten. But riots and political meetings continued. In 1839 fourteen men were killed by soldiers in a riot in Newport, Wales, and many others sent to one of Britain's colonies as prisoners.

135

*Many parts of London and other large cities were very dangerous,
particularly after dark. It was for this reason that the first regular police force
was established by Sir Robert "Bob" Peel, after whom the new police were
nicknamed "bobbies".*

The government's severe actions showed how much
it feared that the poor might take power, and
establish a republic.

The government was saved partly by the skill of
Robert Peel, the Prime Minister of the time. Peel
believed that changes should be made slowly but
steadily. He was able to use the improved economic
conditions in the 1840s to weaken the Chartist
movement, which slowly died. In 1846 he
abolished the unpopular Corn Law of 1815, which
had kept the price of corn higher than necessary.
Not only had this made life hard for those with
little money, but it had brought their employers,
the growing class of industrialists, into conflict with
the landlord class.

These industrialists neither wished to pay higher
wages, nor employ an underfed workforce. In this

way, Peel's decision to repeal the Corn Law was a
sign of the way power was passing out of the hands
of the eighteenth-century gentry class. These had
kept their power in the early years of the
nineteenth century. But now power decisively
passed into the hands of the growing number of
industrialists and traders.

Besides hunger, crime was the mark of poverty.
Peel had turned his attention to this problem
already, by establishing a regular police force for
London in 1829. At first people had laughed at his
blue-uniformed men in their top hats. But during
the next thirty years almost every other town and
county started its own police force. The new police
forces soon proved themselves successful, as much
crime was pushed out of the larger cities, then out
of towns and then out of the countryside. Peel was
able to show that certainty of punishment was far
more effective than cruelty of punishment.

Britain's success in avoiding the storm of revolution
in Europe in 1848 was admired almost everywhere.
European monarchs wished they were as safe on
their thrones as the British queen seemed to be.
And liberals and revolutionaries wished they could
act as freely as radicals in Britain were able to do.
Britain had been a political model in the eighteenth century, but with the War of Independence
in America and revolution in France interest in
liberalism and democracy turned to these two
countries. Now it moved back to Britain, as a
model both of industrial success and of free
constitutional government. For much of the nineteenth century Britain was the envy of the world.

Family life

In spite of the greater emphasis on the individual
and the growth of openly shown affection, the end
of the eighteenth century also saw a swing back to
stricter ideas of family life. In part, the close family
resulted from the growth of new attitudes to
privacy, perhaps a necessary part of individualism.
It was also the result of the removal, over a period
beginning in the sixteenth century, of the social
and economic support of the wider family and
village community, which had made family life so

"Dinner Hour at Wigan" by Eyre Crowe (1844–1910) gives a fine but romantic view of life in one of Britain's industrial towns. Factory women cannot often have looked so clean or healthy. Some wear wooden soled clogs on their feet, others are barefoot. It is a picture full of interest, and perhaps the most important point of the picture is the companion-ship of women. Women's closest friendships were probably more often made with other women than with their husbands. In the middleground stands a policeman, a reminder of authority and that authority was male.

much more public. Except for the very rich, people no longer married for economic reasons, but did so for personal happiness. However, while wives might be companions, they were certainly not equals. As someone wrote in 1800, "the husband and wife are one, and the husband is that one". As the idea of the close family under the "master" of the household became stronger, so the possibility for a wife to find emotional support or practical advice outside the immediate family became more limited. In addition, as the idea of the close family slowly spread down the social order, an increasing number of women found their sole economic and social usefulness ended when their children grew up, a problem that continued into the twentieth century. They were discouraged from going out to work if not economically necessary, and also encouraged to make use of the growing number of people available for domestic service.

This return to authority exercised by the head of the family was largely the result of three things. These were fear of political revolution spreading from France, of social change caused by industrial revolution in Britain, and the influence of the new religious movements of Methodism and Evangelicalism.

One must wonder how much these things reduced the chance of happy family life. Individualism, strict parental behaviour, the regular beating of children (which was still widespread), and the cruel conditions for those boys at boarding school, all worked against it. One should not be surprised that family life often ended when children grew up. As one foreigner noted in 1828, "grown up children and their parents soon become almost strangers". It is impossible to be sure what effect this kind of family life had on children. But no doubt it made young men unfeeling towards their own wives who, with unmarried sisters, were the responsibility of the man of the house. A wife was legally a man's property, until nearly the end of the century.

In spite of a stricter moral atmosphere in Scotland which resulted from the strong influence of the Kirk, Scottish women seem to have continued a stronger tradition of independent attitudes and plain speaking. In 1830 a Scotswoman called for "the perfect equality of her sex to that of man". Another in 1838 wrote, "It is the right of every woman to have a vote . . . in her county, and more so now that we have got a woman [Queen Victoria] at the head of government." She had a long time to wait.

20 The years of self-confidence

The railway · The rise of the middle classes · The growth of towns and cities · Population and politics · Queen and monarchy · Queen and empire · Wales, Scotland and Ireland

In 1851 Queen Victoria opened the Great Exhibition of the Industries of All Nations inside the Crystal Palace, in London. The exhibition aimed to show the world the greatness of Britain's industry. No other nation could produce as much at that time. At the end of the eighteenth century, France had produced more iron than Britain. By 1850 Britain was producing more iron than the rest of the world together.

Britain had become powerful because it had enough coal, iron and steel for its own enormous industry, and could even export them in large quantities to Europe. With these materials it could produce new heavy industrial goods like iron ships and steam engines. It could also make machinery which produced traditional goods like woollen and cotton cloth in the factories of Lancashire. Britain's cloth was cheap and was exported to India, to other colonies and throughout the Middle East, where it quickly destroyed the local cloth industry, causing great misery. Britain made and owned more than half the world's total shipping. This great industrial empire was supported by a strong banking system developed during the eighteenth century.

The railway

The greatest example of Britain's industrial power in the mid-nineteenth century was its railway system. Indeed, it was mainly because of this new form of transport that six million people were able to visit the Great Exhibition, 109,000 of them on one day. Many of them had never visited London

before. As one newspaper wrote, "How few among the last generation ever stirred beyond their own villages. How few of the present will die without visiting London." It was impossible for political reform not to continue once everyone could escape localism and travel all over the country with such ease.

In fact industrialists had built the railways to transport goods, not people, in order to bring down the cost of transport. By 1840 2,400 miles of track had been laid, connecting not only the industrial towns of the north, but also London, Birmingham and even an economically unimportant town like Brighton. By 1870 the railway system of Britain was almost complete. The canals were soon empty as everything went by rail. The speed of the railway even made possible the delivery of fresh fish and raspberries from Scotland to London in one night.

In 1851 the government made the railway companies provide passenger trains which stopped at all stations for a fare of one penny per mile. Now people could move about much more quickly and easily.

The middle classes soon took advantage of the new opportunity to live in suburbs, from which they travelled into the city every day by train. The suburb was a copy of the country village with all the advantages of the town. Most of the London area was built very rapidly between 1850 and 1880 in response to the enormous demand for a home in the suburbs.

"Home Sweet Home" by Walter Sadler shows a prosperous home in about 1850. The branches of holly decorating the mirror, mantelpiece and picture tell us that it is Christmas, but it is before the age of greetings cards. Sitting either side of the fireplace are the grandparents, enjoying the family scene. Mother plays the piano, while the father and children sing. The eldest daughter has been reading, possibly aloud to give her grandparents pleasure. Beside the grandmother stands a round frame on which someone has been doing embroidery work. On the floor is a "Turkey carpet", probably a British machine-made copy of the more expensive handwoven carpets from Turkey.

Poor people's lives also benefited by the railway. Many moved with the middle classes to the suburbs, into smaller houses. The men travelled by train to work in the town. Many of the women became servants in the houses of the middle classes. By 1850 16 per cent of the population were "in service" in private homes, more than were in farming or in the cloth industry.

The rise of the middle classes

There had been a "middle class" in Britain for hundreds of years. It was a small class of merchants, traders and small farmers. In the second half of the eighteenth century it had increased with the rise of industrialists and factory owners.

In the nineteenth century, however, the middle class grew more quickly than ever before and included greater differences of wealth, social position and kinds of work. It included those who worked in the professions, such as the Church, the law, medicine, the civil service, the diplomatic service, merchant banking and the army and the navy.

Isambard Kingdom Brunel (1806–1859) was a middle-class man who represented the height of British engineering success and the leadership of the middle classes in national life. In 1833 he oversaw the construction of the Great Western Railway. In 1838 he designed the first steamship to cross the Atlantic regularly. In 1845 he built the Great Britain, the first large ship to be made of iron with a screw propeller.

"Capital and Labour", a cartoon from Punch *magazine. A gentleman relaxes comforted in the knowledge that the sufferings of the poor have at least given his family and himself such luxury. Below, in the background, child labourers can be seen toiling along the galleries of a coal mine.*

It also included the commercial classes, however, who were the real creators of wealth in the country. Industrialists were often "self-made" men who came from poor beginnings. They believed in hard work, a regular style of life and being careful with money. This class included both the very successful and rich industrialists and the small shopkeepers and office workers of the growing towns and suburbs.

In spite of the idea of "class", the Victorian age was a time of great social movement. The children of the first generation of factory owners often preferred commerce and banking to industry. While their fathers remained Nonconformist and Liberal, some children became Anglican and Tory. Some went into the professions. The very successful received knighthoods or became lords and joined the ranks of the upper classes.

Those of the middle class who could afford it sent their sons to feepaying "public" schools. These schools aimed not only to give boys a good education, but to train them in leadership by taking them away from home and making their living conditions hard. These public schools provided many of the officers for the armed forces, the colonial administration and the civil service.

The growth of towns and cities

The escape of the middle classes to the suburbs was understandable. The cities and towns were overcrowded and unhealthy. One baby in four died within a year of its birth. In 1832 an outbreak of cholera, a disease spread by dirty water, killed 31,000 people. Proper drains and water supplies were still limited to those who could afford them.

In the middle of the century towns began to appoint health officers and to provide proper drains and clean water, which quickly reduced the level of disease, particularly cholera. These health officers also tried to make sure that new housing was less crowded. Even so, there were many "slum" areas for factory workers, where tiny homes were built very close together. The better town councils provided parks in newly built areas, as well as libraries, public baths where people could wash, and even concert halls.

Some towns grew very fast. In the north, for example, Middlesbrough grew from nothing to an iron and steel town of 150,000 people in only fifty years. Most people did not own their homes, but rented them. The homes of the workers usually had

Mr Gladstone speaking in the House of Commons, 1882. Each party sat on either side of the Speaker (seated back right) and the central table. The Speaker's responsibility was to ensure the orderly conduct of parliamentary business. To help him, a line along the floor (running under the feet of one of Gladstone's colleagues) marks the boundary each MP had to stay behind on each side of the House. This was to avoid angry arguments becoming fights. The two lines are two swordlengths' distance apart. The silver mace on the table is a symbol of royal authority.

only four small rooms, two upstairs and two downstairs, with a small back yard. Most of the middle classes lived in houses with a small garden in front, and a larger one at the back.

Population and politics

In 1851, an official population survey was carried out for the first time. It showed that the nation was not as religious as its people had believed. Only 60 per cent of the population went to church. The survey also showed that of these only 5.2 million called themselves Anglicans, compared with 4.5 million Nonconformists and almost half a million Catholics. Changes in the law, in 1828 and 1829, made it possible, for the first time since the seventeenth century, for Catholics and Nonconformists to enter government service and to enter Parliament. In practice, however, it remained difficult for them to do so. The Tory–Anglican alliance could hardly keep them out any longer. But the Nonconformists naturally supported the Liberals, the more reformist party. In fact the Tories held office for less than five years between 1846 and 1874.

In 1846, when Sir Robert Peel had fallen from power, the shape of British politics was still unclear. Peel was a Tory, and many Tories felt that his repeal of the Corn Laws that year was a betrayal of Tory beliefs. Peel had already made himself very unpopular by supporting the right of Catholics to enter Parliament in 1829. But Peel was a true representative of the style of politics at the time. Like other politicians he acted independently, in spite of his party membership. One reason for this was the number of crises in British politics for a whole generation after 1815. Those in power found they often had to avoid dangerous political, economic or social situations by taking steps they themselves would have preferred not to take. This was the case with Peel. He did not wish to see Catholics in Parliament, but he was forced to let them in. He did not wish to repeal the Corn Laws because these served the farming interests of the Tory landowning class, but he had to accept that the power of the manufacturing middle class was growing greater than that of the landed Tory gentry.

Peel's actions were also evidence of a growing acceptance by both Tories and Whigs of the

Much of London still looks as it did in the closing years of the nineteenth century. "St Pancras Hotel and Station from Pentonville Road: Sunset" by John O'Connor (1884) shows St Pancras as it was meant to be seen, a temple to Victorian values towering above the surrounding houses. St Pancras, built by George Gilbert Scott, is one of London's finest "Gothic revival" buildings.

economic need for free trade, as well as the need for social and political reform to allow the middle class to grow richer and to expand. This meant allowing a freer and more open society, with all the dangers that might mean. It also meant encouraging a freer and more open society in the countries with which Britain hoped to trade. This was "Liberalism", and the Whigs, who were generally more willing to advance these ideas, became known as Liberals.

Some Tories also pursued essentially "Liberal" policy. In 1823, for example, the Tory Foreign Secretary, Lord Canning, used the navy to prevent Spain sending troops to her rebellious colonies in South America. The British were glad to see the liberation movement led by Simon Bolivar succeed. However, this was partly for an economic reason. Spain had prevented Britain's free trade with Spanish colonies since the days of Drake.

Canning had also been responsible for helping the Greeks achieve their freedom from the Turkish empire. He did this partly in order to satisfy romantic liberalism in Britain, which supported Greek freedom mainly as a result of the influence of the great poet of the time, Lord Byron, who had visited Greece. But Canning also knew that Russia, like Greece an orthodox Christian country, might

use the excuse of Turkish misrule to take control of Greece itself. Canning judged correctly that an independent Greece would be a more effective check to Russian expansion.

From 1846 until 1865 the most important political figure was Lord Palmerston, described by one historian as "the most characteristically mid-Victorian statesman of all." He was a Liberal, but like Peel he often went against his own party's ideas and values. Palmerston was known for liberalism in his foreign policy. He strongly believed that despotic states discouraged free trade, and he openly supported European liberal and independence movements. In 1859–60, for example, Palmerston successfully supported the Italian independence movement against both Austrian and French interests. Within Britain, however, Palmerston was a good deal less liberal, and did not want to allow further political reform to take place. This was not totally surprising, since he had been a Tory as a young man under Canning and had joined the Whigs at the time of the 1832 Reform Bill. It was also typical of the confusing individualism of politics that the Liberal Lord Palmerston was invited to join a Tory government in 1852.

After Palmerston's death in 1865 a much stricter "two party" system developed, demanding greater loyalty from its membership. The two parties, Tory (or Conservative as it became officially known) and Liberal, developed greater party organisation and order. There was also a change in the kind of men who became political leaders. This was a result of the Reform of 1832, after which a much larger number of people could vote. These new voters chose a different kind of MP, men from the commercial rather than the landowning class.

Gladstone, the new Liberal leader, had been a factory owner. He had also started his political life as a Tory. Even more surprisingly Benjamin Disraeli, the new Conservative leader, was of Jewish origin. In 1860 Jews were for the first time given equal rights with other citizens. Disraeli had led the Tory attack on Peel in 1846, and brought down his government. At that time Disraeli had strongly supported the interests of the landed gentry. Twenty years later Disraeli himself changed the outlook of the Conservative Party, deliberately increasing the party's support among the middle class. Since 1881 the Conservative Party has generally remained the strongest.

Much of what we know today as the modern state was built in the 1860s and 1870s. Between 1867 and 1884 the number of voters increased from 20 per cent to 60 per cent of men in towns and to 70 per cent in the country, including some of the working class. One immediate effect was the rapid growth in party organisation, with branches in every town, able to organise things locally. In 1872 voting was carried out in secret for the first time, allowing ordinary people to vote freely and without fear. This, and the growth of the newspaper industry, in particular "popular" newspapers for the new half-educated population, strengthened the importance of popular opinion. Democracy grew quickly. A national political pattern appeared. England, particularly the south, was more conservative, while Scotland, Ireland, Wales and the north of England appeared more radical. This pattern has generally continued since then. The House of Commons grew in size to over 650 members, and the House of Lords lost the powerful position it had held in the eighteenth and early nineteenth centuries. Now it no longer formed policy but tried to prevent reform taking place through the House of Commons.

Democracy also grew rapidly outside Parliament. In 1844 a "Co-operative Movement" was started by a few Chartists and trade unionists. Its purpose was self-help, through a network of shops which sold goods at a fair and low price, and which shared all its profits among its members. It was very successful, with 150 Co-operative stores by 1851 in the north of England and Scotland. By 1889 it had over 800,000 members. Co-operative self-help was a powerful way in which the working class gained self-confidence in spite of its weak position.

After 1850 a number of trade unions grew up, based on particular kinds of skilled labour. However, unlike many European worker struggles, the English trade unions sought to achieve their goals through parliamentary democracy. In 1868 the first congress of trade unions met in Manchester, representing 118,000 members. The following year the new Trades Union Congress established a parliamentary committee with the purpose of achieving worker representation in Parliament. This wish to work within Parliament rather than outside it had already brought trade unionists into close co-operation with radicals and reformist Liberals. Even the Conservative Party tried to attract worker support. However, there were limits to Conservative and Liberal co-operation. It was one thing to encourage "friendly" societies for the peaceful benefit of workers. It was quite another to encourage union campaigns using strike action. During the 1870s wages were lowered in many factories and this led to more strikes than had been seen in Britain before. The trade unions' mixture of worker struggle and desire to work democratically within Parliament led eventually to the foundation of the Labour Party.

During the same period the machinery of modern government was set up. During the 1850s a regular civil service was established to carry out the work of government, and "civil servants" were carefully chosen after taking an examination. The system still exists today. The army, too, was reorganised, and from 1870 officers were no longer able to buy their commissions. The administration of the law was reorganised. Local government in towns and counties was reorganised to make sure of good government and proper services for the people. In 1867 the first move was made to introduce free and compulsory education for children. In fact social improvement and political reform acted on each other throughout the century to change the face of the nation almost beyond recognition.

Queen and monarchy

Queen Victoria came to the throne as a young woman in 1837 and reigned until her death in 1901. She did not like the way in which power seemed to be slipping so quickly away from the monarchy and aristocracy, but like her advisers she was unable to prevent it. Victoria married a German, Prince Albert of Saxe-Coburg, but he died at the age of forty-two in 1861. She could not get over her sorrow at his death, and for a long time refused to be seen in public.

This was a dangerous thing to do. Newspapers began to criticise her, and some even questioned the value of the monarchy. Many radicals actually believed the end of monarchy was bound to happen as a result of democracy. Most had no wish to hurry this process, and were happy to let the monarchy die naturally. However, the queen's advisers persuaded her to take a more public interest in the business of the kingdom. She did so, and she soon became extraordinarily popular. By the time Victoria died the monarchy was better loved among the British than it had ever been before.

One important step back to popularity was the publication in 1868 of the queen's book *Our life in the Highlands*. The book was the queen's own diary, with drawings, of her life with Prince Albert at Balmoral, her castle in the Scottish Highlands. It delighted the public, in particular the growing middle class. They had never before known anything of the private life of the monarch, and they enjoyed being able to share it. She referred to the Prince Consort simply as "Albert", to the

Queen Victoria in her sixty-eighth year, 1887. Because of the growth of parliamentary government she was less powerful than previous sovereigns. However, as queen and empress, she ruled over more lands and peoples than any previous sovereigns. Furthermore, she enjoyed the respect and affection of her British subjects.

Prince of Wales as "Bertie", and to the Princess Royal as "Vicky". The queen also wrote about her servants as if they were members of her family.

The increasingly democratic British respected the example of family life which the queen had given them, and shared its moral and religious values. But she also touched people's hearts. She succeeded in showing a newly industrialised nation that the monarchy was a connection with a glorious history. In spite of the efforts of earlier monarchs to stop the spread of democracy, the monarchy was now, quite suddenly, out of danger. It was never safer than when it had lost most of its political power.

"We have come to believe that it is natural to have a virtuous sovereign," wrote one Victorian. Pure family morality was an idea of royalty that would have been of little interest to the subjects of earlier monarchs.

Queen and empire

Britain's empire had first been built on trade and the need to defend this against rival European countries. After the loss of the American colonies in 1783, the idea of creating new colonies remained unpopular until the 1830s. Instead, Britain watched the oceans carefully to make sure its trade routes were safe, and fought wars in order to protect its "areas of interest". In 1839 it attacked China and forced it to allow the profitable British trade in opium from India to China. The "Opium Wars" were one of the more shameful events in British colonial history.

After about 1850 Britain was driven more by fear of growing European competition than by commercial need. This led to the taking of land, the creation of colonies, and to colonial wars that were extremely expensive. Fear that Russia would advance southwards towards India resulted in a disastrous war in Afghanistan (1839–42), in which one army was completely destroyed by Afghan forces in the mountains. Soon after, Britain was fighting a war in Sindh, a part of modern Pakistan, then another against Sikhs in the Punjab, in northwest India.

The Russian danger also affected south Europe and the Middle East. Britain feared that Russia would destroy the weak Ottoman Empire, which controlled Turkey and the Arab countries. This would change the balance of power in Europe, and be a danger to Britain's sea and land routes to India. When Russia and Ottoman Turkey went to war Britain joined the Turks against Russia in Crimea in 1854, in order to stop Russian expansion into Asiatic Turkey in the Black Sea area.

It was the first, and last, time that newspapers were able to report freely on a British war without army control. They told some unwelcome truths; for example, they wrote about the courage of the ordinary soldiers, and the poor quality of their officers. They also reported the shocking conditions in army hospitals, and the remarkable work of the nurse Florence Nightingale.

In India, the unwise treatment of Indian soldiers in British pay resulted in revolt in 1857. Known in Britain as the "Indian Mutiny", this revolt quickly became a national movement against foreign rule, led by a number of Hindu and Muslim princes. Many of these had recently lost power and land to the British rulers. If they had been better organised, they would have been able to throw the British out of India. Both British and Indians behaved with great violence, and the British cruelly punished the defeated rebels. The friendship between the British and the Indians never fully recovered. A feeling of distrust and distance between ruler and ruled grew into the Indian independence movement of the twentieth century.

In Africa, Britain's first interest had been the slave trade on the west coast. It then took over the Cape of Good Hope at the southern point, because it needed a port there to service the sea route to India.

Britain's interest in Africa was increased by reports sent back by European travellers and explorers. The most famous of these was David Livingstone, who was a Scottish doctor, a Christian missionary and an explorer. In many ways, Livingstone was a "man of his age". No one could doubt his courage, or his honesty. His journeys from the east coast into "darkest" Africa excited the British. They greatly admired him. Livingstone discovered areas of Africa unknown to Europeans, and "opened" these areas to Christianity, to European ideas and to European trade.

Christianity too easily became a tool for building a commercial and political empire in Africa. The governments of Europe rushed in to take what they could, using the excuse of bringing "civilisation" to the people. The rush for land became so great that European countries agreed by treaty in 1890 to divide Africa into "areas of interest". By the end of

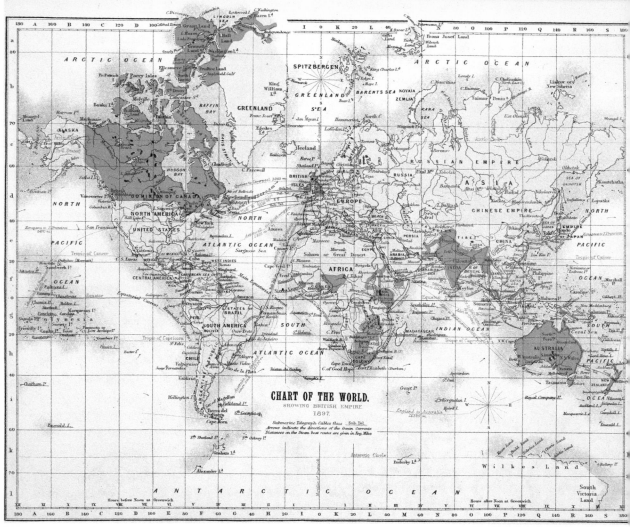

Our Empire Atlas, 1897, clearly shows Britain's strategic control of much of the world. Although not marked as such, Egypt and the Sudan were also colonies in practice. The extent of Britain's colonial possessions doubled during the nineteenth century. Britain's appetite for new possessions towards the end of the century was a sign of its nervousness concerning the growth of other European world powers, particularly France and Germany. Although Britain became rich partly through her colonial possessions, defending them eventually proved too great a strain on Britain's economy.

the century, several European countries had taken over large areas of Africa. Britain succeeded in taking most.

In South Africa Britain found that dealing with other European settlers presented new problems. The Dutch settlers, the Boers, fought two wars against the British at the end of the century, proving again, as the Crimean War had done, the weaknesses of the British army. The Boers were defeated only with great difficulty.

The real problems of British imperial ambition, however, were most obvious in Egypt. Britain, anxious about the safety of the route to India

Britain had to use an increasing number of soldiers to defend its growing empire. The battle of Isandhlwana in south Africa in 1879 was a humiliating defeat. Britain did not expect its soldiers to be defeated by black African Zulus.

through the newly dug Suez Canal, bought a large number of shares in the Suez Canal company.

When Egyptian nationalists brought down the ruler in 1882, Britain invaded "to protect international shipping". In fact, it acted to protect its imperial interest, its route to India. Britain told the world its occupation of Egypt was only for a short time, but it did not leave until forced to do so in 1954. Involvement in Egypt led to invasion and takeover of the Sudan in 1884, a country two-thirds the size of India. Like other powers, Britain found that every area conquered created new dangers which in turn had to be controlled. In all these countries, in

Sixty years a queen, Victoria celebrates her Diamond Jubilee. Immediately behind her stands her son and successor, Edward VII, and his own son and successor, George V, stands on his left. Victoria is acclaimed queen and empress by the many different colonial peoples under her rule.

India, Africa and elsewhere, Britain found itself involved in a contradiction between its imperial ambition and the liberal ideas it wished to advance elsewhere. Gladstone's view that "the foreign policy of England should always be inspired by a love of freedom" seemed to have little place in the colonies. In the twentieth century this contradiction was a major reason for the collapse of the empire.

There was another reason for the interest in creating colonies. From the 1830s there had been growing concern at the rapidly increasing population of Britain. A number of people called for the development of colonies for British settlers as an obvious solution to the problem. As a result, there was marked increase in settlement in Canada, Australia and New Zealand from the 1840s onwards. The settlers arrived to take over the land and to farm it. In all three countries there had been earlier populations. In Canada most of these were pushed westwards, and those not killed became part of the "white" culture. In Australia British settlers killed most of the aboriginal inhabitants, leaving only a few in the central desert areas. In New Zealand the Maori inhabitants suffered less than in either Canada or Australia, although they still lost most of the land.

The white colonies, unlike the others, were soon allowed to govern themselves, and no longer depended on Britain. They still, however, accepted the British monarch as their head of state. The move towards self-government was the result of trouble in Canada in 1837. A new governor, Lord Durham, quickly understood the danger that Canada might follow the other American colonies into independence. His report established the principle of self-government, first for the white colonies, but eventually for all British possessions. It prepared the way from empire to a British "Commonwealth of Nations" in the twentieth century.

By the end of the nineteenth century Britain controlled the oceans and much of the land areas of the world. Most British strongly believed in their right to an empire, and were willing to defend it against the least threat. This state of mind became known as Jingoism, after a famous Music Hall song of 1878:

> We don't want to fight, but, by jingo if we do,
> We've got the ships, we've got the men, we've
> got the money too.

But even at this moment of greatest power, Britain had begun to spend more on its empire than it took from it. The empire had started to be a heavy load. It would become impossibly heavy in the twentieth century, when the colonies finally began to demand their freedom.

Wales, Scotland and Ireland

As industrialisation continued, the areas at the edge of British economic power became weaker. Areas in Wales, Scotland and Ireland were particularly affected.

Wales had fewer problems than either Scotland or Ireland. Its population grew from half a million in 1800 to over two million by 1900, partly because the average expectation of life doubled from thirty to sixty. In south Wales there were rich coal mines which quickly became the centre of a rapidly growing coal and steel industry. In their search for work, a huge number of people, between two-thirds and three-quarters of the total Welsh population, moved into the southeast corner of the country. By 1870 Wales was mainly an industrial society.

This new working-class community, born in southeast Wales, became increasingly interested in Nonconformist Christianity and radicalism. It created its own cultural life. In many mining villages brass bands were created, and these quickly became symbols of working-class unity. Other people joined the local Nonconformist chapel choir, and helped to create the Welsh tradition of fine choral singing. Wales was soon a nation divided between the industrialised areas and the unchanged areas of old Wales, in the centre and north.

The parliamentary reforms of the nineteenth century gave Wales a new voice. As soon as they were allowed to vote, the Welsh workers got rid of the Tories and the landowning families who had represented them for 300 years.

Scotland was also divided between a new industrialised area, around Glasgow and Edinburgh, and the Highland and Lowland areas. Around the two great cities there were coal mines and factories producing steel and iron, as well as the centre of the British shipbuilding industry on the River Clyde. Like Wales, Scotland became strongly Liberal once its workforce gained voting rights.

The clearances in the Highlands continued. In the second half of the century it became more profitable to replace the sheep with wild deer, which were hunted for sport. Many old clan lands were sold to new landowners who had no previous connection with the Highlands, and who only occasionally visited their estates. The Highlands have never recovered from the collapse of the clan system, either socially or economically. It is probable that the Highland areas would have become depopulated anyway, as people moved away to find work in the cities. But the way in which it happened was not gentle, and left a bitter memory.

The Irish experience was worse than that of Scotland. In the nineteenth century, an increasing number of Protestant Irish turned to England as a protection against the Catholic inhabitants. To the Catholics, however, most Irish Protestants were a reminder that England, a foreign country, was still as powerful in Ireland as it had been in 1690. The struggle for Irish freedom from English rule became a struggle between Catholic and Protestant. The first great victory for Irish freedom was when Catholics were allowed to become MPs in 1829. In fact in Ireland this decision was accompanied by a repression of civil and political liberties. Even so, the fact that a Catholic could enter Parliament increased Irish national feeling.

But while this feeling was growing, Ireland suffered the worst disaster in its entire history. For three years, 1845, 1846 and 1847, the potato crop, which was the main food of the poor, failed. Since the beginning of the century, the population had risen quickly from five to eight million. In these three years 1.5 million (about 20 per cent) died from hunger. At the same time Ireland had enough wheat to feed the entire population, but it was grown for export to England by the mainly Protestant landowners. The government in London failed to realise the seriousness of the problem.

Many Irish people had little choice but to leave. At least a million left during these years, but many more followed during the rest of the century because of the great poverty in Ireland. Most settled in the United States. Between 1841 and 1920 almost five million settled there. Some went eastwards to the towns and cities of Britain. Many helped to build Britain's railways.

Many Scottish Highlanders and Irish were driven off their land in the nineteenth century. The Irish suffered worst of all. After the terrible potato famine of 1845, there were other years of poor harvest, notably in the years 1877–79, but many landlords refused to lower rents during this time. Many families, like the one shown in this photograph, were locked out of their homes as they could no longer pay rent. Most of them made their way to the United States of America, where Irish Americans still remember how their ancestors were treated.

The Irish population has still not yet grown to the same level. Today it is less than five million (three million in the Republic of Ireland, 1.5 million in Northern Ireland), only a little more than half what it was in 1840. Emigration from Ireland continues.

The Irish who went to the United States did not forget the old country. Nor did they forgive Britain. By 1880 many Irish Americans were rich and powerful and were able to support the Irish freedom movement. They have had an influence on British policy in Ireland ever since.

Meanwhile, Charles Parnell, a Protestant Irish MP, demanded fuller rights for the Irish people, in particular the right to self-government. When most Irish were able to vote for the first time in 1885, eighty-six members of Parnell's Irish party were elected to Parliament. Most Liberals supported Parnell, but the Tories did not and Ireland did not gain the right to self-government, or "home rule", until thirty years later. But then Britain's war with Germany delayed it taking place, and by the time the war ended Irish nationalists had decided they could only win their freedom by fighting for it.

21 The end of an age

Social and economic improvements · The importance of sport · Changes in thinking · The end of "England's summer" · The storm clouds of war

Social and economic improvements

Between 1875 and 1914 the condition of the poor in most of Britain greatly improved as prices fell by 40 per cent and real wages doubled. Life at home was made more comfortable. Most homes now had gas both for heating and lighting. As a result of falling prices and increased wages, poor families could eat better food, including meat, fresh milk (brought from the countryside by train) and vegetables. This greatly improved the old diet of white bread and beer.

In 1870 and 1891 two Education Acts were passed. As a result of these, all children had to go to school up to the age of thirteen, where they were taught reading, writing and arithmetic. In Scotland there had been a state education system since the time of the Reformation. There were four Scottish universities, three dating from the Middle Ages. In Wales schools had begun to grow rapidly in the middle of the century, partly for nationalist reasons. By the middle of the century Wales had a university and a smaller university college. England now started to build "redbrick" universities in the new industrial cities. The term "redbrick" distinguished the new universities, often brick-built, from the older, mainly stone-built universities of Oxford and Cambridge. These new universities were unlike Oxford and Cambridge, and taught more science and technology to feed Britain's industries.

Nature study in an elementary school, 1908. In 1870 it became the duty of local authorities to establish schools at the expense of local ratepayers. They were authorised to compel attendance. During the next twenty years schools were built and the attendance of most, if not all, children achieved at elementary level.

The face of the towns had greatly changed in the middle years of the century. The organised improvement of workers' homes, of factory conditions, public health and education had all come fast, once the Victorians had developed the administrative and scientific means. Sidney Webb, an early socialist, amusingly described the pride of the new town authorities, or municipalities, which carried out these changes:

> The town councillor will walk along the municipal pavement, lit by municipal gas and cleansed by municipal brooms with municipal water and, seeing by the municipal clock in the municipal market, that he is too early to meet his children coming from the municipal school ... will use the national telegraph system to tell them not to walk through the municipal park, but ... to meet him in the municipal reading room.

It was easy to see the physical changes such as the growth of towns and cities and villages. It was less easy to see the social changes. But in fact, power had moved from the shires to the towns. At the beginning of the nineteenth century the country squire could use his power to rule the village, send children to work in the workhouse, and enclose common land for his own use. By 1900 he was a harmless reminder of an earlier age. JPs lost all their local government and administrative powers in 1888, and could now only make judgements in very small cases. New county councils took their place, which were made up of elected men and women, with a staff of administrators to carry out their decisions, a system which still operates today.

The authority of the Church was also weakened. In the country, the village priest no longer had the power he had had a century earlier. Churches were now half empty, because so many people had gone to live in the towns, where they stopped going to church. By 1900 only 19 per cent of Londoners went regularly to church. Those who did usually lived in richer areas. This remains true today, when under 10 per cent are regular churchgoers.

Why did the poor no longer go to church? One reason was that the Church of England offered them no help with the problems of their daily lives. Staying away from church was also a kind of rebellion against the ruling establishment with which the Church was still closely connected. In the village, many people had gone to church because they were forced to do so by the squire, who probably employed them. In the great cities of industrial Britain they were free, and they chose to stay away.

They were also attracted by other ways of spending their Sundays. By the 1880s, for the first time, working people could think about enjoying some free time. Apart from museums, parks, swimming

The seaside became the place where everyone wished to go on holiday. Different seaside towns around the country attracted different classes. Scarborough in Yorkshire, illustrated here, attracted the middle classes. On the west coast Blackpool, Lancashire, attracted lower income families.

Cricket was a gentleman's game in which others could also join in as "players". The division between "gentlemen" (the ruling establishment) and "players" (of lower social status) was a clear statement of the divide between classes in Britain at the end of the century. However, cricket was an important bridge between classes, where respect was given to those who played well, regardless of class. It was partly for this reason, and also because it was a game which mixed team work with individual excellence, that the game became a symbol of fair play in national life. Shameful behaviour in politics or in public life was frequently described in the press as "not cricket".

pools and libraries recently opened in towns, the real popular social centre remained the alehouse or pub. Thousands of these were built in the new suburbs.

From the middle of the century many people had started to use the railway to get to work. Now they began to travel for pleasure. The working class went to the new seaside holiday towns. The middle class enjoyed the countryside, or smaller seaside resorts of a more expensive kind. But for both, the seaside was a place where families could take holidays together.

The invention of the bicycle was also important. For the first time people could cycle into the countryside, up to fifty miles from home. It gave a new freedom to working-class and middle-class people, who met each other for the first time away from work. More importantly, it gave young women their first taste of freedom. Up till then they had always had an older woman as a companion to make sure that nothing "happened" when they met men. Now these young women had a means of escape, and escape they did.

The importance of sport

By the end of the nineteenth century, two sports, cricket and football, had become of great interest to

the British public. Cricket, which had started as a "gentleman's" sport, had become an extremely popular village game. Although it had first developed in the eighteenth century, it was not until a century later that its rules were organised. From 1873 a county championship took place each year. Cricket was a game which encouraged both individual and team excellence and taught respect for fair play. As one Englishman said at the time, "We have a much greater love of cricket than of politics." Cricket was successfully exported to the empire: to the West Indies, India, Pakistan, Ceylon, Australia and New Zealand. But while it was popular in Wales, it never had the same popularity in Scotland.

Britain's other main game, football, was also organised with proper rules in the nineteenth century. As an organised game it was at first a middle-class or gentleman's sport, but it quickly became popular among all classes. Football soon drew huge crowds who came to watch the full-time professional footballers play the game. By the end of the nineteenth century almost every town between Portsmouth on the south coast of England and Aberdeen in northeast Scotland had its own football, or "soccer" team. These often encouraged local loyalties. Sometimes they symbolised something more. In Glasgow Celtic was supported by the thousands of Irish immigrants and other

Catholics, while Rangers was supported by Protestants. But at this time there was no violence. Crowds were well behaved. Britain also exported football abroad, as young commercial travellers took the game with them, particularly to Europe and to South America.

Changes in thinking

The most important idea of the nineteenth century was that everyone had the right to personal freedom, which was the basis of capitalism. This idea had spread widely through the book *Enquiry into the Wealth of Nations*, written by the Scotsman Adam Smith in the eighteenth century. After Adam Smith, several capitalist economists argued that government should not interfere in trade and industry at all. Fewer laws, they claimed, meant more freedom, and freedom for individuals would lead to happiness for the greatest number of people. These ideas were eagerly accepted by the growing middle class.

However, it soon became very clear that the freedom of factory owners to do as they pleased had led to slavery and misery for the poor, not to happiness or freedom. By 1820 more and more people had begun to accept the idea that government must interfere to protect the poor and the weak. The result was a number of laws to improve working conditions. One of these, in 1833, limited the number of hours that women and children were allowed to work. Another law the same year abolished slavery throughout the British Empire. While this set a new example internationally, factory owners were quick to point out that while slave owners were compensated for the loss of slave labour, they were not compensated for the new limits on labour in Britain.

Such laws did not make British factories perfect places in which to work, and many factory owners did their best to avoid obeying them. But by the end of the century, few people thought it was wrong for the government to interfere in factory conditions, health in towns, and education for children. People now saw these as government duties.

As so often happens, government policy was influenced by individual people. At the beginning of the century Robert Owen, a factory owner in Scotland, gave his workers shorter working hours. He built his factory in the countryside, away from the fog and dirt of the cities, and provided good housing nearby, and education for the workers' children. Owen was able to prove that his workers produced more in less time than those forced to work long hours. Owen also encouraged trade unions, and supported the Tolpuddle Martyrs. Owen's ideas and example began to spread. Other reformers, like the Quaker, Arthur Cadbury, famous for his Birmingham chocolate factory, built first-class housing for their workers.

In spite of men like Owen, improvements were slow. By the end of the century, 30 per cent of the

Most of the poorer classes lived in unhealthy conditions in small, damp "back-to-back" houses, with few open spaces. As the middle classes moved out to better suburbs, parts of the city centres became areas of poverty, like this street in Newcastle in 1880.

nation was still extremely poor. It was an uncomfortable fact for the most powerful nation on earth. Again, it was individual people who led the fight against this problem. William Booth started a new religious movement, the Salvation Army, to "make war" on poverty. His book *In Darkest England and the Way Out* was a reminder that while the British called Africa "the dark continent", areas of possibly greater "darkness" were just down the road in their own towns.

Literature was influenced by the new mood of change. In the middle of the century Charles Dickens attacked the rich and powerful for their cruelty towards the weak and unfortunate in society. Painting too was affected. A century earlier it had been the great landowning aristocracy who had bought paintings and paid artists. In the nineteenth century it was the mainly urban middle class, and to please them, artists painted different subjects, such as sentimental scenes of the countryside, and paintings which told a moral story. But some painted industrial scenes which raised questions about the new society Britain had created. "Pre-Raphaelite" painters looked back to the pre-industrial medieval and classical worlds with fresh and romantic eyes. Later on in the century, many of the first socialists in Britain were writers or artists. Some of these belonged to the "Arts and Crafts Movement", whose members turned away from the new middle-class values, and looked to pre-industrial handcraft and to nature for inspiration.

Above all, Victorian society was self-confident. This had been shown in the Great Exhibition in 1851. British self-confidence was built not only upon power but also upon the rapid scientific advances being made at the time. In 1857 Charles Darwin published *The Origin of Species*. His theory of evolution, based upon scientific observation, was welcomed by many as proof of mankind's ability to find a scientific explanation for everything. But for churchgoing people, who were mostly to be found among the middle classes, the idea that all animals, including human beings, had developed from more simple creatures shook this self-confidence and led to a crisis in the Church. Most of the churchgoing

population believed every word of the Bible. They found it difficult to accept Darwin's theory that the world had developed over millions of years, and had not been created in six days in the year 4004 BC. Even less acceptable was the idea that over a period of thousands of years man had developed from the ape. The battle between "faith" and "reason" lasted for the rest of the century.

There was one dangerous result of Darwin's book. Some of those who accepted his ideas began to talk of "advanced" and "inferior" races. These ideas soon influenced Britain's imperial policy. Several European countries already shared the view that for reasons of religion and "higher" civilisation, they could justify their colonial policy. But the idea of racial or genetic superiority was a new one, from which the colonised peoples could not hope to escape. They could accept Christianity and could become "more civilised", but they could not change their race.

Today it is difficult to understand how these ideas could have been accepted. But at the time there was little doubt among most of the British that Britain was the most advanced of the "advanced" races, with a duty to govern the "inferior" races.

The end of "England's summer"

At the beginning of the twentieth century people did not, of course, realise that they were living at the end of an age. There was still a general belief in the "liberal idea", that the nation could achieve steady economic and social improvement as well as democracy without revolution. Things for Britain could only get better and better.

A growing demand for reform led "New Liberal" governments to try to improve social conditions. In 1907 they provided free school meals, to improve the health of Britain's children. The following year they started an old age pensions scheme. It was an astonishing new idea that government should prevent the old from starving or becoming homeless. In 1909 Labour Exchanges were opened, where those without work could look for jobs. Two years later all working people were made to pay for "national insurance". It was another new idea that those unable to earn money through sickness or unemployment would be helped by the state.

The New Liberals had begun to establish what became the "welfare state". By doing so, they made important changes to the free capitalism of the nineteenth century. Government, said the Liberals, had a duty to protect the weak against the strong. As in the gentlemanly sport of cricket, the Liberals believed that even within capitalism there had to be "fair play".

In 1911 another important political event occurred. The Liberal drive for reform, both in Irish politics and in social affairs at home, was extremely unpopular with most Conservatives, who had a majority in the House of Lords. They used this majority to stop many of the bills introduced by the Liberal government in the Commons in the years 1906–10. The battle of wills between the two Houses produced a crisis when the Liberals tried to introduce a new budget in 1909 which was intended to increase the taxes paid by the rich, particularly the large landowners. The Lords turned down the new budget. The new king, George V, put an end to the crisis by warning that he would create enough new Liberal lords to give the Liberals a majority. The Lords gave in. One result of the dispute was that taxation was increasingly seen as a social matter as well as an economic one.

The crisis, however, was not only about money, or about reform. There was a constitutional disagreement. The Conservatives still favoured a two-house parliamentary system, but they now recognised that the Lords would have to be changed. The Liberals wanted one strong house, with the powers of the Lords so weakened that it could not prevent the will of the Commons from being carried out. The result of this constitutional debate was the Parliament Act of 1911. Like much of British political development it resulted from a compromise, but one in which the Liberals won most of what they wanted. The House of Lords lost its right to question financial legislation passed in the Commons. Its powers in all other matters were limited. It could no longer prevent legislation but only delay it, and for not more than two years. The system still operates.

In the same year, for the first time, the Commons agreed that MPs should be paid. This was a far more important step than it might seem, for it meant that men of low income could now become MPs. In 1906 a new "Labour" party had managed to get twenty-nine representatives elected to Parliament. It was clear to even the most conservative-minded that socialists should work inside the parliamentary system rather than outside it. The dangers of political evolution were far less than those of revolution.

The storm clouds of war

By the end of the century it had become clear that Britain was no longer as powerful as it had been. In 1885 a book entitled *England* noted "we have come to occupy a position in which we are no longer progressing, but even falling back . . . We find other nations able to compete with us to an extent such as we have never before experienced." In Europe Germany was now united and had become very strong. Its economic prospects were clearly greater than Britain's. Like the USA it was producing more steel than Britain, and it used this to build strong industries and a strong navy.

Why did Britain lose the advantages it had over other countries at the time of the Great Exhibition of 1851? There seem to be a number of reasons. Other countries, Germany particularly, had greater natural wealth, including coal and iron, and wheat-producing lands. Most British people invested their money abroad rather than in building up home industry. British workers produced less than those in other countries, and Britain was behind other countries in science and technology, as well as in management skills, and did little to change this. Public schools, the private system of education for the richer middle class, did not encourage business or scientific studies. Britain had nothing to compare with the scientific and technical education of Germany. Finally, the working class, used to low pay for long hours, did not feel they were partners in manufacture.

The balance of power in Europe that had worked so well since Waterloo was beginning to collapse. The

British believed that the long period of peace had been the result of Britain's authority in world affairs. This authority came from Britain's imperial and economic power. By 1880 the British merchant fleet was four times larger than it had been in 1847, when it was already the world leader. More than two out of every three tons of shipping passing through the Suez Canal was British. By 1880, too, Britain led the world in telegraphic communications, with lines to almost every part of the world. London was beyond doubt the centre of the growing international financial system. But in spite of such things, Britain found that Germany, France and the USA were increasingly competing with her. Britain was not used to being so strongly challenged.

Suddenly Britain realised that it no longer ruled the seas quite so assuredly, and that others had more powerful armies and more powerful industries. As a result of the growth of international trade Britain was less self-sufficient, and as a result of growing US and German competition started to trade more with the less developed and less competitive world. This experience increased its sense of political uncertainty. Britain had been surprised and shocked by the way in which almost the whole of Europe had taken the part of the Boers against Britain during the South African war, 1899–1902. It was a sharp reminder that friendship in Europe did matter, and that Britain was no longer able to persuade other countries how to behave in quite the same way that it had fifty years earlier. It had to reach agreement with them. Between 1902 and 1907 Britain made treaties or understandings of friendship with France, Japan and Russia. It failed to reach agreement with the Ottoman Empire, and with the country it feared most, Germany.

The danger of war with Germany had been clear from the beginning of the century, and it was this which had brought France and Britain together. Britain was particularly frightened of Germany's modern navy, which seemed a good deal stronger than its own. The government started a programme of building battleships to make sure of its strength at sea. The reason was simple. Britain could not possibly survive for long without food and other essential goods reaching it by sea. From 1908 onwards Britain spent large sums of money to make sure that it possessed a stronger fleet than Germany. Britain's army was small, but its size seemed less important than its quality. In any case, no one believed that war in Europe, if it happened, would last more than six months.

By 1914 an extremely dangerous situation had developed. Germany and Austria-Hungary had made a military alliance. Russia and France, frightened of German ambitions, had made one also. Although Britain had no treaty with France, in practice it had no choice but to stand by France if it was attacked by Germany.

A dreadful chain of events took place. In July 1914 Austria-Hungary declared war on its neighbour Serbia following the murder of a senior Austrian Archduke in Sarajevo. Because Russia had promised to defend Serbia, it declared war on Austria-Hungary. Because of Germany's promise to stand by Austria-Hungary, Russia also found itself at war with Germany. France, Russia's ally, immediately made its troops ready, recognising that the events in Serbia would lead inevitably to war with Germany. Britain still hoped that it would not be dragged into war, but realised only a miracle could prevent it. No miracle occurred.

In August 1914 Germany's attack on France took its army through Belgium. Britain immediately declared war because it had promised to guarantee Belgium's neutrality by the treaty of 1838. But Britain went to war also because it feared that Germany's ambitions, like Napoleon's over a century earlier, would completely change the map of Europe. In particular Britain could not allow a major enemy power to control the Low Countries. Gazing sadly across St James's Park from his room in the Foreign Office, Sir Edward Grey, the Foreign Secretary, remarked, "The lamps are going out all over Europe. We shall not see them lit again in our lifetime." In a sense the "lamps" went out for ever. For what neither Britain, nor Germany, nor anyone else realised was that after the war no one, not even the winners, would be able to return to life as it had been before.

The twentieth century

22 Britain at war

The First World War • The rise of the Labour Party • The rights of women • Ireland • Disappointment and depression • The Second World War

At the start of the twentieth century Britain was still the greatest world power. By the middle of the century, although still one of the "Big Three", Britain was clearly weaker than either the United States or the Soviet Union. By the end of the seventies Britain was no longer a world power at all, and was not even among the richest European powers. Its power had ended as quickly as Spain's had done in the seventeenth century.

One reason for this sudden decline was the cost and effort of two world wars. Another reason was the cost of keeping up the empire, followed by the economic problems involved in losing it. But the most important reason was the basic weaknesses in Britain's industrial power, and particularly its failure to spend as much as other industrial nations in developing its industry.

Now, near the end of the century, Britain has lost much of its earlier self-confidence, but no one is sure what the reasons for this are. Some argue that the workforce is lazy, or that the trade unions are

An advertisement for the London Underground in 1908 offers the twentieth-century dream for many British people. As the "tube" reached out into the countryside, new suburbs were built. Here, so the advertisement suggested, a family could live in a suburban house in the "mock" Tudor style, suggestive of a past age of national glory, with their own garden. The husband waters the flowers, while his wife and child prepare wool for knitting. It is a scene that suggests both domestic happiness and also a middle-class property-owning democracy. It is an extremely clever advertisement, for it has lost none of its appeal eighty years later.

too powerful, or that there are not enough good managers. Others blame the immigrants who have settled in Britain from the old colonies since the Second World War. No one doubts that Britain is living in an age of uncertainty.

Britain still has some valuable advantages. The discovery of oil in the North Sea has rescued the nation from a situation that might have been far worse. And in electronics and technology Britain is still a world competitor.

A nation's story is not, or should not be, solely about wealth or power, but about the quality of the community's existence. Britain's loss of power need not damage that quality, unless this is measured only in material terms.

The First World War

Germany nearly defeated the Allies, Britain and France, in the first few weeks of war in 1914. It had better trained soldiers, better equipment and a clear plan of attack. The French army and the small British force were fortunate to hold back the German army at the River Marne, deep inside France. Four years of bitter fighting followed, both armies living and fighting in the trenches, which they had dug to protect their men.

Apart from the Crimean War, this was Britain's first European war for a century, and the country

The awfulness of war: one of Britain's 750,000 dead in the First World War.

was quite unprepared for the terrible destructive power of modern weapons. At first all those who joined the army were volunteers. But in 1916 the government forced men to join the army whether they wanted to or not. A few men, mainly Quakers, refused to fight. For the first time, a government accepted the idea that men had the right to refuse to fight if they believed fighting to be wrong. But the war went on, and the number of deaths increased. On 1 July 1916 Britain attacked German positions on the River Somme. By the evening it had lost 20,000 dead and 40,000 wounded. In fact, five months of fighting from 1 July 1916 cost Britain 400,000, France 200,000 and Germany 500,000 dead and wounded. At Passchendaele, the following year, the British army advanced five miles at the cost of another 400,000 dead and wounded. Modern artillery and machine guns had completely changed the nature of war. The invention of the tank and its use on the battlefield to break through the enemy trenches in 1917 could have changed the course of the war. It

would have led to fewer casualties if its military value had been properly understood at the time.

In the Middle East the British fought against Turkish troops in Iraq and in Palestine, and at Gallipoli, on the Dardanelles. There, too, there were many casualties, but many of them were caused by sickness and heat. It was not until 1917 that the British were really able to drive back the Turks.

Somehow the government had to persuade the people that in spite of such disastrous results the war was still worth fighting. The nation was told that it was defending the weak (Belgium) against the strong (Germany), and that it was fighting for democracy and freedom.

At the same time popular newspapers, using large print, memorable short sentences and emotional language, encouraged the nation to hate Germany, and to want Germany's destruction. National feelings were even stronger in France, which had already been badly defeated by Germany in 1871. As a result, when Germany offered to make peace at the end of 1916, neither the British nor the French government welcomed the idea. Both were prisoners of the public feelings they had helped to create.

The war at sea was more important than the war on land, because defeat at sea would have inevitably resulted in British surrender. From 1915 German submarines started to sink merchant ships bringing supplies to Britain. At the battle of Jutland, in 1916, Admiral Jellicoe successfully drove the German fleet back into harbour. At the time it was said, with some truth, that Admiral Jellicoe was the only man on either side who could have lost the war in a single afternoon. If Germany's navy had destroyed the British fleet at Jutland, Germany would have gained control of the seas around Britain, forcing Britain to surrender. In spite of this partial victory German submarines managed to sink 40 per cent of Britain's merchant fleet and at one point brought Britain to within six weeks of starvation. When Russia, following the Bolshevik revolution of 1917, made peace with Germany, the German generals hoped for victory against the

Allies. But German submarine attacks on neutral shipping drew America into the war against Germany. The arrival of American troops in France ended Germany's hopes, and it surrendered in November 1918.

By this time Britain had an army of over five million men, but by this time over 750,000 had died, and another two million had been seriously wounded. About fifty times more people had died than in the twenty-year war against Napoleon. Public opinion demanded no mercy for Germany.

In this atmosphere, France and Britain met to discuss peace at Versailles in 1919. Germany was not invited to the conference, but was forced to accept its punishment, which was extremely severe. The most famous British economist of the time, John Maynard Keynes, argued that it was foolish to punish the Germans, for Europe's economic and political recovery could not take place without them. But his advice was not accepted.

Apart from hatred of Germany, there was great sorrow for the dead. The destruction had been terrible. As one young soldier wrote shortly before he himself died, "Everywhere the work of God is spoiled by the hand of man." Wives had lost their husbands, children had lost their fathers, parents had lost their sons. It was natural for a nation in these circumstances to persuade itself that the war had somehow been worth it. Those who died in battle have been remembered ever since in these words:

> They shall grow not old, as we that are left grow
> old:
> Age shall not weary them, nor the years
> condemn.
> At the going down of the sun and in the morning
> We will remember them.
>
> "For the Fallen", Laurence Binyon 1869–1943

There was also anger about the stupidity of war, best expressed by Britain's "war poets". As the most famous of them, Wilfred Owen, wrote, shortly before he himself died on the battlefield, "My subject is War, and the pity of War." The poems written by young poet–soldiers influenced public opinion, persuading many that the war had been an act against God and man. "Never again" was the feeling of the nation when it was all over.

When peace came there were great hopes for a better future. These hopes had been created by the government itself, which had made too many promises about improved conditions of life for soldiers returning from the war. As soon as the war had ended, the government started a big programme of building homes and improving health and education. But there was far less progress than people had been led to hope for.

The rise of the Labour Party

An important political development during the war was the rapid growth of the Labour Party. Although it was formally established in 1900, its beginnings dated from 1874, as part of the trade union movement. The trade unions themselves had grown enormously, from two million members to five million by 1914, and eight million by 1918. In that year, for the first time, all men aged twenty-one and some women over thirty were allowed to vote. The number of voters doubled from eight to sixteen million people, most of whom belonged to the working class.

As a result of these changes, the Labour Party, which had won twenty-nine seats in the 1906 election, won fifty-seven seats in 1918, 142 seats in 1922, and 191 seats in 1923. The following year the first Labour government was created. The Labour Party, however, was not "socialist". Its leaders were, or had become, members of the middle classes. Instead of a social revolution, they wanted to develop a kind of socialism that would fit the situation in Britain. This was partly because Labour's leaders did not wish to frighten the voters. It was also because middle-class thinkers before the war had almost completely failed to interest the working class in socialist ideas. In fact Karl Marx, who spent most of his life in Britain studying and writing, was almost unknown except to a few friends. Both he and his close friend Friedrich Engels, who owned a factory in Manchester, had little hope of the British working classes becoming truly socialist. In 1885 Engels had written of the trade unionists: "The fools want to reform society to suit themselves, but not reform themselves to suit the development of society." Most working-class people wished to improve their financial situation and to enjoy the advantages of the middle class without becoming involved in socialist beliefs. The trade unions and the Labour movement had been shaped by the experiences of the nineteenth century. They did not believe they could bring down the existing form of government, and in any case they wanted to change things by accepted constitutional means, in Parliament. This was partly because they were supported not only by the working class but also by radicals already in Parliament.

By 1914 the socialist Beatrice Webb could write: "The landslide in England towards social democracy proceeds steadily, but it is the whole nation that is sliding, not one class of manual workers." That slide has continued for most of this century. As a result, the effect on Britain of the 1917 Bolshevik revolution in Russia was not as great as many feared it would be. Enough people were interested in Marxism to establish a Communist Party, but the Labour Party firmly refused to be connected with it. However, Marxism stirred a deep-seated fear in the Conservative Party, which has continued to see evidence of Marxist Socialism behind the Labour Party, the trade unions and strike action.

As a result of Labour's success in 1924, the Liberal Party almost completely disappeared. Liberals with traditional capitalist ideas on the economy joined the Conservative Party, while most Liberal "reformers" joined the Labour Party.

The rights of women

In 1918, some women over the age of thirty gained the right to vote after a long, hard struggle. John Stuart Mill, a radical thinker, had tried unsuccessfully to include votes for women in the 1867 Reform Bill. The industrial revolution had increased the power of men, and their feelings about property. Karl Marx noticed that the factory-owning Englishman's attitude of "chivalry" to women had not prevented them from forcing women to work like slaves in their factories and workhouses.

A man thought of his wife and daughters as his property, and so did the law. It was almost impossible for women to get a divorce, even for those rich enough to pay the legal costs. Until 1882, a woman had to give up all her property to her husband when she married him. And until 1891, husbands were still allowed by law to beat their wives with a stick "no thicker than a man's thumb", and to lock them up in a room if they wished. By 1850, wife beating had become a serious social problem in Britain. Men of all classes were able to take sexual advantage of working women. Women were probably treated worse in Britain than in any other industrialising European country at this time.

After 1870 the situation, particularly for middle-class women, began to improve. Women were allowed to vote and to be elected to borough or county councils. A very small number started to study at Oxford and Cambridge in separate women's colleges. But while they were allowed to follow the same course of study as men, they could not receive a degree at the end. Middle-class women became increasingly determined to have equal rights.

Working-class women were more interested in their legal rights concerning working conditions, and they found support in the trade union movement. In 1888 the policy of the unions was that "where women do the same work as men, they should receive equal pay". It was nearly another century before this principle became law. Female membership of the unions increased, but it was not always easy to persuade working men to respect the equal rights of their wives, particularly in times of unemployment.

In 1897 women started to demand the right to vote in national elections. Within ten years these women, the "suffragettes", had become famous for the extreme methods they were willing to use. Many politicians who agreed with their aims were shocked by their violent methods and stopped

Suffragettes arrested after "attacking" Buckingham Palace, May 1914. Suffragettes caused great feelings of hostility by their lawless acts, but they believed that it was only by acting in such a way that they could gain the attention of the nation. The First World War interrupted their campaign.

supporting them. However, if they had not been willing to shock the public, the suffragettes might not have succeeded.

The war in 1914 changed everything. Britain would have been unable to continue the war without the women who took men's places in the factories. By 1918 29 per cent of the total workforce of Britain was female. Women had to be given the vote. But it was not until ten years later that the voting age of women came down to twenty-one, equal with men.

The liberation of women took other forms. They started to wear lighter clothing, shorter hair and skirts, began to smoke and drink openly, and to wear cosmetics. Married women wanted smaller families, and divorce became easier, rising from a yearly average of 800 in 1910 to 8,000 in 1939. Undoubtedly many men also moved away from Victorian values. Leading writers like D.H. Lawrence, Aldous Huxley, James Joyce and Virginia Woolf freely discussed sexual and other sensitive matters, which would have been impossible for earlier generations.

Once women could vote, many people felt that they had gained full and equal rights. But there was still a long battle ahead for equal treatment and respect both at work and at home. The struggle for full women's rights is one of the most important events in recent British social history, and its effects continue to be felt.

Ireland

Before the beginning of the First World War the British government had agreed to home rule for Ireland. It was afraid, however, that the Protestants in the north would start a civil war in Ulster if home rule was introduced. For this reason, when war began in 1914, the government delayed the introduction of home rule, and called on Irishmen to join the army. Many thousands did, encouraged by their MPs, who hoped that this show of loyalty would help Ireland win self-government when the war ended.

There was another group of Irishmen, however, who did not see why they should die for the British, who had treated Ireland so badly. They did not only want home rule, but full independence. At Easter 1916, these republicans rebelled in Dublin. They knew they could not win, but they hoped their rising would persuade other Irishmen to join the republican movement. The "Easter Rising" was quickly put down, and most Irish disapproved of it. But the British executed all the leaders, which was a serious mistake. The public was shocked, not only in Ireland, but also in London. Irish Americans were also angry, just at the moment when America had joined Britain in the war against Germany.

In the 1918 elections the republicans won in almost every area except Ulster. Instead of joining the British parliament, however, they met in their own new parliament, the Dail in Dublin, and announced that Ireland was now a republic. Irishmen joined the republic's army, and guerrilla fighting against the British began. As a result the British government decided to make peace. In 1921 it agreed to the independence of southern Ireland. But it also insisted that Ulster, or Northern Ireland as it became known, should remain united with Britain.

The Anglo-Irish Treaty of 1921 led to civil war between the Irish themselves. By this treaty the new "Irish Free State" accepted continued British use of certain ports, the sovereignty of the British Crown, and most important of all, the loss of Northern Ireland, which remained under British control. The pro-Treaty forces won, and the republicans, who insisted that all Ireland, including Northern Ireland, should be an independent republic, were defeated. But a group of republicans formed a new party, Fianna Fail, which won the election of 1932 and the new Prime Minister, Eamon de Valera, began to undo the Treaty and in 1937 declared southern Ireland a republic. The British Crown was now no longer sovereign in Ireland.

Ireland and Britain today find themselves in the strange position of being entirely separate states, but by agreement their citizens are not considered foreigners in one another's country. Within the Republic of Ireland the majority have continued to believe that all Ireland should one day be united, but without the use of force. A minority, however, has remained since 1921 ready and willing to use violent means to achieve a united Ireland.

Disappointment and depression

The men who had fought in such terrible conditions during the war had been promised a land "fit for heroes". But this promise could not easily be kept, even by the popular new Labour Party.

Alongside the social effects of the war were far-reaching economic ones. The cost of the war had led to an enormous increase in taxation, from 6 per cent of income in 1914 to 25 per cent in 1918. The demands of the war had also led to a doubling in the size of the civil service, and greater government control of national life. It was inevitable that there should be increasing disagreement between workers and the government. Just before the war in 1914 there had been an outbreak of strikes. Immediately after the war there were further serious strikes, and in 1919 and 1921 soldiers were used to break these strikes, and force men back to work.

In 1926 discontent led to a general strike by all workers. The reasons for the strike were complicated, but the immediate cause was a coalminers' strike. An earlier miners' strike in 1921 had been defeated and the men had returned to work bitterly disappointed with the mine owners' terms. In 1925 mine owners cut miners' wages and

another miners' strike seemed inevitable. Fearing that this would seriously damage the economy, the government made plans to make sure of continued coal supplies. Both sides, the government and the Trades Union Congress (representing the miners in this case), found themselves unwillingly driven into opposing positions, which made a general strike inevitable. It was not what the TUC had wanted, and it proved deeply damaging to everyone involved.

The general strike ended after nine days, partly because members of the middle classes worked to keep services like transport, gas and electricity going. But it also ended because of uncertainty among the trade union leaders. Most feared the dangers both to their workers and the country of "going too far". The miners struggled on alone and then gave up the strike. Many workers, especially the miners, believed that the police, whose job was to keep the law, were actually fighting against them. Whether or not this was true, many people remembered the general strike with great bitterness. These memories influenced their opinion of employers, government and the police for half a century.

It is possible to argue that Britain missed an opportunity to reform the economic structure of the country after the war. But instead of careful planning, businessmen were allowed to make quick profits, particularly in the cotton mills, the shipyards and engineering industries. But perhaps there was little the government could do to control the situation, as it was not in control of economic forces. All over Europe and America a serious economic crisis, known as "the depression", was taking place. It affected Britain most severely from 1930 to 1933, when over three million workers were unemployed.

In Germany the depression was even more severe, and it destroyed Britain's second most important market from before the war. John Maynard Keynes's warning – that if Germany did not recover then neither would its European trading partners – became horribly true. Far worse, the economic collapse of Germany led to the rise of Adolf Hitler.

Because the worst effects of the depression in Britain were limited to certain areas, the government did not take the situation seriously enough. The areas most affected by the depression were those which had created Britain's industrial revolution, including Clydeside, Belfast, the industrial north of England and southeast Wales. The working class in these areas still lived in poor conditions. Men and women could not expect to live as long as people in richer areas, and more babies died in the first year of life. There was little hope for these people because almost no one was willing to invest the large amounts of money needed to get industry working again. The Labour Party was no better at dealing with the situation than the Conservatives.

It is surprising that Britain avoided a serious political crisis in the 1920s. The unfairness of the situation was so obvious to working-class people, who had neither political nor economic power. Two-thirds of the wealth of the nation was in the hands of only 400,000 people, less than 1 per cent of the population. In other European countries economic crisis and social unrest had led to great changes. In Russia there had been the Bolshevik revolution. Powerful new Nazi and Fascist governments were taking over in Germany, Italy, Austria and Spain, while France also faced political crisis. Britain's reasonably calm political life was proof of an astonishing level of popular agreement about the basis of government which did not seem to exist in many parts of Europe.

In the 1930s the British economy started to recover, especially in the Midlands and the south. This could be seen in the enormous number of small houses which were being built along main roads far into the countryside.

This new kind of development depended on Britain's growing motor industry, which was based in the Midlands. In the nineteenth century, towns had been changed by the building of new homes near the railway. Now the country around the towns changed as many new houses were built along main roads suitable for motoring. Middle-class people moved out even further to quieter new

The despair of unemployment. This fine photograph is simply entitled "Street scene in Wigan". In Lancashire clogs were still the usual footwear for the working class until after the Second World War.

suburbs, each of which was likely to have its own shops and a cinema. Unplanned suburbs grew especially quickly around London, where the underground railway system, the "tube", had spread out into the country. It seemed as if everyone's dream was to live in suburbia.

Economic recovery resulted partly from the danger of another war. By 1935 it was clear that Germany, under its new leader Adolf Hitler, was preparing to regain its position in Europe, by force if necessary. Britain had done nothing to increase its fighting strength since 1918 because public opinion in Britain had been against war. The government suddenly had to rebuild its armed forces, and this meant investing a large amount of money in heavy industry. By 1937 British industry was producing weapons, aircraft and equipment for war, with the help of money from the United States.

The Second World War

The people of Britain watched anxiously as German control spread over Europe in the 1930s. But some had foreseen this dangerous situation. They believed that the reasons for German expansion could be found in the harsh peace terms forced on Germany by the Allies in 1919, and the failure to involve it in the post-war political settlement. In 1920 the Allies had created the League of Nations which, it was hoped, would enable nations to co-operate with each other. Although the League did not forbid war, its members agreed to respect and preserve the borders and territory of all other members. But in 1935 Italy invaded Abyssinia (Ethiopia), a fellow member of the League. Britain and France were anxious to win Italy's co-operation against Hitler, who was illegally rearming Germany, and therefore decided against taking action against Italy as the rules of the League required them to do. This failure to use the League's authority had serious results. Italy's Fascist leader, Benito Mussolini, and Hitler realised that Britain and France lacked the will to make sure the standards the League demanded of its members were followed.

For the next four years Germany, Italy and their ally in the Far East, Japan, took advantage of this weakness to seize territory of interest to them. There was good evidence that the demands of Germany could not be satisfied. But in order to avoid war in 1938, the British Prime Minister, Neville Chamberlain, accepted and co-operated in the takeover of German-speaking parts of Czechoslovakia by Germany. Chamberlain returned from meeting Hitler in Munich. He reassured Britain that he had Hitler's written promise that Germany had no more territorial ambitions, in the memorable words, "peace for our time". Six months later Germany occupied the rest of Czechoslovakia. Britain, realising that war was inevitable, gave a guarantee of support to Poland if Germany invaded.

Chamberlain was widely blamed for his "appeasement" of Germany. But he expressed the feelings of many people in Britain, to avoid war at all costs. As one of his opponents, Ernest Bevin,

generously said in 1941, "If anyone asks me who was responsible for the British policy leading up to the war, I will, as a Labour man myself, make the confession and say, 'All of us.' We refused absolutely to face the facts."

In September 1939 Germany invaded Poland, and Britain entered the war. The British felt again that they were fighting for the weaker nations of Europe, and for democracy. They had also heard about the cruelty of the Nazis from Jews who had escaped to Britain.

Few people realised how strong the German army was. In May 1940 it attacked, defeating the French in a few days, and driving the British army into the sea. At Dunkirk, a small French port, the British army was saved by thousands of private boats which crossed the English channel. Dunkirk was a miraculous rescue from military disaster, and Britain's new Prime Minister, Winston Churchill, persuaded the nation that it was a victory of courage and determination at Britain's darkest hour. Although the army had lost almost all its weapons in France, Churchill told the nation there could be no thought of surrender or peace negotiation: "we shall defend our island, whatever the cost may be, we shall fight on the beaches, we shall fight on the landing grounds, we shall fight in the fields and in the streets, we shall fight on the hills; we shall never surrender.... until in God's good time the New World, with all its power and might, sets forth to the liberation and rescue of the Old." And he offered his countrymen nothing but "blood, toil, tears and sweat."

Everyone in Britain expected Germany to invade, but the British air force won an important battle against German planes in the air over Britain. This, however, did not prevent the German air force from bombing the towns of Britain. Almost one and a half million people in London were made homeless by German bombing during the next few months. Once again Churchill brilliantly managed to persuade a nation "on its knees" that it would still win.

The war had begun as a traditional European struggle, with Britain fighting to save the "balance

*Winston Churchill at his desk,
March 1944.*

of power" in Europe, and to control the Atlantic Ocean and the sea surrounding Britain. But the war quickly became worldwide. Both sides wanted to control the oil in the Middle East, and the Suez Canal, Britain's route to India. In 1941 Japan, Germany's ally, attacked British colonial possessions, including Malaya (Malaysia), Burma and India. As a result, Britain used soldiers from all parts of its empire to help fight against Germany, Italy and Japan. But the weakness of Britain was obvious to the whole world when its army surrendered Singapore to Japan, described by Churchill as the worst surrender in British history.

In 1941 Germany and Japan had made two mistakes which undoubtedly cost them the war. Germany attacked the Soviet Union, and Japan attacked the United States, both quite unexpectedly. Whatever the advantages of surprise attack, the Axis of Germany, Italy and Japan had now forced onto the battlefield two of the most powerful nations in the world.

Britain could not possibly have defeated Germany without the help of its stronger allies, the Soviet Union and the United States. By 1943 the Soviet army was pushing the Germans out of the USSR, and Britain had driven German and Italian troops out of North Africa. Italy surrendered quickly following Allied landings in July 1943. In 1944

Britain and the United States invaded German-occupied France. They had already started to bomb German towns, causing greater destruction than any war had ever caused before. Such bombing had very doubtful military results. Dresden, a particularly beautiful eighteenth-century city, and most of its 130,000 inhabitants, were destroyed in one night early in 1945. In May 1945, Germany finally surrendered. In order to save further casualties among their own troops, Britain and the United States then used their bombing power to defeat Japan. This time they used the new atomic bombs to destroy most of Nagasaki and Hiroshima, two large Japanese cities. Over 110,000 people died immediately and many thousands more died later from the after-effects.

It was a terrible end to the war, and an equally terrible beginning to the post-war world. But at the time there was great relief in Britain that the war had finally ended. It had lasted longer than the First World War, and although less than half as many British troops had died this time, the figures of over 303,000 soldiers and 60,000 civilians in air raids was a very heavy price to pay for the mistakes of the inter-war years. The Soviet Union, Germany and Japan paid a fair more terrible price, as did ethnic groups like the Jewish and gypsy peoples, several million of whom were deliberately killed.

23 The age of uncertainty

The new international order · The welfare state · Youthful Britain · A popular monarchy · The loss of empire · Britain, Europe and the United States · Northern Ireland · Scotland and Wales · The years of discontent · The new politics · Britain: past, present and future

The new international order

During the war the Allies had started to think of ways in which a new world order could replace the failed League of Nations. Even before it joined the war against the Axis powers, the United States had agreed an "Atlantic Charter" with Britain. The basis of this new charter was US President Roosevelt's "Four Freedoms": freedom of speech and expression; freedom of worship; freedom from fear; and freedom from want.

At the end of the war the victorious Allies created the United Nations, which expressed the ideas of the Atlantic Charter. The Allies formed themselves into a "Security Council", into which they invited some less powerful nations. They hoped that the success of wartime alliance could be carried into peacetime. But this depended on a continuing feeling of common purpose, which no longer existed. The idea of the four allies (Soviet Union, United States, France and Britain) working together for the recovery of central Europe collapsed. Europe became divided into two, the eastern part under communist Soviet control, the western part under a capitalist system protected by US power.

In 1948–9 the Soviet Union tried to capture West Berlin by stopping all road and rail traffic to it, and it was only saved by a huge airlift of essential supplies from the West, which lasted almost one year. As a result of the struggle for West Berlin, opposing alliances were formed: the North Atlantic Treaty Organization of the Western nations, and the Warsaw Pact of the Eastern bloc.

In 1950 the United Nations faced new difficulties in the Far East. Troops of North Korea, which was under Soviet control invaded South Korea, which was under US control. British troops formed part of the United Nations force which defended South Korea. Only fear on both sides limited the level and extent of the war. But while Britain became more fearful of Soviet intentions, it also became more unhappy with the forceful attitude of its ally, the United States.

British foreign policy was not only concerned with the danger from the Soviet Union. It was also concerned with finding a new part to play in a fast-changing world, and getting used to changing relations with its friends, particularly with the United States, with the European countries, and with members of the Commonwealth, a new association of former British possessions.

Britain still considered itself to be a world power, and this confidence was strengthened by three important technical developments in the 1950s which increased its military strength. These developments were in research into space, in the design of nuclear weapons, and in the design of intercontinental ballistic missiles. Britain's leadership in nuclear power resulted in the development of nuclear weapons. But it also led to the building of the first nuclear energy power station in the world in 1956. All these military and scientific developments drew Britain more closely to the United States, both for political and financial reasons.

However, by the early 1960s Britain was increasingly interested in joining the new European Community (EC). Britain wanted to join the Community because of the realisation that it had lost political power internationally, and because of a growing desire to play a greater part in European politics.

It was in Egypt that Britain's weakening international position was most obvious. Until 1956 Britain had controlled the Suez Canal, but in that year Egypt decided to take it over. Britain, together with France and Israel, attacked Egypt. But the rest of the world, in particular the United States loudly disapproved of Britain's action, and forced Britain to remove its troops from Egypt. Until Suez, Britain had been able to deal with the United States and the Soviet Union as an equal, but after Suez this was no longer possible. From now on, Britain was viewed in a new light, not only by the two Great Powers, but also by many weaker countries in Asia and Africa, particularly by the Arab countries. They began to challenge Britain's authority more openly. Even more importantly, Suez opened a painful debate inside Britain, in which politicians tried to define Britain's new international role after such a humiliating political defeat.

The welfare state

In 1918 there had been a wish to return to the "good old days". There was no such feeling during the Second World War, when Winston Churchill had told the nation, "We are not fighting to restore the past. We must plan and create a noble future." At the end of the war many reforms were introduced, both by Conservative and Labour Party ministers. Most of them agreed that there were social wrongs in British life which had to be put right. The reforms introduced were based on the "New Liberal" reforms which had been carried out just before the First World War. But they went much further, and it could be said that the whole

nation, Conservative and Labour, had moved politically to the left. This move was one of the greatest achievements of the British labour movement, and its effect was felt for the next thirty years.

In 1944, for the first time, the government promised free secondary education for all, and promised to provide more further and higher education. In 1946 a Labour government brought in a new National Health Service, which gave everyone the right to free medical treatment. Two years later, in 1948, the National Assistance Act provided financial help for the old, the unemployed and those unable to work through sickness. Mothers and children also received help.

Progress in these areas was the result of new ideas about basic human rights. Important citizens' rights, particularly freedom of speech, had been firmly established in the seventeenth and eighteenth centuries. Political rights, particularly the right to vote, and to vote secretly, developed during the nineteenth century. In the twentieth century people began to demand basic social rights, such as the right to work, the right to proper health care, and the right to care in old age. *The Times* newspaper wrote in 1940: "If we speak of democracy we do not mean democracy which maintains the right to vote but forgets the right to work and the right to live."

The Labour government went further, taking over control of credit (the Bank of England), power (coal, iron and steel), and transport (railways and airlines). These acts were meant to give direction to the economy. But only 20 per cent of British industry was actually nationalised, and these nationalised industries served private industry rather than directed it. Nationalisation was a disappointment. Even the workers in the nationalised industries did not feel involved in making them succeed, as the planners had hoped. Strikes in the nationalised industries were as big a problem as they were in privately owned industries.

As a result of the changes which gave importance to people's happiness and wellbeing, the government became known as "the welfare state".

The Royal Festival Hall was among the best of 1950s architecture. It was built as part of the Festival of Britain celebration in 1951, one hundred years after the Great Exhibition. But its real importance was to mark the end of the hardships caused by the war. It was a popular celebration of national recovery, with a new concert hall on London's South Bank and a funfair further upstream at Battersea.

For the next quarter century both the Conservative and Labour parties were agreed on the need to keep up the "welfare state", in particular to avoid unemployment. Britain became in fact a social democracy, in which both main parties agreed on most of the basic values, and disagreed mainly about method. The main area of disagreement was the level of nationalisation desirable for the British economy to operate at its best.

However, although the welfare state improved many people's lives, it also introduced new problems. Government administration grew very fast in order to provide the new welfare services. Some people objected to the cost, and claimed that state welfare made people lazy and irresponsible about their own lives.

Youthful Britain

Like much of post-war Europe, Britain had become economically dependent on the United States. Thanks to the US Marshall Aid Programme, Britain was able to recover quickly from the war.

Working people now had a better standard of living than ever before. There was enough work for everyone. Wages were about 30 per cent higher than in 1939 and prices had hardly risen at all.

People had free time to enjoy themselves. At weekends many watched football matches in large new stadiums. In the evenings they could go to the cinema. They began to go away for holidays to low-cost "holiday camps". In 1950, car production was twice what it had been in 1939, and by 1960 cars were owned not only by richer people but by many on a lower income. It seemed as if the sun shone on Britain. As one Prime Minister said, "You've never had it so good," a remark that became famous.

It was also the age of youth. Young people had more money in their pockets than ever before, now that wages for those just starting work had improved. The result was that the young began to influence fashion, particularly in clothing and music. Nothing expressed the youthful "pop" culture of the sixties better than the Beatles, whose music quickly became internationally known. It was no accident that the Beatles were working-class boys from Liverpool. They were real representatives of a popular culture.

Young people began to express themselves in other ways. They questioned authority, and the culture in which they had been brought up. In particular they rebelled against the sexual rules of Christian society. Some young people started living together without getting married. In the early 1960s the number was small, perhaps only 6 per cent, but it grew to 20 per cent within twenty years. Improvements in birth control made this more open sexual behaviour possible. Divorce became much easier, and by 1975 one marriage in three ended in divorce, the highest rate in Europe. Older people were frightened by this development, and called the new youth culture the "permissive society". Perhaps the clearest symbol of the permissive age was the mini skirt, a far shorter skirt than had ever been worn before.

But there was a limit to what the permissive society was prepared to accept. Two cabinet ministers, one in 1963, the other in 1983, had to leave the government when their sexual relationships outside marriage became widely known. Public disapproval could still be unexpectedly strong.

A popular monarchy

During the twentieth century the monarchy became more popular than ever before. George V, the grandson of Victoria, had attended the first football Cup Final match at Wembley Stadium, and royal attendance became an annual event. On Christmas Day, 1932, he used the new BBC radio service to speak to all peoples of the Commonwealth and the empire. His broadcast was enormously popular, and began a tradition. In 1935 George V celebrated his Silver Jubilee, and drove through crowded streets of cheering people in the poorest parts of London. "I'd no idea they felt like that about me," he said, "I'm beginning to think they must really like me for myself." To his own great surprise, George V had become a "people's king".

However, in 1936 the monarchy experienced a serious crisis when George V's son, Edward VIII, gave up the throne in order to marry a divorced woman. Divorce was still strongly disapproved of at that time, and the event showed how public opinion now limited the way the royal family could act in private life. At the time it caused much discussion, and has remained a matter for heated argument.

The Beatles were an example of the new popular culture. They came from an ordinary suburb of Liverpool, and quickly became world famous for their music from 1964 onwards.

During the Second World War George VI, Edward's brother, became greatly loved for his visits to the bombed areas of Britain. He and his wife were admired for refusing to leave Buckingham Palace even after it also had been bombed. Since 1952, when Elizabeth II became queen, the monarchy has steadily increased in popularity.

The loss of empire

At the end of the First World War, the German colonies of Africa, as well as Iraq and Palestine in the Middle East, were added to Britain's area of control. Its empire was now bigger than ever before, and covered a quarter of the entire land surface of the world.

There were already signs, however, that the empire was coming to an end. At the 1919 peace conference US President Woodrow Wilson's disapproval of colonialism resulted in Britain's latest territorial gains being described as "mandated" from the League of Nations. Britain had to agree to help these territories towards self-government. The real questions were how long this would take, and how much Britain would try to control the foreign policies of these territories even after self-government had been achieved. In fact it took longer than the populations of some of these areas had been led to hope, and by 1945 only Iraq was independent, and even here Britain had a strong influence on its foreign policy.

The United Nations Charter in 1945 also called for progress towards self-government. It seemed hardly likely in this new mood that the British Empire could last very long. This feeling was strengthened by the speed with which Britain had lost control of colonial possessions to Japan during the war.

In India there had been a growing demand for freedom during the 1920s and 1930s. This was partly because of the continued mistrust and misunderstanding between the British rulers and the Indian people, well described in E.M. Forster's novel *A Passage to India*, published in 1924. But it was also the result of a growing nationalist movement, skilfully led by Mahatma Gandhi, which successfully disturbed British rule. By 1945 it

was clear that British rule in India could no longer continue. It was impossible and extremely expensive to try to rule 300 million people without their co-operation. In 1947 the British finally left India, which then divided into a Hindu state and a smaller Muslim state called Pakistan. Britain also left Palestine, where it was unable to keep its promises to both the Arab inhabitants and the new Jewish settlers. Ceylon became independent the following year.

For most of the 1950s Britain managed to keep its other possessions, but after Suez it began to give them up. On a visit to Africa in 1960 Prime Minister Macmillan warned of a "wind of change blowing through the Continent." On his return to London he began to speed up plans to hand over power. This was partly because of the rapid growth of local independence movements, but also because of a change in thinking in Britain itself. Most people no longer believed in Britain's right to rule. Between 1945 and 1965 500 million people in former colonies became completely self-governing. In some countries, like Kenya, Cyprus and Aden, British soldiers fought against local people. Other countries became independent more peacefully.

On the whole, however, the ending of Britain's empire was a highly successful process, carried out in spite of some who opposed surrendering power, however costly this might be. It compared well with the bloody events which occurred when both France and Belgium pulled out of their colonies. This successful retreat resulted partly from the great skill of Prime Ministers and those they chose for the difficult job of handing over power in each colony. But it was also the result of the quality of its colonial administrators, particularly those in junior positions. In spite of the great wrongs of colonial rule, many of these administrators had the highest ideals of duty and service. It was largely due to their work that the newly independent countries felt they wanted to remain on friendly terms with Britain.

Britain tried to hold onto its international position through its Commonwealth, which all the old colonies were invited to join as free and equal members. This has been successful, because it is based on the kind of friendship that allows all members to follow their own policies without interference. At the same time, it allows discussion of international problems in a more relaxed atmosphere than is possible through the United Nations. It was with the help of the Commonwealth that Zimbabwe finally moved peacefully from rebellion by the whites to independence and black majority rule.

Britain also tried to keep its influence by a number of treaties with friendly governments in the Middle East and in southeast Asia. But most ex-colonies did not wish to be brought into such arrangements, either with Britain or with any other powerful country.

By 1985 Britain had few of its old colonial possessions left, and those it still had were being claimed by other countries: Hong Kong by China, the Falklands/Malvinas by Argentina, and Gibraltar by Spain. In 1982 Britain went to war to take back the Falklands after an Argentinian invasion. In spite of the great distance involved, British forces were able to carry out a rapid recapture of the islands. The operation was very popular in Britain, perhaps because it suggested that Britain was still a world power. But Britain's victory made an eventual solution to the problem more difficult, and possession of the islands extremely expensive. The war itself had cost £900 million, but the total cost of defending the island since 1982 had risen to £3 billion by 1987.

Britain, Europe and the United States

It was, perhaps, natural that Britain was unable to give proper attention to its relations with Europe until it was no longer an imperial power. Ever since the growth of its trade beyond Europe during the seventeenth century, Britain had ceased to be fully active in Europe except at moments of crisis. As long as Europe did not interfere with Britain's trade, and as long as the balance of power in Europe was not seriously disturbed, Britain could happily neglect European affairs.

At the end of the eighteenth century Napoleonic France drew Britain further into European politics

than it had been, perhaps, since the Hundred Years war. In 1815 Britain co-operated with the other European powers to ensure peace, and it withdrew this support because it did not wish to work with the despotic powers then governing most of Europe. For the rest of the century, European affairs took second place to empire and imperial trade.

After the First World War it was natural that some Europeans should try to create a European union that would prevent a repetition of war. A few British people welcomed the idea. But when France proposed such an arrangement in 1930, one British politician spoke for the majority of the nation: "Our hearts are not in Europe; we could never share the truly European point of view nor become real patriots of Europe. Besides, we could never give up our own patriotism for an Empire which extends to all parts of the world . . . The character of the British people makes it impossible for us to take part seriously in any Pan-European system."

Since then Britain has found it difficult to move away from this point of view. After the Second World War the value of European unity was a good deal clearer. In 1946 Churchill called for a "United States of Europe", but it was already too late to prevent the division of Europe into two blocs. In 1949 Britain joined with other Western European countries to form the Council of Europe, "to achieve greater unity between members", but it is doubtful how far this aim has been achieved. Indeed, eight years later in 1957, Britain refused to join the six other European countries in the creation of a European Common Market. Britain was unwilling to surrender any sovereignty or control over its own affairs, and said it still felt responsibility towards its empire.

It quickly became clear that Britain's attitude, particularly in view of the rapid loss of empire, was mistaken. As its financial and economic difficulties increased, Britain could not afford to stay out of Europe. But it was too late: when Britain tried to join the European Community in 1963 and again in 1967, the French President General de Gaulle refused to allow it. Britain only became a member in 1973, after de Gaulle's retirement.

After becoming a member in 1973, Britain's attitude towards the European Community continued to be unenthusiastic. Although trade with Europe greatly increased, most British continued to feel that they had not had any economic benefit from Europe. This feeling was strengthened by the way in which Prime Minister Margaret Thatcher argued for a better financial deal for Britain in the Community's affairs. The way in which she fought won her some admiration in Britain, but also anger in many parts of Europe. She welcomed closer co-operation in the European Community but only if this did not mean any lessening of sovereignty. Many Europeans saw this as a contradiction. Unless member states were willing to surrender some control over their own affairs, they argued, there could be little chance of achieving greater European unity. It is not surprising therefore that Britain's European partners wondered whether Britain was still unable "to take part seriously in any Pan-European system."

De Gaulle's attitude to Britain was not only the result of his dislike of "*les Anglo-Saxons*". He also believed that Britain could not make up its mind whether its first loyalty, now that its empire was rapidly disappearing, was to Europe or to the United States.

Britain felt its "special relationship" with the United States was particularly important. It was vaguely believed that this relationship came from a common democratic tradition, and from the fact that the United States was basically Anglo-Saxon. Neither belief was wholly true, for the United States since 1783 had been a good deal more democratic than Britain, and most US citizens were not Anglo-Saxons. Even Britain's alliance with the United States was very recent. In 1814 British troops had burnt down the US capital, Washington. In the middle of the nineteenth century most British took the part of the South in the American Civil War. By the end of the century the United States was openly critical of Britain's empire.

Britain's special relationship rested almost entirely on a common language, on its wartime alliance with the United States and the Cold War which followed it. In particular it resulted from the close relationship Winston Churchill personally enjoyed with the American people.

After the war, Britain found itself unable to keep up with the military arms race between the United States and the Soviet Union. It soon gave up the idea of an independent nuclear deterrent, and in 1962 took American "Polaris" nuclear missiles for British submarines. The possession of these weapons gave Britain, in the words of one Prime Minister, the right "to sit at the top of the table" with the Superpowers. However, Britain could only use these missiles by agreement with the United States and as a result Britain was tied more closely to the United States.

Other European countries would not have felt so uneasy about the close ties between the United States and Britain if they themselves had not disagreed with the United States concerning the Soviet Union and other foreign policy matters. Ever since 1945 the United States and the political right in Britain were more openly hostile to the Soviet Union. The Europeans and the British political left were, on the whole, just as suspicious of Soviet intentions, but were more anxious to improve relations. However, even under Labour governments, Britain remained between the European and American positions. It was natural, therefore, that under Thatcher, who was more firmly to the right than any Conservative Prime Minister since the war, British foreign policy was more closely linked to that of the United States, particularly with regard to the Soviet Union. This was most clearly shown when, after the Russians invaded Afghanistan, Britain joined the United States in boycotting the Moscow Olympics in 1980. Britain sided with the United States in other foreign policy matters too, which alarmed its European partners. In 1986, for example, it allowed US aircraft to use British airfields from which to attack the Libyan capital, Tripoli. One thing was clear from these events. Britain still had not made up its mind whether its first political loyalty lay across the Atlantic, or in Europe.

Troops on the front line in Belfast, Ulster. When the conflict broke out in 1969 police faced civil rights protesters. After the IRA started its campaign of shootings and bombings, the Ulster police was unable to maintain authority unassisted and the British army was drawn into the fight. Civilian protesters and rioters became younger and younger, making it harder for the army and police to keep control. The use of force against twelve-year-old demonstrators looked bad on television. Those who believed Britain should continue to govern Northern Ireland saw the conflict as a security struggle, while those who believed Ulster should become part of the Republic of Ireland saw it as a liberation struggle.

Northern Ireland

When Ireland was divided in 1921, the population of the new republic was only 5 per cent Protestant. But in Ulster, the new province of Northern Ireland, 67 per cent of the people were Protestant. For many years it seemed that almost everyone accepted the arrangement, even if some did not like it.

However, many people in Northern Ireland considered that their system of government was unfair. It was a self-governing province, but its government was controlled by the Protestants, who feared the Catholics and kept them out of responsible positions. Many Catholics were even unable to vote.

Suddenly, in 1969, Ulster people, both Catholics and Protestants, began to gather on the streets and demand a fairer system. The police could not keep control, and republicans who wanted to unite Ireland turned this civil rights movement into a nationalist rebellion against British rule.

In order to keep law and order, British soldiers were sent to help the police, but many Catholics saw them as a foreign army with no right to be there.

Violence has continued, with bomb attacks and shootings by republicans, which the British army tried to prevent. In 1972 the Northern Ireland government was removed and was replaced with direct rule from London. Since then, Britain has been anxious to find a solution which will please most of the people there, and offer peace to everyone.

In 1985 Britain and Ireland made a formal agreement at Hillsborough that they would exchange views on Northern Ireland regularly. This agreement was bitterly opposed by Protestant political leaders in the province. But their failure to put a stop to the Hillsborough Agreement resulted in a growing challenge from those Protestants who wanted to continue the struggle outside Parliament and possibly in a military form.

The future of Northern Ireland remains uncertain. The Catholic population is increasing slightly faster than the Protestant one, but there are unlikely to be more Catholics than Protestants for a very long time. Meanwhile young people in Northern Ireland cannot remember a time when there was peace in the province.

Scotland and Wales

In Scotland and Wales, too, there was a growing feeling by the 1970s that the government in London had too much power. In Wales, a nationalist party, Plaid Cymru, the party of "fellow countrymen", became a strong political force in the 1970s. But Welsh nationalism lost support in 1979 when the people of Wales turned down the government's offer of limited self-government. Almost certainly this was because many of them did not welcome wider official use of the Welsh language. In spite of the rise of Plaid Cymru, the Welsh language was actually spoken less and less. In 1951 29 per cent of the Welsh population spoke Welsh. By 1981 this figure had fallen to 19 per cent, even though Welsh was used for many radio and television programmes, and in schools.

In Scotland, the Scottish Nationalist Party (SNP) showed its growing popularity by increasing its percentage of the national vote from 20 per cent to 30 per cent during 1974. The SNP became the second party in Scotland, pushing the Conservatives into third place. When Scotland was offered the same limited form of self-government as Wales, just over half of those who voted supported it. But the government decided that 54 per cent of those who voted was not a big enough majority, and to the anger of the SNP it abandoned the self-government offer. As a result the SNP itself collapsed at the next election, losing nine of its eleven seats. But like Plaid Cymru in Wales, the SNP remained active in Scottish politics. In both countries most people continued to support the Labour Party, partly in protest against mainly Conservative England. Although in Wales Welsh was declining, and although in Scotland only a very few people still spoke Gaelic, the different political and cultural life of Celtic Wales and Scotland seemed unlikely to disappear.

The years of discontent

During the 1950s and 1960s Britain remained a European leader economically as well as politically. But Britain suddenly began to slip rapidly behind its European neighbours economically. This was partly

The discovery of oil in commercial quantities in the North Sea provided welcome help to Britain when its traditional sources of income were in decline in the 1970s. The construction of oil rigs provided work for thousands of shipbuilders for whom there were no more ships to build. By the early 1980s, however, no more oil rigs were required and unemployment followed. In addition, much of Britain's income from oil was lost on unemployment benefit for the three million or so people out of work.

Concorde, the result of Anglo-French co-operation, was the most advanced civil jet airliner in the world. But it was too expensive, no one wished to buy it, and it was a commercial failure. It was only used by the French and British national airlines.

the result of a new and unpleasant experience, a combination of rising prices and growing unemployment. Governments were uncertain about how to solve the problem, and no longer agreed that the state had a responsibility to prevent unemployment.

How real were Britain's economic problems? Most people's wealth had continued to grow. By the end of the 1970s four-fifths of homes had their own telephones and refrigerators, and two-thirds owned their own homes and cars.

Compared with its European neighbours, however, Britain was certainly doing less well. In 1964 only West Germany of the six European Community countries produced more per head of population than Britain. Thirteen years later, however, in 1977, only Italy produced less. Britain eventually joined the European Community in 1973, hoping that it would be able to share the new European wealth. By 1987 this had not yet happened, and Britain has continued to slip behind most other European countries. The British Ambassador in Paris wrote in 1979, "today we are not only no longer a world power, but we are not in the first rank as a European one . . . We talk of ourselves without shame as being one of the least prosperous countries in Europe . . . If present trends continue, we shall be overtaken . . . by Italy and Spain well before the end of the century." And he pointed out that for the first time in three hundred years the average individual income in Britain was well below that in France. France itself, however, made a great economic recovery in the seventies. Some believed that Britain could do the same.

Britain also experienced new social problems, particularly after the arrival of immigrants in Britain. All through British history there have been times when large numbers of immigrants have come to settle in the country. But until recently these people, being Europeans, were not noticeably different from the British themselves. In the fifties, however, the first black immigrants started to arrive from the West Indies, looking for work. By 1960 there were 250,000 "coloured" immigrants in Britain and also the first signs of trouble with young whites.

Later, Asian immigrants started to arrive from India and Pakistan and from East Africa. Most immigrants lived together in poor areas of large cities. Leicester's population became 16 per cent immigrant, Wolverhampton and Bradford about 8 per cent each. By 1985 there were about five million recent immigrants and their children out of a total population of about fifty-six million. By 1985, too, almost half this black population had been born in Britain. Even so, there were still white people who, in the words of one newspaper, "go on pretending . . . that one day the blacks can somehow be sent 'home', as though home for most of them was anywhere else but Britain."

As unemployment grew, the new immigrants were sometimes wrongly blamed. In fact, it was often the immigrants who were willing to do dirty or unpopular work, in factories, hospitals and other workplaces. The relationship between black immigrants and the white population of Britain was not easy. Black people found it harder to obtain employment, and were often only able to live in the worst housing. The government passed laws to prevent unequal treatment of black people, but also to control the number of immigrants coming to Britain.

The old nineteenth-century city centres in which black immigrants had settled were areas with serious physical and economic problems. In the 1980s bad housing and unemployment led to riots in Liverpool, Bristol and London, worse than any seen in Britain since the nineteenth century. Black people were blamed for causing these riots, but they were in fact mainly the result of serious and longstanding economic difficulties, which affected the black population living in the old city centres more than the white.

There were other signs that British society was going through a difficult period. The Saturday afternoon football match, the favourite entertainment of many British families, gradually became the scene of frightening and often meaningless violence. British football crowds became feared around the world. In 1984 an English crowd was mainly responsible for a disaster

Immigrants from different Commonwealth countries tended to live together in particular districts. In Southall, west London, many Punjabis, Gujaratis and Sikhs from India settled down, opening shops and becoming successful in trade.

at a match in Brussels in which almost forty people were killed. People were shocked and ashamed, but still did not understand the reason for the violence. The permissive society and unemployment were blamed, but the strange fact was that those who started the violence were often well-off members of society with good jobs.

Women, too, had reasons for discontent. They spoke out increasingly against sexism, in advertising, in employment and in journalism. They protested about violence against women and demanded more severe punishment for sexual crimes. They also tried to win the same pay and work opportunities as men. This new movement resulted from the growth in the number of working women. Between 1965 and 1985 the number of wives with jobs increased from 37 per cent to 58 per cent. In 1975 it became unlawful to treat women differently from men in matters of employment and pay. But this law was not fully enforced, and it continued to be harder for women to take a full part in national life.

Unemployment increased rapidly at the end of the 1970s, reaching 3.5 million by 1985. In many towns, 15 per cent or more of the working population was out of work. Unemployment was highest in the industrial north of England, and in Belfast, Clydeside and southeast Wales, as it had been in the 1930s depression. Things became worse as steel mills and coal mines were closed. In 1984 the miners refused to accept the closing of mines, and went on strike. After a year of violence during which miners fought with the police the strike failed.

The defeat of the miners showed how much power and confidence the trade unions had lost. This was partly because they faced a government determined to reduce the power of the unions. But it was also because they seemed unable to change themselves to meet changed circumstances, and they seemed afraid of losing their power.

Inflation had made the situation more difficult. Between 1754 and 1954, prices had multiplied by six. Then, they multiplied by six again in the space of only thirty years, between 1954 and 1984. In such circumstances it proved almost impossible to make sure that all workers felt that they were fairly paid.

Industrial problems also increased the differences between the "comfortable" south and the poorer north. It is easy to forget that this division already existed before the industrial revolution, when the north was poorer and had a smaller population. The large cities and towns built during the industrial revolution have had great difficulty in creating new industries to replace the old.

The new politics

Few of the problems of the 1980s were entirely new. However, many people blamed them on the new Conservative government, and in particular, Britain's first woman Prime Minister, Margaret Thatcher. Thatcher had been elected in 1979 because she promised a new beginning for Britain. The need for such a break with the past had been widely recognised for some years. As a result the old Conservative–Labour agreement on the guiding principles of the welfare state had already broken down. In the Conservative Party there had been a strong movement to the right, and in the Labour Party there had been a similarly strong move to the left. Both moved further away from the "centre" of British politics than they had done in living memory.

This basic change in British politics caused a major crisis for the Labour Party. Labour was no stranger to internal conflict, nor to these conflicts being damagingly conducted in public. In the 1930s the party had turned against its own first Prime Minister, Ramsay MacDonald, when he formed a national government with the Conservatives to handle the financial crisis of 1931. Four years later it had again been split between its traditional anti-war members and those who recognised the Nazi danger. In 1959 Labour had again publicly disagreed about two issues, nationalisation and nuclear weapons, which a large section of the party

Margaret Thatcher, the longest serving Prime Minister of the twentieth century. Her style and her views appealed to many British people who had lost confidence in the welfare state and in the direction the nation had taken. In some ways she was the first genuine leader the nation had had since Churchill, the politician on whom she consciously modelled herself. In spite of the fact that over half the nation disagreed with her policies, they were unable to vote her out of office.

wished to give up, whether other nuclear armed nations did so or not. This time, however, the disagreements between the party's left and right were far more damaging. The 1979 election result was the worst defeat since 1931. Worse, however, was to follow, and as the bitter conflict continued, many people ceased to believe in the party's ability to govern itself, let alone the country.

Labour suffered a further blow when four senior right-wing members left the party to form their own "Social Democratic Party" in 1981, in alliance with the small but surviving Liberal Party. For some years the Liberal Party had been calling for a change in the electoral system. It had good reason to do so. In 1974 the Liberals had received 20 per cent of the national vote but only 2 per cent of the seats in Parliament. By March 1982 the new "Alliance" was gaining ground both from the Conservative and Labour parties.

Margaret Thatcher had come to power calling on the nation for hard work, patriotism and self-help. She was not, however, a typical Conservative. As one of her ministers said, "I am a nineteenth-century Liberal, and so is Mrs Thatcher. That's what this government is about." There was much truth in the remark, for she wanted free trade at home and abroad, individual enterprise and less government economic protection or interference. However, she was more of a Palmerston than a Gladstone. She wanted more "law and order" but was a good deal less willing to undertake the social reform for which later nineteenth-century Liberals were noted.

Not everyone in the Conservative Party was happy about the change in policy. The discontented members became known as "wets", one of whom argued that "people . . . must at least feel loyalty to the state. This loyalty will not be deep unless they gain from the state protection and other benefits", and he warned against the state's "failure to create a sense of community". Thatcher, however, ignored these views, saying that she "could not waste time having any internal arguments."

By the beginning of 1982 the Conservative government had become deeply unpopular in the country. However, by her firm leadership during the Falklands War Thatcher captured the imagination of the nation, and was confidently able to call an election in 1983.

As expected, Thatcher was returned to power with a clear majority of 144 seats in the 650-seat Parliament. It was the greatest Conservative victory for forty years. In part Thatcher's victory was a result of the "Falklands factor". Far more, however, it was the result of a split opposition vote, between Labour and the Alliance, and the continued weakness of the Labour Party, which suffered its worst result since the early 1920s. Once again the Alliance had the disappointment of gaining 26 per cent of the national vote, but only 3.5 per cent of the seats in Parliament. A clear majority had voted against the return of a Conservative government, showing dissatisfaction with Thatcher's policies. It was not difficult to see why this was so.

Thatcher had promised to stop Britain's decline, but by 1983 she had not succeeded. Industrial production since 1979 had fallen by 10 per cent, and manufacturing production by 17 per cent. By 1983, for the first time since the industrial revolution, Britain had become a net importer of manufactured goods. There was a clear economic shift towards service industries. Unemployment had risen from 1.25 million in 1979 to over 3 million.

However, Thatcher could claim she had begun to return nationalised industries to the private sector, that she had gone even further than she had promised. By 1987 telecommunications, gas, British Airways, British Aerospace and British Shipbuilders had all been put into private ownership. She could also claim that she had broken the power of the trade unions, something else she had promised to do. In fact, the trade unions had been damaged more by growing unemployment than by government legislation. She could be less confident about increased law and order. In spite of increasing the size of the police force, there was a falling rate of crime prevention and detection. In addition, the rough behaviour of the police in dealing with industrial disputes and city riots had seriously damaged their reputation.

The most serious accusation against the Thatcher government by the middle of the 1980s was that it had created a more unequal society, a society of "two nations", one wealthy, and the other poor. According to these critics, the divide cut across the nation in a number of ways. The number of very poor, who received only a very small amount of government help, increased from twelve million in 1979 to over sixteen million by 1983. In the meantime, reductions in income tax favoured the higher income earners.

The division was also geographical, between prosperous suburban areas, and neglected inner city areas of decay. Although the government sold many state-owned houses and flats to the people who lived in them, it also halved the number of new houses it built between 1981 and 1985, a period in which the number of homeless people increased.

London's docklands. From the eighteenth century until the 1950s the inhabitants of these areas worked in London's busy docks. Then the docks died, and remained empty until the 1980s when the whole area was redeveloped. Young professionals from outside the area moved into the new housing (foreground) because it was close to the banks and financial institutions (background) in which they worked. Although redevelopment brought new wealth to the area, some of the old low-incomed dockland community who saw no benefit for themselves moved out.

More importantly, people saw a divide between the north and south of the country. Ninety-four per cent of the jobs lost since 1979 had been north of a line running from the Wash, on the east coast, to the Bristol channel in the west. People were aware of growing unemployment in the "depressed" areas, and fewer hopes of finding a job. Indeed, by 1986 41 per cent of those unemployed had been out of work for over a year, compared with only 25 per cent in 1979. As a result, it was not surprising that Labour continued to be the stronger party in the north, and in other depressed areas. In the more heavily populated south, the Alliance replaced Labour as the main opposition party.

The black community also felt separated from richer Britain. Most blacks lived in the poor inner city areas, not the richer suburbs, and unemployment among blacks by 1986 was twice as high as among the white population.

In spite of these problems, Thatcher's Conservative Party was still more popular than any other single party in 1987. In the national elections that year, the Conservative Party was returned to power with a majority of 102 seats. This was partly because since 1979 personalities had become politically more important. Thatcher was seen as more determined and more convincing than the Labour or Alliance leaders. It was also because the opposition to Conservative policy remained split between Labour and the Alliance, and it appeared permanently so.

There were other reasons why the Conservative Party, with only 43 per cent of the national vote, won so convincingly. Its emphasis on personal wealth and property ownership had begun to change the way many traditional Labour supporters voted. It may be that many lower income people living in the Midlands and south shifted their loyalties to the right. On the other hand, in Scotland the Conservatives lost half their seats, mainly to Labour or the Scottish National Party, an indication of the increased sense of division between richer and poorer Britain, and an indication that Scottish radicalism was as strong as ever.

Thatcher's victory caused concern for both opposition parties. Labour had done better than many had expected. However, it still had to face the fact that Thatcher's policies were creating a society which seemed decreasingly interested in Labour philosophy, and it had to decide how it could make this philosophy more attractive without giving up its principles. The Alliance also faced serious problems. It had done worse than expected, calling into question its claim to replace the two-party system with a three-party one. It now seemed that it would take two or three national elections before this question, and the connected question of proportional representation, would be decided.

The 1987 election brought some comfort, however, to two underrepresented groups. In 1983 only nineteen (3 per cent) of the 650 members of Parliament had been women, almost the lowest proportion in western Europe. In 1987 this figure more than doubled to forty-one women MPs (6.5 per cent), a figure which suggested that the political parties realised that without more women representatives they might lose votes. Blacks and Asians, too, gained four seats, the largest number they had ever had in Parliament, although like women they remained seriously underrepresented.

Britain: past, present and future

By the late 1980s most British people felt that the future was full of uncertainty. These doubts resulted from disappointment with lost economic and political power. Many people looked back to the "Swinging Sixties" as the best ten years Britain had had this century.

However, people were divided concerning the nation's future possibilities. Some, those who had voted for Thatcher, were optimistic. They believed that material wealth was vital for national renewal, and that economic success was about to happen.

Others were unhappy with the direction the nation was taking. They believed that the emphasis on material wealth encouraged selfishness, and a retreat from an ideal of community to a desire for personal gain. They were worried by the weakening of the welfare state, particularly in the educational and health services.

The government said much about maintaining "traditional values", particularly law and order. Respect for the law, it argued, was rooted in British tradition. It also spoke of a return to Victorian values. On the other hand, its opponents argued that the tradition of broad popular agreement on the management of the nation's affairs was in grave danger. Neither side was wholly right in its claim. For example, the Conservative argument forgot that in the past, the law had been frequently broken not only by criminals but also by those for whom it was oppressive, like the Tolpuddle Martyrs. It forgot, too, that the Victorians had valued not only enterprise and hard work but had also cared about social reform to assist the weaker members of society. In the same way, when Labour accused the Conservatives of putting broad national agreement in danger, it forgot that its own party origins lay with the radicals who stood against accepted national political practice. But such awkward facts were easily placed on one side, and the political parties appealed to "history", as this fitted their view of modern Britain and the glorious future they offered if the people supported them.

There was nothing new in this. People have always looked at history in the way that suited their system of beliefs. In 1988 Britain celebrated two major anniversaries, the defeat of the Spanish Armada in 1588, and the Glorious Revolution in 1688. One was about Britain's successful military and foreign policy, the other about its successful constitutional development. The popular view is that both were truly glorious events. However, the truth is less

The royal family celebrates the wedding of Prince Andrew and Sarah Ferguson. In the 1980s the royal family became "world property" in a way it had not been before. Members of the royal family became the subject of journalistic investigation, both in their public and private lives, and began to mirror television "soap operas" in their entertainment value.

simple. The Spanish Armada was defeated more by the weather than by the English navy, the Spanish navy became stronger rather than weaker after 1588, and the war with Spain seriously damaged the economy of England. Nevertheless, the defeat of the Armada has remained a symbol of Britain's seafaring success. It was given particular importance in the late nineteenth century, when British world-wide command of the seas was at its height. By 1988 it was harder to think in the same way, because British foreign policy had shrunk in recent years, with a decline in its interests beyond Europe and the United States.

There was also something slightly uncomfortable about celebration of the Glorious Revolution. The Glorious Revolution was about the sovereignty of Parliament in the nation's affairs. But not everyone was happy with parliamentary life by 1988. Was its constituency system truly democratic? Was Parliament itself too powerful? There was another

reason for discomfort. The Glorious Revolution had been a disaster for Ireland. In 1988 there was a reminder of this side of Britain's history in the conflict in Northern Ireland, where even the Protestant "Loyalists" were unhappy with rule by the Westminster Parliament. In Scotland, Wales, and parts of England, too, there were people who disliked the centralised power of Westminster, which had increased in the Thatcher years.

Britain has more living symbols of its past than many countries. It still has a royal family and a small nobility. Its capital, cities and countryside boast many ancient buildings, castles, cathedrals, and the "stately homes" of the nobility. Every year there are historical ceremonies, for example the State Opening of Parliament, the Lord Mayor's Show, or the meeting of the Knights of the Garter at Windsor each St George's Day. It is easy to think these symbols are a true representation of the past. Britain's real history, however, is about the whole people of Britain, and what has shaped them as a society. This means, for example, that the recent story of black and Asian immigration to Britain is as much a part of Britain's "heritage" as its stately homes. Indeed more so, since the immigrant community's contribution to national life lies mainly in the future.

When looking at Britain today, it is important to remember the great benefits from the past. No other country has so long a history of political order, going back almost without interruption to the Norman Conquest. Few other countries have enjoyed such long periods of economic and social wellbeing.

It is also important, however, to remember the less successful aspects of the past. For example, why did the political views of the seventeenth-century Levellers or nineteenth-century Chartists, which today seem so reasonable, take so long to be accepted? Why did the women's struggle to play a fuller part in national life occur so late, and why was it then so difficult and painful? Why is there still a feeling of division between the north and south of Britain? Is Britain, which in many ways has been a leader in parliamentary democracy, losing that position of leadership today, and if so, why?

The questions are almost endless, and the answers are neither obvious nor easy. Yet it is the continued discussion and reinterpretation of the past which makes a study of Britain's history of value to its present and its future.

Index

Aberdeen 56, 61, 153
Adam, Robert 116
Adelard of Bath 99
Africa (see also west, south,
    north and east Africa) 4,
    145–8, 169, 172
Africa Company 75
Agincourt 43, 53, 54
Albert, Prince Consort 144
aldermen 13
Alexander, King of Scots 30
Alfred, King 15, 16
Alliance, Liberal and Social
    Democratic 179–182
Allies (1939–45) 166–168
America see also South America,
    United States and Canada 16,
    31, 69, 73, 74, 81, 97, 99,
    105, 112, 113, 123, 128, 142,
    145, 148, 154, 161, 163, 164
    Civil War 174
    War of Independence 112,
        134, 136
Anne, Queen 87, 88, 96, 97,
    107
Angles 11, 20, 21, 85
Anglican Church see Church of
    England
Anglo-Irish 32
Anglo-Saxons 7, 12–15, 18,
    23, 35, 37, 39, 40, 45
    language 64
Anglo-Irish Treaty (1921) 163
Anselm, Archbishop of Canter-
    bury 29
Aquitaine 26, 44
Arab countries 145, 169
Arbroath, Declaration of (1320)
    33
Argentina 173
Armada, Spanish 43, 54, 73–
    74, 98, 182–3
army, British 92–3, 97, 109,
    112, 113, 128–9, 145–6, 159–
    60, 166–7, 172, 173, 175
Arthur, King 6, 45, 65, 75
Arthur, Prince of Wales 75
Arts and Crafts Movement 155
Atlantic Charter 168
Augustine, St 13, 14
Auld Alliance 43, 44, 56, 77,
    96
Australia 75, 116, 132, 148,
    153
Austria 27, 109, 131, 142, 165
Austria-Hungary 157
Avignon, popes of 49
Axis, (1939–45) 166–168

BBC 171
Bacon, Francis 99
Bacon, Roger 99
Balkans 132
Balliol, John de 32–33
Bank of England 108, 169

Bannockburn, battle of (1314)
    33, 43
Baptists 99
barrows (burial mounds) 4
Bath 99, 116
Bayeux Tapestry 17
Beaker people 5, 6
Beatles 170–1
Bede, the Venerable 11, 14, 15,
    99
Becket, Thomas, Archbishop of
    Canterbury 23, 29, 64
Bedford, John duke of 53
    duke of 117
Belfast 165, 175, 178
Belgic tribes 7
Belgium 44, 68, 128, 129, 132,
    157, 160
Bevin, Ernest 166
Birmingham 12, 84, 107, 114,
    128, 134, 138, 154
Black Death (1348) 46
Black Prince 45, 48
Blenheim, battle of (1704) 97
Boadicea 8, 9
Boers 146, 157
Boleyn, Anne 68, 69, 70
Bolsheviks, Bolshevism 160,
    162, 165
Bonaparte see Napoleon
Booth, William 155
Boru, Brian 20
Boston Tea Party 112
Bosworth, battle of (1485) 55,
    56, 68
Boyle, Robert 99
Boyne, battle of the (1690) 97
Bradford 134, 177
Bretigny, Treaty of (1360) 44
Bretons 53, 55
Bristol 74, 103, 106, 125, 177
Britain, Great, new state of
    (1707) 96
Brittany 44
Britons, Ancient 21
Bronze Age 6–7
Bruce, Robert 32–3
Brunel, Isambard Kingdom 139
Buckingham 134
    duke of 55
    Buckingham Palace 172
Bunyan, John 99
burgh, borough 16
Burgundy, duke of 44, 53, 55
Burghley, Lord 80
Burke, Edmund 112–3, 128
Burma 167
Byron, Robert 142

cabinet government 108
Cadbury, Arthur 154
Cadiz 74
Caernarfon 32, 52
Caesar, Julius 7, 8
Calais 44, 53, 60

Caledonia 9
Calvin, John 69
Cambridge 41, 55, 61, 65, 100,
    151, 162
Canada 109, 112, 116, 148
canals 103, 123
Canning, Lord 142
Canon law 35
Canterbury 13, 29
    Archbishops of 14, 28, 30, 49,
        89
Cape Colony 131
Catherine of Aragon 69, 70, 71
Catholicism, Catholics (see also
    Church) 70–73, 76, 77, 85,
    88, 89, 94–6, 97, 108, 113,
    114, 141, 149, 154
Cavaliers (Royalists) 91
Caxton, William 65, 75
Celts, Celtic culture 6–14, 18–
    21, 31, 32, 45, 56
Ceylon 131, 153, 172
Chamberlain, Neville 166
Charles I 86, 88–93
Charles II 93–95, 100, 101
Charles V (of Spain) 59, 70
Charles Edward, Prince (Bonny
    Prince Charlie) 111, 113
charters of freedom 40
Chartists 135, 136, 143, 184
Chatham, William Pitt the
    Elder, Lord 109, 112
Chaucer, Geoffrey 64, 65, 85,
    99
China 145, 173
Christianity 13–15, 17, 19, 23,
    145
Church 13, 16, 23, 28, 29–30,
    35, 36, 41, 49, 53, 61, 62, 65,
    69, 70, 85, 94–95, 99, 105,
    152, 155
    Celtic Church 14, 15, 21, 32
    Church of England 69, 88,
        93–5, 99, 123, 124, 139, 140,
        141, 152
    Roman Church see also
        Catholicism 14
Churchill, Winston Spencer
    166–69, 174
civil law 35
Civil War (1642–45) 90, 91,
    95
clans 21, 32, 56, 77, 113, 116
Cnut, King 16
coffeehouses 104
Coke, Sir Edward 88
Columba, St 20, 21
Commons, House of 31, 61, 79,
    80, 87, 88, 92, 125, 135, 141,
    143, 156
Cold War 174
Commonwealth, British 148,
    168, 171, 172, 173
communism 162
Concorde 176

Conservative Party 143, 156–7,
    162, 169–70, 174, 176, 179,
    180–1, 182
Co-operative Movement 143
Copenhagen, battle of
    (1801) 128
Corn Law 136, 141
Cornwall 4, 5, 7, 11
Corresponding Society 128
Crécy, battle of (1346) 44
Crimea 145, 146, 159
Cromwell, Oliver 91, 92–4, 99,
    104
Cromwell, Richard 93
Cromwell, Thomas 68, 70
Culloden, battle of (1746) 111,
    113, 116
Cyprus 172
Czechoslovakia 166

Dail (Irish parliament) 163
Danegeld 16
Danelaw 16, 36
Danes see also Vikings 16, 17,
    36
Dardanelles 160
Darnley, Lord 78
Darwin, Charles 155
David, King of Scots 44
Defoe, Daniel 109
Denmark 15
Derry (see also Londonderry) 76
Dickens, Charles 131, 132, 155
Disraeli, Benjamin 143
Domesday Book 25, 34, 36–37,
    70
Dorset 5, 6, 8, 134
Drake, Sir Francis 73–4, 109,
    142
Druids 8, 19
Dublin 20, 32, 97, 113, 163
Dunkirk 166
Durham, Lord 148
Dutch 73, 75, 87, 97

earl 13
east Africa 177
East Anglia 12, 48, 92
East India Company 75, 97, 110
East Indies 75, 108
Easter Rising (1916) 163
Eastland Company 75
Edinburgh 21, 44, 56, 61, 113,
    116, 149
Education Acts 151
Edward the Confessor 16–17,
    18, 34
Edward I 30–4, 39, 43, 52, 57
Edward II 32–3, 43, 51
Edward III 33, 44, 45, 48–9,
    51, 61, 64
Edward IV (Duke of York) 55,
    56
Edward V 55
Edward VI 70, 71, 77, 79

Edward VII *148*
Edward VIII 171
Egypt 128, 146, 147, 169
eisteddfods 76
Einstein, Albert 100
Eleanor of Aquitaine 26
Elizabeth I 67, 70, 72–4, 76,
  77, 79–80, 84, 87, 89, 118
Elizabeth II 172
empire, British 74–5, 107, 129,
  145–8, 171–2, 174
electoral politics 110, 134, 143,
  161–3, 176, 180–2
enclosures 81–2, 107, 116–7,
  118
Engels, Friedrich 161–2
Erasmus 85
Ethelred, King 16
Eton College 55, 65
Europe 3, 4, 5, 6, 7, 8, 10, 13,
  15, 29, 31, 40, 41, 43, 59, 68,
  69, 73, 88, 97, 101, 103, 114,
  117, 120, 121, 123, *127*, 128–
  9, 131, 132, 136, 138, 145,
  155–7, 159, 161, 164, 165,
  166–8, 170–1, 173, 174, 175,
  183
Evangelicalism 137

Factory Act, First (1833) 125
Falklands 173, 180
family life 62–3, 84–5, 105,
  119–20, 136–7
Far East 109, 166, 168
Fairfax, General 91
fascists, fascism 165–6
Fawkes, Guy 89
feudalism 23–5, 28, 31, 32, 33,
  39, 43
Fianna Fail 164
First World War (1914–18)
  159–61, 163, 167, 169, 172,
  173
Flanders 44, 48, 60, 61
Flemings 40, 48, 56, 83
Flodden, battle of (1513) 77
Fox, Charles James 128
France (and the French) 15, 16,
  17, 26, 27, 28, 29, 30, 31, 32,
  34, 39, 40, 43, 44, 49, 52, 53,
  56, 61, 67, 68, 69, 72, 73, 77,
  78, 93, 96, 97, 98, 107, 108–
  10, 113, 121, 123, 125–9,
  131, 132, 134, 136, 137, 138,
  142, 157, 159–61, 165, 166–
  8, 173
  French language 41, 64
Franks 9, 15
Frederick of Prussia 111
French Revolution 125, 128–
  129, 134
Frobisher, Martin 73
Fry, Elizabeth 125

Gallipoli 160
Gandhi, Mahatma 172
Garter, Order of the 45
  Knights of the 183
Gascony 40, 44, 53
Gaul 8, 9
Gaulle, General de 173

Gaunt, John of 51, 55
general strike (1926) 164
Geoffrey of Monmouth 5
Geoffrey Plantagenet, duke of
  Anjou 26
George I 107, 108
George III 109, 110–1, 113
George V *148*, 156, 171
George VI 172
Germanic groups 9–11
Germany 14, 15, 39, 69, 78,
  132, 143, 150, 156–7, 159–
  61, 164, 165–7, 172
  German language 108
Gibraltar 97, 173
Gladstone, William *141*, 143,
  148, 180
Glasgow 56, 61, 107, 116, 134,
  149, 153
Glorious Revolution 95, 108,
  182–3
Glyndwr, Owain 52
government, Saxon 12
  Viking 16
  early Middle Ages 23, 31,
  34–5
  late Middle Ages 57
  Tudor 69, 79–80
  Stuart 94–5
  eighteenth century 108–9
  nineteenth century 136
  twentieth century 155–6,
  169–70, 179–82
  local government 12, 13, 57–
  8, 61, 72, 82–3, 152–3
Great Exhibition (1851) 138,
  155–6, *170*
Greeks 142
Gregory the Great, Pope 13
Grey, Sir Edward 157
Grey, Lady Jane 71
Grey, Lord 134
Gruffydd ap Llewelyn 18
guilds 40–41, 76

Hadrian, Emperor 9
Halley, Edmund 100
Hanseatic League 68
Harold, King 17
Harvey, William 99
Hastings, battle of (1066) 12,
  17
Hawkins, Sir John 73, 74
Hanover 96, 107, 110
Hebrides 21
henges 5, 6
Henry I 25, 26, 29, 31, 34, 35,
  99, 108
Henry II 22, 26, 27, 29, 32, 35,
  36
Henry III 30, 35
Henry IV (duke of Lancaster)
  50–3, 55
Henry V 53, *54*
Henry VI 53, 55, 65
Henry VII (Tudor) 55, 57, 67–
  9, 73, 75, 77–9
Henry VIII 67, 68–70, 73, 75–
  7, 79, 82, 84, 87
Highlanders 21, 77, 96, *111*,
  113, 149–50

Highlands, Scottish 20, 22, 32,
  56, 116
hillforts 6, 7, 8
Hillsborough Agreement (1985)
  175
Hitler, Adolf 164, 165–6
Holland *see also* Netherlands and
  Low Countries 95, 97, 117
Holy Land 25
Holy Roman Empire 68, 69, 98
homage 24–25
Hong Kong 173
Hooke, Robert 99
Howard, Catherine 68
Huguenots 99
Hundred Years War 44, 53, 56,
  68, 173

Ice Age 3, 4
immigration, immigrants 39,
  40, 98, 177, *178*, 184
India 75, 97, 109, *110*, 117,
  129, 138, 145–8, 153, 167,
  172, 177–8
Indian Mutiny 145
Industrial Revolution 107, 121–
  9, 137, 162, 178, 180
industry 48, 84, 121–3, *130*,
  136, 154, 162, 164, 165, 169,
  178, 180
Ireland (and the Irish) 5, 7, 8,
  9, 14, 15, 18, 19–21, 32, 43,
  74–6, 90, 93, 96, 97, 104,
  113, 143, 149–50, 153, 163,
  175, 183
Irish Free State 163
Iron Age 6
Israel 169
Italy 68, 79, 142, 165–7, 177

Jacobinism 128
Jacobites 108, 113
James I (of Scotland) 56
James II (of Scotland) 56
James III (of Scotland) 56
James IV (of Scotland) 77
James V (of Scotland) 77
James VI (of Scotland) and I (of
  England) 77, 78, 87–90, 93,
  96, 98
James VII (of Scotland) and II
  (of England) 94–97, 108, 113
James III, the Old
  Pretender 108
Jellicoe, Admiral 160
Jews 39, 99, 114, 143, 166–7
  Exchequer of 39
jingoism 148
John, King 27–8, 29–30, 37
Johnson, Samuel 114
Jonson, Ben 85
jury system 36
Justice, Chief 88
justices of the peace (JPs) 61,
  62, 80, 81, 82, 83, 104, 151
Jutes 11, 85
Jutland, battle of (1916) 160

Katherine of Valois 53
Kells, The Book of 19

Kent *3*, 11, 13, 48, 63, 71, 103
Kenya 172
Keynes, John Maynard 161, 164
Kirk, the Scottish 77, 78, 88–
  9, 96, 137
Korea, North and South 168

Labour Exchanges 155
Labour movement 125, 162,
  169
Labour Party 143, 156, 159,
  161–2, 164, 169–70, 176,
  179, 180, 182
Lancashire 114, 123, 138, *152*,
  165
Lancastrians 52, 55
Langland, William 64
Latin 8, 15, 41, 49
Laud, William 89
law and justice 15, 35–6, 61,
  68, 110
  schools 61
League of Nations 166, 168,
  172
Leicester 9, 177
  earl of 30
Leinster 19, 20
Levant Company 75
Levellers 93, 98, 184
Liberals 128, 134, 140, 141,
  142, 143, 149, 150, 155–6,
  162, 179, 180
Lindisfarne Gospel 14
Liverpool 107, 111, 114, 171,
  177
Llewelyn ap Gruffydd *30*, 32
Locke, John 95
Lollardy 49–50
London 9, 10, 15, 16, 17, 21,
  28, 41, 71, 81, 82, 84, 91, 95,
  103, 111, 113, 114, 115, 117,
  118, 128, 134, 138, 165–7,
  172, 175
  Docklands 181
  Tower of *43*, 55, *82*, 85, 111,
  Underground *158*
Londonderry 76, 96, 97
longbow 44
Lord Mayor of London 41
  Lord Mayor's Show 183
Lord Protector 92, 93
Lords, House of 31, 40, 79, 80,
  92, 93, 134, 143, 156
Louis XIV (of France) 93, 97,
  99
Low Countries *see also* Holland,
  Netherlands 39, 40, 68, 128,
  157
Lowlands, Scottish 20, 56, 90,
  113, 116, 149
Loyalists, Ulster 183
Luddites 123

MacDonald, Ramsay 179
Macmillan, Harold 172
Magna Carta (1215) 28, 29, 30,
  31, 88
Malaya (Malaysia) 167
Malplaquet, battle of (1709) 97
Manchester 84, 107, 114, 123,
  134, 143, 161

manor 13
March, earl of 51, 52
Margaret of Scotland 33
Margaret, daughter of Henry VII 77
Marlborough, duke of 97
Marlee, William 99
Marlowe, Christopher 85
Marshall Aid Programme 170
Marx, Karl 161, 162
Mary, queen of Scots 72, 77, 78
Mary Stuart, queen 95–6
Mary Tudor, queen 70–2, 73, 79
Matilda, Queen 26, 71
Mayflower 99
Mediterranean 48, 97, 131, 132
Merchant Adventurers 60, 75
Mercia 12
Methodism, Methodists 107, 121, 124–5, 137
middle classes 61, 125, 139, 140, 143, 152, 156, 161–2, 164, 165
Middle East 138, 145, 160, 167, 172, 173
Midlands 11, 85, 107, 114, 122, 123, 133, 134, 165, 182
Mill, John Stuart 162
Milton, John 99
Montfort, Simon de 30, 31
More, Sir Thomas 68, 85
Muslims 25, 27, 145, 172
Mussolini, Benito 166

Napoleon Bonaparte 107, *127*, 128–9, 131, 157, 161
Napoleonic Wars 125–9, 132, 173
Naseby, battle of (1645) 91
National Assistance Act (1948) 169
navy 73–75, 107, 109, *127*, 128–9, 131, 157, 160
Nelson, Horatio Lord *126–7*, 128–9
Nightingale, Florence 145
National Health Service 169
Neolithic 4, 5
Netherlands *see also* Holland, Low Countries 56, 68, 73, 85, 97, 98
New Liberals 155–6, 169
New Stone Age *see* Neolithic
New Zealand 148, 153
Newcastle 40, 84, 103, *154*
duke of 115
newspapers 101, 111–12, 145, 160, 169
Newton, Sir Isaac 100
Nonconformists 95, 99, 114, 120, 125, 140, 141, 149
Norman 13, 16, 17, 20, 23, 25, 26, 31, 32, 35, 37, 38, 39, 52, 184
Normandy 16, 17, 25, 28, 34, 37, 40, 44, 53
Norsemen 21
North Africa 4, 167

North Atlantic Treaty Organisation (NATO) 168
Northern Ireland *see also* Ulster 150, 163, 164, 175, 183
Northumbria 12, 14, 20
Nottingham 12, 37, 91, 128
Norway 15, 21, 39

Ockham, William of 99
Offa, king of Mercia 12, 14
Dyke 12, 18
Opium Wars 145
Orange Lodges 113
Orange *see* William of
ordeal, trial by 35–6
Orkney Islands 4, 5, 21
Orleans, duke of 43
Ottoman Empire *see also* Turkey 145, 157
Oudenarde, battle of (1708) 97
Owen, Robert 154
Oxford 40, 41, 49, 61, 65, 99, 100, 151, 162
Oxfordshire 83

Paine, Tom 112, 128
Pakistan 142–3, 177
Pale 32
Palestine 160, 172
Palmerston 142–3, 180
Parliament *see also* Commons and Lords 28, 30–1, 39, 43, 47, 61, 67, 69, 70, 71, 76, 79, 82, 87, 88–90, 91, 92–6, 107, 108, 110, 111, 114, 117, 125, 134, 141, 143, 156, 161–2, 163, 180, 182–3
Parliament Act of 1911 156
Members of (MPs) 79, 80, 88, 92, 93, 94, 95, 110, 117, 135, 143, 149, 156, 161, 179–82
Speaker of 80
State Opening of 183
Parnell, Charles 150
Parr, Catherine 70
Passchendaele, battle of (1917) 160
Peasants' Revolt 48–9, *50*
Peel, Sir Robert 136, 141, 142, 143
Penn, William 105, 119
People's Charter (1838) 135
Philip II (of Spain) 71, 72, 73, 74, 79
Picts 20, 21
Pilgrim Fathers 99
Pilgrimage of Grace (1539) 82
Pitt the Elder, William *see* Chatham
Pitt the Younger, William *127*, 128
Plaid Cymru 176
Plantation, origins 108
Prime Minister, origins 108
Poitiers, battle of (1356) 44
police 136, 164, 180
Poor Laws 83, 118, 132
Pope, Alexander 100
population 10, 38, 46, 48, 80–1, 84, 103, 114–5, 131, 133, 134, 141, 149, 150

potato famine (1845–7) 149
Pre-Raphaelites 155
Presbyterians 89, 95, 105
Protectorate 93, 104
Protestantism, Protestants 69–72, 76, 77–79, 85, 89, 90, 93, 95, 96, 97, 98–9, 105, 107, 113, 149, 150, 154, 174, 175, 183
Prussia 109, 129, 131
Puritans 84, 92–5, 98, 120, 125
Pyrenees 26

Quakers 98, 99, *102*, 105, 114, 115, 119, 154, 160
Quebec 109

radicals 112, 128, 134, 135, 143, 149, 162
railway 138–9
Raleigh, Sir Walter 74, 85
Ramillies, battle of (1706) 97
Reform Bill (1832) 134, 142, 143
(1867) 167
Reformation 68, 69–72, 76, 77–79, 85, 105
Renaissance, 12th century 41
15th/16th century 79, 85
Richard I (Coeur de Lion) 27–8, 40, 53
Richard II 51
Richard III, duke of Gloucester 55, 57
Right, Petition of (1628) 89
Rights, Bill of (1689) 95
Robert of Normandy 25, 26
Romans 4, 6, 7–10, 13, 15
Rome *see also* Church, Roman 33, 49, 79
Roundheads 91
Royal Society 99, 100
Royalists 91
rural life 10, 12–13, 37–38, 47, 57, 60, 80–81, 116–8
Russia *see also* Soviet Union 3, 6, 20, 129, 131, 132, 142–3, 157, 160, 162, 165, 174

St Paul's Cathedral 100
Salvation Army 155
Sarajevo 157
Saxons 9, 11–17, 21, 23, 32, 35, 37, 75, 85
Scandinavia 39, 75, 78
schools, boarding 120, 137
elementary *151*
grammar 41, 85
public 140, 156
Scotland (and Scots) 4, 5, 7, 8, 9, 11, 14, 18, 20–21, 23, 32, 43–4, 48, 52, 56, 61, 67, 72–3, 75, 88–9, 90, 92, 93, 95, 96, 98, 105, 113, 114, 116, 134, 138, 143, 149, 151, 153, 154, 176, 182–3
Scottish Nationalist Party 176, 182
Second World War (1939–45) 101, 159, 166–7, 169, 173

Settlement, Act of (1701) 96
Seymour, Jane 70
Shakespeare, William 55, 85
Sheffield 114, 128, *133*, 134
shires 12, 31
shire reeve (sheriff) 12
Sidney, Algernon 95
Sidney, Sir Philip 85
Singapore 131, 167
slavery 74, 97, 120, 125, 154
Smith, Adam 154
Social Democratic Party 179
Somme, battle of the (1916) 160
South Africa 157, 146
South America *see also* America 73, 74, 109
South Sea Company (and Bubble) 108
Soviet Union *see also* Russia 159, 167, 168, 174
Spain 67, 68, 69, 71, 72, 73, 77, 78, 84, 85, 97, 98, 109, 128, 129, 142, 159, 165, 173, 177
Speenhamland Act (1795) 118
Spenser, Edmund 76, 85
Staple, Company of the 60
Star Chamber, Court of 68
Stephen of Blois 26
Stonehenge *2*, 5, 6
Strathclyde 20
Stuarts 87–105, 107, 108, 113
Sudan *146*, 147
Suez Canal 147, 157, 167, 169, 172
suffragettes 162–3
Supremacy, Act of (1534) 69

Tara 5, 19
Test Act (1673) 94
Thatcher, Margaret 174, 179, 183
Thirty Years War (1618–48) 88, 101
Tolpuddle Martyrs 134, 154, 182
Tories *see also* Conservative Party 94–5, 107–8, 113, 128, 134, 140, 141, 142, 143, 149, 150
town and city life 8, 9, 16, 39, 40, 41, 57–9, 61, 82, 103, 114, 140
trade unions 125, 134–5, 143, 159, 161, 162, 164
Trades Union Congress 143, 164
Trafalgar, battle of (1805) *126–7*, 128
Troyes 53
Tudors 65, 67–86, 87, 104, 105, 117, *159*
Tull, Jethro 117
Turkey *see also* Ottoman Empire 131, 132, 142, 145, 160
Tyler, Wat 48, 49, *50*

Ulster 5, 18, 19, 76, 90, 97, 113, 163, 175

Union Act, England and
  Scotland (1707) 96
United Nations 168, 172, 173
  Security Council 168
United States *see also*
  America 35, 149, 150, 156,
  157, 159, 165–7, 168, 169–
  70, 173, 174, 183
universities 41, 56, 61, 65, 151
Utrecht, Treaty of (1713) 97

Valera, Eamon de 164
Versailles, Treaty of (1919) 161
Victoria, Queen 137, 138, 144,
  148, 171
Vikings 15–17, 20, 21, 32, 39,
  85
voting *see* electoral politics

Wales (and the Welsh) 3, 4, 5,
7, 11, 12, 13, 14, 18, 19, 21,
23, 31, 32, 43, 44, 48, 52, 61,
75, 76, 79, 81, 114, 134, 135,
143, 149, 151, 153, 165, 175,
178, 183
  Prince of *30, 32, 52, 75,* 144
Wallace, William 33, 52
Walpole, Robert 108–9
Warsaw Pact 168
Waterloo, battle of (1815) 129,
  156
Watt, James 121, 123
Webb, Beatrice 162
Webb, Sidney 152
Wedgwood, Josiah 123
welfare state 155–6, 169–70
Wellington, duke of 128–9
Wesley, John 123–5
Wessex 12, 15, 17, 21
west Africa *107,* 109

West Indies 97, 108–9, 117,
  125, 153, 177
Westminster 15, 16, 17, 23, 25,
  34, 35, *51,* 90, 117, 183
Whigs 94, 95, 108, 110, 128,
  134, 141, 142
Whitby, Synod of (663) 14, 21
Wilkes, John 110–2, 125
Wilkinson, John 121
William I (the Conqueror) 17,
  23, 25, 28, 29, 34, 36
William II, Rufus 25, 29
William of Orange 87, 95, 97,
  113
Wilson, Woodrow 172
Winchester 9, 25, 34, 64
Windsor 45, 183
Witan 12, 16
Wolsey, Cardinal 69, 70
women 8, 60, 62–3, 84–5,

105, 119–20, 135, 137, 161,
  162–3, 178, 182, 184
working classes 149, 153, 156,
  161, 162, 164, 165, 171
Wren, Sir Christopher 100, *101*
Wyatt, Thomas 71
Wycliffe, John 49, 61
Wykeham, William of 65

yeomanry regiments 128
yeomen 47, 58, 81, 84, 104,
  128
York 9, 10, 23, 30, 123
  duke of 55
Yorkists 52, 55
Yorkshire 4, 37, 48, *70,* 114,
  152

Zimbabwe 173
Zulus 147